WRITING WITHOUT RULES

HOW TO WRITE & SELL A NOVEL WITHOUT GUIDELINES, EXPERTS, OR (OCCASIONALLY) PANTS

JEFF SOMERS

WRITER'S DIGEST
BOOKS

WritersDigest.com
Cincinnati, Ohio

For more resources for writers, visit www.writersdigest.com.

21 20 19 18   5 4 3 2 1

Distributed in the U.K. and Europe by F+W Media International
Pynes Hill Court, Pynes Hill, Rydon Lane
Exeter, EX2 5AZ, United Kingdom
Tel: (+44) 1392-797680, Fax: (+44) 1626-323319
E-mail: postmaster@davidandcharles.co.uk

Library of Congress Cataloging-in-Publication Data

ISBN-13: 978-1-4403-5292-8

Edited by Cris Freese and Amy Jones
Designed by Craig Ramsdell and Alexis Estoye
Production coordinated by Debbie Thomas

DEDICATION

To Danette, whose love for me is as inexplicable as it is miraculous.

ACKNOWLEDGMENTS

When I was a young man partial to baseball caps and regrettable choices in beer, I met a beautiful woman who agreed to go out with me despite my tragic, losing struggle with a mega-cowlick so huge and sentient it had its own name: The Fin. The date was going well despite The Fin and my habit of leaping up to dance every time The Macarena came on the jukebox (surprisingly often), until the subject of how, exactly, I planned to make my fortune came up and I admitted to aspiring to write novels. The fact that my future wife stayed for the rest of that date was nothing if not a miracle (or the direct result of the thirteen tequila fanny bangers she had ordered over the course of the meal). Many years later when I told my wife about my plan to write a book composed of my wit and wisdom regarding the business of writing and selling novels, she resisted the urge to express her sincere doubt about my ability to do so, causing my heart to grow three sizes that day.

When I burst into my agent's office one cold February day after day drinking at a nearby bar for several hours, I was initially suspicious of her suggestion that I consider writing this book, because it sounded like work. I countered with an idea to simply take every email I'd ever written and collect them into a manuscript and call it a post-post-post-modern novel, but she rejected that idea and insisted I could write and sell a great book about writing and selling books. This book would literally not exist without her counsel, encouragement, and liberal office cocktails policy.

I continue to be surprised at how many people at Writer's Digest still return my calls and emails. Jessica Strawser and Tyler Moss bought articles from me and then improved them dramatically with their feedback, and challenged me to come up with more irresistible pitches. All of that made me think about writing in a new way and forged my path to this book. And when the book was written, Cris Freese and Amy Jones worked their tails off to run it through a Brilliance Machine and make it better than it was, while Jessica Farris helped me come up with smart ways to promote and sell the darn thing.

I have over 1,400 rejection notes on file at home. Every one of them, every piece of negative feedback, every bad review has pushed me to prove them all wrong and sell the next story, the next novel, the next article. Because if I'm going to get revenge on all those people I'm going to need to be, like, Bond Villain rich.

Speaking of Bond Villain rich: A sincere thank you to every person who has ever purchased one of my books or stories, or bought a magazine or anthology because it contained my work. And to everyone who bought this book (or will as soon as they finish reading this line and walk to the checkout): Thanks, you just bought me a drink!

ABOUT THE AUTHOR

Jeff Somers (www.jeffreysomers.com) was born in Jersey City, New Jersey, although the city has purged all evidence of his residency and refuses to discuss him. He wrote his first novel at the age of nine and was sent to a deprogramming camp by his parents, who were worried he would never become rich enough to support them.

He has published nine novels, including the Avery Cates Series of noir-science fiction novels from Orbit Books (www.avery-cates.com), the darkly hilarious crime novel *Chum* from Tyrus Books, and most recently tales of blood magic and short cons in the Ustari Cycle, including the novel *We Are Not Good People* and the novellas *Fixer*, *The Stringer*, *Last Best Day*, and *The Boom Bands* from Pocket Gallery (www.wearenotgoodpeople.com). He has published over thirty short stories, including "Ringing the Changes," which was selected for inclusion in *Best American Mystery Stories 2006*, "Sift, Almost Invisible, Through," which appeared in the anthology *Crimes by Moonlight* edited by Charlaine Harris, and "Three Cups of Tea," which appeared in the anthology *Hanzai Japan*. He also writes about books for Barnes and Noble and ThoughtCo.com and about the craft of writing for Writer's Digest, which published his book on the craft of writing *Writing Without Rules* in 2018 (that is, this book you are currently reading, so this should really be the least surprising thing about this entire About the Author section).

He lives in Hoboken, New Jersey with his wife, The Duchess, and their many, many cats. The Duchess considers him dimwitted enough to require constant supervision. The cats consider him to be warm furniture. Jeff considers pants to always be optional.

TABLE OF CONTENTS

PART I: WRITING A NOVEL
HOW TO DO IT WITHOUT BREAKING A SWEAT OR PUTTING ON PANTS

PART II: SELLING A NOVEL
HOW TO MAKE A DIME
(SADLY, PROBABLY LITERALLY)

INTRODUCTION

EVERYTHING I NEEDED TO KNOW ABOUT WRITING AND PUBLISHING I LEARNED IN HIGH SCHOOL

When I was sixteen years old I was pretty much the ideal of the Matthew-Broderick-in-*War-Games* KGB recruitment profile. I was smart enough that school was really easy, but also uninterested and bored, so my grades were awful. I wore huge plastic-rim glasses that people often took for humorous props. I dressed like a middle-aged Parrothead[1] and spent more time playing an elaborate computer-based statistical model baseball game with my friends than actually playing baseball.[2] It's frankly surprising I *wasn't* recruited by the KGB—except it's entirely possible they tried and I proved too myopic and distracted to even notice.

---

1 You may be tempted to google this term if you're not familiar with the musical subculture of Jimmy Buffett fans. You will be disappointed if you do.

2 Were my friends and I massive unrepentant nerds? We were. The game was called *Microleague Baseball*, and we actually played real-time games against each other, recorded wins and losses, and had playoffs and a World Series. We did this for years. We would then order Blimpie for lunch, go out and play basketball, come back and vomit, and play more video games. My childhood was glamorous.

I also wrote a lot. My story as a writer is depressingly common: I loved to read as a kid and started writing at a very young age, then discovered a passion for it. A lot of writers like to think that passion and an obsession with reading and writing makes them special, but we all have the same basic story: Books got us through our low times, we wanted to tell our own stories, we all (probably) wore glasses with lenses so large and thick we could see the future and thus write stories about it to astound and amaze.

UNCONVENTIONAL TIP

Writing and reading as much as you can is often (and correctly) prescribed for aspiring writers. When it comes to reading, there is no right or wrong—read anything, read everything, and don't worry about whether you have "good taste" in books. Reading feeds the machine no matter what kind of books we're talking about. On the other hand, writing all the time isn't a goal unto itself. *Finishing* things is just as important. We'll discuss this in more detail later in the book.

When I was sixteen, I had already written several terrible, derivative science-fiction and fantasy stories. I had a can't-lose method that I'll teach you right now: I took an already-published book, like *The Lord of the Rings*, and rewrote it, deleting 90 percent of the nuance and detail and changing all the names.[3]

Hey, writing is a learning process.

At sixteen, though, I had a breakthrough and I wrote what I consider to be my first more or less original novel. It was titled *White Rabbit* and it was about a spy for a galactic civilization who had been trained and augmented to be able to change his appearance through total control over every muscle and ligament and tendon in his body.[4] He stumbles on a mysterious packet of information that soon causes the whole universe to chase him, and later he finds himself on a planet where magic

---

3 This is not a drill. In my first "novel" I had creatures called Twabbots. And, yes, I feel shame.

4 I said "original," not "good."

works. There was a reason for that last bit, but I forget what it was now. It doesn't matter; I don't think it was a good novel, but I did manage to sell it in my junior year of high school.[5]

Well, *sell* is a strong word. I never got paid any money, and very likely never would have. The publisher was a one-man micropress out in California, and although I signed a contract, he never even finished the editing process. I did spend two years or so telling everyone I would soon be a best-selling author and thus they could take their dire warnings about getting an education and making plans for the future and stuff them, which made me incredibly popular among my parents' friends.[6]

What did I learn from this humiliating experience? On a personal level, nothing, as I was and remain disturbingly confident in my own awesomeness, as well as proud of my inability to grow in any sort of emotional sense. On a professional level, I learned something incredibly valuable: *Publishing a book doesn't require competence, organization, or good spelling.*

So, *White Rabbit*. The book was written on a manual typewriter. Yes, I am that old, although part of my fetish for manual typewriters is sexual in nature, which also explains why I continued to doggedly pound out (see what I did there?) first drafts on my ancient Remington portable up until about 2005. This also means that *White Rabbit* wasn't revised in any way. You read that right. I took a steaming first draft fresh from the typewriter, covered in correction fluid, made a dozen photocopies at my father's office without telling him,[7] and mailed them out to publishers without even bothering to proofread the thing.

---

5 I attended St. Peter's There but for the Grace of God Academy along with my older brother, who I will call Yan in order to protect the little dignity he has left. It was a Jesuit institution, and Yan was so smart that every teacher I encountered would talk about him in awed tones and then jokingly wonder out loud whether I was half as smart as him. By the end of my time there no one was joking any more.

6 And then spent the next two years meekly trying to pretend I'd never told anyone that I'd sold a book, because by that point no one believed a word I said. I briefly considered changing my name. Many possible names were considered, including Malachi the Magnificent, Pierre Mon Dieu, and, simply, Igor.

7 This was payback for the time my father took my very first, ninety-page novel and photocopied it at his job and passed it out to everyone. One of his co-workers took pity on me and copyedited

Not only that—the photocopies I sent out were mysteriously lacking pages 85, 89, 93, and 142.

Not only *that*, but the cover letter I wrote was hilarious—if you're me. For just about everyone else in the universe, not so much. I assigned code names to potential editors and myself. Why sixteen-year-old Jeff

18 June 1989

Jeffrey Somers

Dear Mr. Somers (alias Sic-Sic etc.):

Despite your none-too-flattering assignment of the name "Tweedeldum" to me (which, by the way, should be spelled "Tweedledum"), I rejected my initial impulse to assume the persona of the Red Queen and shout "Off with his head!" or at least "Off with his manuscript!" and have started reading your novel. Despite your rather tenuous command of English spelling and punctuation, I like it. At least, so far. Unfortunately, I have had to stop reading it because page 85 is missing. So also are pages 89, 93 and 142. Kindly send them so I may get on with the yarn.

Press has been inactive for the past two years, and there were not supposed to be any listings in current directories. Suddenly, I am getting short stories and novels from all over the place. These are all being generated by the same listing... I know this because they all come with the wrong zipcode; my zip is 91320, not 91330. By a peculiar coincidence, I had decided to reactivate Press shortly before these started arriving. I am going to try again, in a somewhat new fashion, to see if I can manage not to lose money publishing SF. There's just too much good stuff out there to ignore. I would appreciate knowing where you found my listing, so I can try an correct that zipcode for their next edition. Also, please enclose your phone number... I tried to get it from Information but they say you are unlisted. If your novel keeps up its pace and hold on my attention, I would be interested in publishing it.

Sincerely,
Cheshire Cat

the book, noting that, among other failures, I hadn't used any quote marks, commas, or colons. I tried to claim I was following the Cormac McCarthy method, but he noted the fact that I was eleven at the time and refused to believe me.

thought this was a good idea is a mystery to present-day Jeff. My code name was (and I am not making this up—it *actually happened*) Sic Sic by the Seaside and the editor's code name was always Tweedledum.

Yes, I called editors who I wanted to publish my book Tweedledum. Not only that, I misspelled *Tweedledum* as *Tweedeldum*.

And despite all that, someone tried to publish it. The editor who tried, valiantly, to publish *White Rabbit* even referred to my "rather tenuous command of English spelling and punctuation" in their acceptance letter.[8] So, let me recap. When submitting this manuscript to real, actual publishers, I did the following:

- sent a raw first draft
- sent out a manuscript with missing pages and numerous typos
- wrote a ridiculous cover letter in which I more or less insulted (and very likely freaked out) anyone who read it

And it (almost) got published.

Little did I know, but this would set a pattern for the rest of my life. A pattern of goofy incompetence and clueless shortcutting—and unambiguous writing and publishing success. To date I've published dozens of short stories, nine novels, several novellas, one comic book, and countless articles and blog posts on the internet and in print magazines. I actually make a living[9] from my writing, both fiction and nonfiction. And I'm here to tell you I haven't gotten any better at any of the things people will often tell you are required to have a professional writing career—like attention to detail, social media competence, and knowledge of the basic rules of society.

The one thing I am good at? The *writing* part. Being incompetent and clueless doesn't mean I don't work hard at my craft. I write every day. I complete a short story every month, no matter what. I constantly submit short fiction to paying markets, and I am forever plaguing my long-suffering agent with new novels to sell. The fact is, cluelessness isn't laziness: Whether it's writing skills or the more frustrating and elusive promotional and business skills that a modern writing career

---

8 Purely based on what you've read so far, you have no doubt already come to a similar conclusion.

9 If you call this living. My wife does not, citing a distinct and measurable lack of diamonds, black credit cards, and the ability to verbally abuse people financially dependent on us.

requires, I've always been good at figuring things out. It's just that my first (and second, and sometimes third) stabs at anything career-related are often hilarious failures—hilarious failures I think you can learn from.

The conclusion? If an idiot such as myself can write and sell novels, so can you. It really isn't nearly as hard as some folks out there seem to believe. And I'm going to go through every mistake I've made, every superficially poor decision that either worked out just fine or had no impact whatsoever, and every lazy moment that should have had some negative consequences to prove to you that writing anything and selling it for money isn't nearly as hard as it might seem.

A NOTE ON ASSUMPTIONS: Back in high school I had a teacher who communicated almost exclusively in allegory and repeated aphorisms. One of his favorite sayings was "Just because you get wet when it rains doesn't mean that if you're wet it must be raining." While none of us could understand a thing the man said, this one phrase stuck with me, because it's a concise way of reminding yourself that your experience is unique: What works for *you* may not work for *everyone*.

---

10 My agent likes to tell me she swapped another agent three romance novelists and a poet for me.

So, this book is intended to be instructive, and within the pages that follow I will be saying a lot of ridiculous things with an air of wise certainty. While I do think you can learn a lot from my experience as an unconventional novelist, keep in mind that your particular circumstances, personality, or process may render some of my experience invalid for you. In other words, if I write something about how refusing to wear pants to the meetings I attend with my agent and publisher has made me the success I am today (something in my heart of hearts I truly believe, even though I am usually not *quite* inebriated enough to say it out loud), you may find that ditching your trousers doesn't work out quite the way I imply it should.

Mainly what I want you to take away from this book is the idea that there are those in the writing world who try to make writing and publishing a novel seem as mysterious and complicated as possible because it burnishes their accomplishments—but it's really much simpler than all that. Specific techniques or experiences may not be duplicable, but the overall takeaway is that if someone as disorganized and borderline incompetent as *me* can write and sell novels, so can *you*.

PART 1

WRITING A NOVEL

HOW TO DO IT WITHOUT BREAKING A SWEAT OR PUTTING ON PANTS

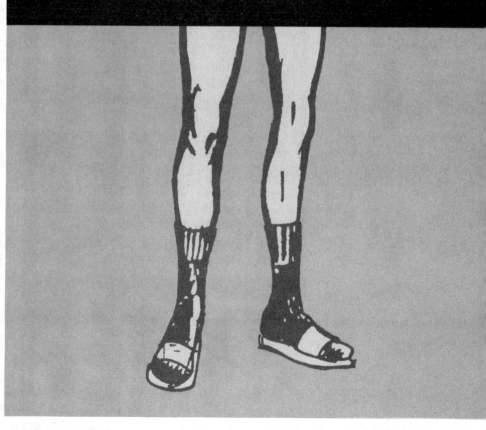

WHAT YOU NEED

My childhood predates most of the things Americans consider to be the bedrock of modern society: smartphones, cable television, easy access to burritos. Back in my day we didn't have fancy things for entertainment—or fancy burritos driven right to your front door by some guy responding to an order you transmitted via app—and so I spent a lot of my time pretending. My brother, Yan, and I entertained ourselves with world-building, usually with a liberal mix of Legos, plastic army men, and aluminum foil shaped into horrific metallic Godzillas. We invaded every room of the house, spinning an infinite yarn of galactic wars, monster-plagued cities, and the brave, doomed paratroopers caught in the branches of the dying Christmas tree and abandoned by their squad.

When my brother was otherwise occupied, I entertained myself with some more good old-fashioned pretending.[1] I would be a drug-addled rock star, using an old tennis racket as a guitar and telling imaginary band mates on stage that I was breaking up the band and going

---

1 I realize this is making my childhood sound like I was born in the eighteenth century. I suppose everyone thinks their childhood was somehow rough and rustic compared to the crazy modern times we live in, but believe me, if you woke up tomorrow and your choices for electronic entertainment was three channels on the TV and Pitfall! on the Atari 2600, you'd be hitting the Legos pretty hard, too.

solo. Or I'd be a world-famous brain surgeon,[2] about to operate on the president just as I notice a twitch in my right hand. In between marathon sessions playing Donkey Kong and reading, I was a lot of things in the privacy of my room. When I got bored with pretending to be a glamorous, highly paid professional, one day I decided to slum it a little and pretend to be a famous writer.[3] So I stole my mother's typewriter.[4]

T.S. Eliot once said that "good writers borrow, but great writers steal." While it's usually understood that Eliot meant "steal" in terms of creativity, trust me when I tell you that when most writers realize how much money they can actually earn from their writing, other definitions of the word steal come to mind.[5]

I didn't intend to steal my mother's typewriter. I was pretending to be an alcoholic, unhappy novelist, and I needed a prop, so I borrowed it—and then I just never gave it back. Here we are forty years later, and I still have it, so I can only assume my mother didn't need to type anything after 1981 or so, which explains a great many things regarding the fact that I don't recall going to school in the 1980s. Or to the doctor.

But I digress. I can't pinpoint the precise moment when I segued from pretending to be a writer to actually writing, but that decision can be laid at the feet of several people, including my old pals C.S. Lewis and J.R.R. Tolkien, because I very much wished there were more Narnia and *Lord of the Rings* novels (so why not write my own!), and Piers Anthony, whose generous Author's Notes at the end of his books demystified novel writing to the point where a snotty ten-year-old kid like me imagined it was easy peasy. And it was, kinda; I wrote my first novel in a few weeks on that typewriter. It was thirty pages long; it was essentially

---

2 Whenever tedious adults would ask me what I wanted to be when I grew up, I always answered brain surgeon, because it sounded impressive and was not an obvious response. Later, when I began to understand the level of math and science I would have to master in order to become the World's Sexiest Brain Surgeon, I changed my response to Donkey Kong Champion of the World.

3 This is what my fellow writers will recognize as Poor Author Humor.

4 It's a beautiful Remington portable manual typewriter circa 1950, a real workhorse. Prior to 2005, every single thing I wrote was at least partially composed on that wonderful machine. Typing on it toned my fingers to the point where I could kill a man just by poking him in the chest.

5 See Footnote 3.

The Fellowship of the Ring, if that novel had been thirty pages long and written in a form of English that didn't require any sort of punctuation.[6]

My only point is simple: At the age of ten, having committed some slight slow-motion larceny in the acquisition of a typewriter,[7] I had the only two things you will ever need to write a novel: a functioning brain and something to write with.

OR, IN MY CASE, A HALF-FUNCTIONING BRAIN

The fact is, writing is one of those creative endeavors that requires almost nothing beyond your creative energy—you don't need collaborators, special equipment, specific training, or special access to anything in order to write a novel. Or, frankly, to publish one. Other creative vocations make it impossible to engage professionally without at least some of those things. Look at the music business: You need years of training (even if you are self-taught), an instrument (often expensive), and equipment, even if we're just talking about a computer with recording software on it and a Bandcamp (https://bandcamp.com) account. You can whittle those requirements down to the bare bones, but it's still more complicated than writing a novel, which really does require nothing more than your imagination and something to write with, even if just a pencil and paper.

And yet, based on the questions I get all the time, people seem to think that writing a novel is a complicated, arduous task that requires not only the right implements, but also the right work space, training, relationships, and lifestyle. Part of this is the fault of film and television that have fetishized writing, in a way; they present writers working like Colin Firth in *Love Actually*, jetting off to an idyllic cottage in

---

6 In yet another a move that would set the tone for the rest of my professional career, when these errors were noted I decided I had made them on purpose and that they constituted a New Way of Doing Things.

7 My poor suffering mother did try to reclaim her typewriter on several occasions, sparking a brief passive-aggressive war that saw the machine relocated multiple times a week. Once I started producing actual material, however, she relented in an effort to either encourage my creativity or (more likely) as part of a complex revenge plot that was forgotten over time—or has yet to detonate.

France to wear ridiculous sweaters and sit by a gorgeous pond, writing on a manual typewriter while sipping delicious teas, his attractive domestic silently falling in love with him.[8]

Part of it is the fault of aspiring writers themselves. You might have heard F. Scott Fitzgerald's famous line about how all Americans imagine they are temporarily embarrassed millionaires; well, all writers imagine they are temporarily embarrassed bestsellers, and we're all vaguely embarrassed at how not arduous writing actually is. I mean, we sit behind a desk and make things up. Sometimes we have to get up before noon and go to the library or ask someone a few questions. It's not literally difficult to write a book, not in the physical sense. So we like to dress it up a little, pretending that writer's block is a thing (a kind of illness that usually implies a very serious headache and possibly death via existential crisis),[9] that we drink too much because of the mental stress of writing (ridiculous; like all sane people, we drink because booze is delicious and transports us to a different state of mind), and that we would be much happier doing anything else because writing is the equivalent of suffering.

UNCONVENTIONAL TIP

A note on research: I debated including research, as it pertains to writing, in this chapter as something unnecessary, simply because it isn't literally required that you know anything about anything in order to write a book; the whole point is that you can make things up. When I began work on *The Electric Church*, I realized I didn't know much about the various brands of automatic weapons in the world; instead of spending some time researching them, I invented my own gun manufacturer, and that allowed me to make up whatever details I wished. My first editor on the original version of that book had a field day with my gun handling, but couldn't say a thing about my depiction of the Roon Model 87a automatic handgun for

---

8 It's a total coincidence that this sentence also perfectly describes the courtship of my wife, The Duchess.

9 See chapter ten.

> the simple fact that it does not actually exist. The point is, research
> is a gray area: necessary, but only to a point.

Bosh, all of it. A lot of very lazy and very disorganized people have written and sold novels. A lot of famous novels have been written in mere days, often solely for the promise of filthy lucre.[10] People have written novels as a response to dares, for spite, and with open disdain for their own creative efforts. Novels have been written in notebooks, on laptops, and even on index cards.[11]

And yet, people will tell you writing is hard to do. A lot of writers offering advice violate my former teacher's axiom about the rain and getting wet, and assume that because they had to do X, Y, and Z to write and publish a novel, then you have to do the same—and they often don't even consider seriously whether X, Y, and Z were really necessary for them, as opposed to being coincidental. The end result is what appears to be a lengthy and ever-growing list of things you absolutely must have to be a writer—a real writer. So, let's do something a bit different and break this down from the other end. Let's make a list of all the things you *don't* need to write a book.

Of course, not needing something doesn't mean you can't use it or benefit from it. Your mileage may vary. But anytime someone says something is required in order to write and sell a novel, they are flat out wrong.[12] You can make your own decisions regarding the necessity of anything listed here—that's fine. Really, it is, but if you show up at one of my readings to drunkenly heckle me about it, that will not be cool.[13]

So, what don't you need?

A Degree. At St. Peter's There but for the Grace of God Academy, everyone was more or less presumed to be college bound. I half-assed my

---

10 Classy example: Fyodor Dostoyevsky wrote *The Gambler* in twenty-six days because he was deeply in debt (from gambling!) and needed to make some quick cash. Nothing beats starvation and ruin when it comes to artistic inspiration.

11 Most notably Vladimir Nabokov, who wrote *Lolita* and other novels using index cards, which he used almost as a primitive hypertext system. His process is fascinating and makes me sleepy when I think about it.

12 With the notable exception of, you know, a novel.

13 I am beginning to suspect this is the only reason anyone shows up for my readings, actually.

way through high school like everything else,[14] and in my senior year I wasn't sure if college was for me. The alternative, however, seemed like a lot of work,[15] so I eventually relented and enrolled.

I was an English major for a few reasons. One, I had already read all the books on the required reading list. Two, it was literally the major with the fewest number of required credits. I made it my mission in life to attend as few lectures as possible while still graduating, because I was an incredibly awful person at that age and had not yet been introduced to the concept of privilege.

I am not proud.[16]

Suffice it to say my bachelor's degree is of dubious value, at best. As part of my heroic effort at doing absolutely nothing, I took as many creative writing courses as I could for reasons both obvious and obscure. On the one hand, I was already writing fiction, so this was a logical move—and the classes were also extremely easy in terms of grades, so it was almost impossible to fail one. But I also took them because I had never experienced feedback from disinterested fellow writers, and I wanted to see what that was like. I learned two very important things. One, if you challenge people to offer criticism, then no matter how much they love your work or find themselves totally neutral toward it, they will find something to criticize, even if it kills them. And two, this means there will always be something wrong with your manuscript.

I had fun in those classes, writing stories and hearing feedback. I still have all the notes one teacher made on my submissions, in fact.[17] But once I managed to squeak out of college with my aforementioned

---

14 It was at that august institution that a classmate introduced me to the MEMO concept: Minimum Effort, Maximum Output. This changed my life. I haven't broken a sweat since I was fifteen, and I immediately began my academic strategy of writing papers about books I had not read or even been in the same room with.

15 Read: Literally.

16 All right, maybe a little—especially of my crowning achievement: Attending just the first day, midterm, and final exam of a 200-level Shakespeare course and getting a solid B. Take that, people who actually care about things!

17 That teacher was Terry Holt, who is an incredible writer. He published one story collection (*In the Valley of the Kings* [W.W. Norton, 2009]) and then decided in middle age to go back to school and get his medical degree. He works as a doctor today. You can draw your own conclusions about writing as a career from this.

dubious English degree, I had only one definitive plan: I wanted to be as far away from a campus as humanly possible for the rest of my life.[18] I have never had any desire to pursue an MFA; frankly, the thought never even occurred to me. I'm not sure I even knew MFA programs existed, but it doesn't matter. I can confidently say that I wouldn't have gone into one even if I had known. And I can confidently say I don't regret it.

UNCONVENTIONAL TIP

MFA programs vary widely in terms of quality, focus, and impact. If you think you'd benefit from one—whether because you think it will improve your writing or because you hope it will introduce you to influential people who will be impressed by your cocktail banter and offer you a book contract they carry with them everywhere for just such a moment—you should do your research. Consider cost, of course, but also location, residency, the faculty, reputation, and how many graduates are actually working as writers, even if they aren't bestsellers. The recent boom in MFA programs is driven in large part by money, just like everything else. A lot of colleges have discovered there are a lot of people willing to take out loans in order to pay for MFA programs ... and so they launch an MFA program. It doesn't mean it's worth it.

MFAs aren't for everyone. Maybe they're for you, and there's certainly nothing wrong with that. People have grown artistically in such programs, made great networking connections, signed with agents, and sold books through MFA programs. Then again, plenty of people have simply accumulated a lot of debt. The point here is that you don't need an MFA to be published, or to be great. MFA programs have existed since the 1930s, and while the number of such programs (and the num-

---

18 Actually, I had two plans. The other involved getting a part-time job; keeping the awful, windowless apartment and my two roommates; and remaining in my college town. The idea was to earn enough money for rent and spend half my day writing. After all, who needed, you know, things? Or food, because beer is a food. This worked well for about a week, and then my general incompetence meant I wasn't earning enough money to pay that rent, and the whole thing devolved into a *Heart of Darkness*-style descent into madness.

ber of people applying to and attending them) has exploded in recent years, they're nothing new, and many incredible writers have sprung from them. Of course, many incredible writers didn't get MFAs: Harper Lee, Jonathan Franzen, Alice Munro, Norman Mailer, me, to name a few. The lesson here is simple: MFAs don't guarantee creative joy, artistic growth, professional success, or better cocktail conversation—and not having an MFA doesn't guarantee anything, either. If you think it'll help, send out those applications. If not, don't sweat it; there are hundreds of paths to publication.

Implements. I'm a pretty simple guy.[19] I like my whiskey neat, my transmissions automatic, and my wardrobe composed of various shades of gray and blue so everything matches. When it comes to writing, I like to keep it as simple as possible: Words going onto a page. I work in two distinct ways: I write short stories longhand in a regular college-ruled notebook, and I type in a vanilla word processor (LibreOffice, if you must know). That's it. Aside from spell-check[20] and a few basic styles, I don't use anything to augment my writing.

UNCONVENTIONAL TIP

The tools you use don't mean anything. George R.R. Martin famously writes his novels on an ancient DOS-based computer that doesn't connect to the Internet, using an obsolete, unsupported word processing program. Why? Because he likes it, and because he's George R.R. Martin and no one can force him to switch to MS Word. This fact doesn't make his universes any less complex, his writing any less marvelous, or *A Song of Ice and Fire* any less groundbreaking. In other words, the specific *feng shui* of your home

---

19 By simple, of course, I mean incredibly lazy. My laziness is legendary even among lazy people. My wife, whom I always refer to as The Duchess (pro tip: Never look her directly in the eyes, or her predator instinct will kick in), once told me she didn't worry about me cheating on her for the simple reason that she knew I was too lazy to manage the minutiae of having an affair. She was not kidding. She was also not wrong.

20 My agent read this line and sent me a note saying "I doubt this completely," which is just hurtful. Accurate, but hurtful. Every manuscript I've ever sent her is absolutely riddled with typos.

> office or the specific software you use to write your book isn't going
> to be stamped on the cover. No one *cares.*

Other writers do. I know this because people ask me about hardware
and software a lot. There are special dedicated word processing devices
so you can type without the Internet to distract you (apparently people
are unaware that the Internet is a thing that can, you know, be turned
off at your discretion). There are software packages like Scrivener, which
is like a word processor designed by Tony Stark, allowing you to not just
type, but to manage metadata, supporting documents, outlines, and a
host of other powerful tools to make organizing and writing your novel
... I dunno, easier? Or more complicated. Some writers swear by Scrivener and other software packages like Tinderbox or Evernote as ways
to keep track of random notes, their plot outlines, the relationships
between their characters, the unwritten backstory, or dozens of other
aspects of the creative process. Some writers replicate this in spread-
sheets or other tools, and of course, a lot of writers do all this work the
old-fashioned way using pieces of paper, Post-it notes, or handwritten
journals. And a lot of these writers are very successful, and that makes
a lot of other writers think all of this stuff is necessary.

It isn't. In fact, I think all this stuff makes writing more difficult and
less fun. I mean, have you ever downloaded the free trial of Scrivener?
It's like trying to learn how to pilot a space shuttle. I didn't become an
author so I could teach myself literary calculus. I became an author to
write books and look cool,[21] like everyone else.

The inherent assumption that all published authors use NASA-level
software and complex organizational systems in order to world-build
and write their novels comes, I think, from the desire to make writing a
profession instead of an artistic calling. There's a tendency to approach
writing like any other career, which means there must be a science to
it: a degree you can get, tools you can buy, systems you can study. But it

---

21 Still working on the latter part, yes, yes, I know, move along.

isn't like any other career.[22] And I am a simple, lazy, lazy man, so I never bothered to do anything more advanced than make up a story, jot a few notes along the way,[23] and then revise out the mistakes and inconsistencies until I'm sick of reading the damn thing. And it's worked for me, so far. Which means it could work just as well for you: Go get something to write with, and start writing. Don't waste time installing software and taking classes to learn that software, only to discover that by the time you get certified in it a whole new paradigm has taken hold and your certifications are useless.

UNCONVENTIONAL TIP

Do not, under any circumstances, become a writer in order to make money. *Can* you make money as a writer? Sure, gobs of it. But the odds are against you. When the average first-time advance on a novel is about $6,500 (spread out over a few years, most likely), the first thing you should do when you sell your first book is probably get a second job.

Agents. I sold my first two novels without an agent, actually: I sold *Lifers* to a small publisher in 1999 for what amounted to a pat on the head and kick in the ass (or, in less technical terms, a $1,000 advance they never quite paid me and a steadily declining rate of correspondence). *The Electric Church* deal came about from a complex chain of events[24] I

---

22 In a recent blog post over at *Boing Boing*, Cory Doctorow made an elegant point when discussing Patreon: "Art is an irrational market; artists make art without regard to the laws of supply and demand." I think that captures the problem with trying to make writing a novel into a replicable science.

23 I have notebooks and pads filled with the mysterious notes of novels past, referring to characters and plot twists I no longer remember or recognize. When I come across these notes, I sometimes wonder if my whole life has been a series of ministrokes.

24 The very compressed version begins in 2004, when I saw an ad for an online publisher seeking science fiction novel pitches. I dug out *The Electric Church*, which I'd been writing off and on since 1993, and polished up a fresh pitch for the novel. They liked it, agreed to publish it, and assigned an editor to work with me. That editor was Lili Saintcrow, just at the start of her own career. When the online publisher went out of business (unsurprisingly, as their business model involved emailing customers one chapter as a PDF every week—one chapter a week!), Lili showed the manuscript to her editor, then at Warner Books, and a book deal was born! Which just goes

wish I'd been brilliant enough to set in motion on purpose.[25] My agent negotiated this deal, and she sold the other four books in that series and four other books for me, so as you read this, Janet, please don't think I am minimizing the incredible benefits that a literary agent of your caliber brings to the pallid, gray life of a humble author.[26]

Readers, if the style of this book changes abruptly, please investigate whether I have been assassinated and replaced by a good-looking middle-aged man with a vague resemblance to me. My agent's powers are dark.

UNCONVENTIONAL TIP

Don't forget, if you sell a book without an agent's help you can still get an agent's help. Having a contract in hand can make you more attractive to agents, possibly, and getting that contract reviewed and, just as important, negotiated is one of the smartest things you can do. If agents passed on the manuscript but sent back thoughtful responses indicating it was close, checking in to see if they want to take you on as a client and help nail down your deal is a very good idea. You can get a load of great information about identifying and contacting literary agents from The Guide to Literary Agents blog (www.writersdigest.com/editor-blogs/guide-to-literary-agents), and you can find out a lot about potentially interested agents from Publishers Marketplace (http://publishersmarketplace.com). The Writer's Market (http://writersmarket.com), of course, remains the gold standard for thorough information about agents (and publishers).

---

to demonstrate what I call Jeff's Law: You gotta get your work out there for the random forces of the universe to work in your favor.

25 It would have required a time machine and a Ph.D. in causality and temporal mechanics. Instead, as I always have, I relied on my natural charm and general cluelessness to alchemically combine into success. Look up *shambolic* in the dictionary and there will be a visual representation of my career.

26 Primarily free cocktails and savage assessments of my fashion choices, head-spinning publishing gossip involving people I've never met and can't identify, and constant promises of golden toilets delivered right to my door—promises that have proved to be hollow, so far.

The thing is, you certainly don't need an agent to write a book and probably will have some trouble convincing one to represent you if you haven't actually written one,[27] so my first piece of advice to new writers is not to worry about getting an agent until you have written a book that you think people will clamor to read. Agents sell the books you write, and while their writing advice in the form of revision notes and feedback and general marketing savvy can be priceless, they aren't necessary to the process of writing.

Once you have a book? Well, the thing is, these days you don't need an agent to just sell the damn thing. Self-publishing has become so easy and refined—though it is not in any way new, it just has a new hat in the form of digital marketplaces and print-on-demand magic—that you can absolutely, 100 percent sell that book to everyone who loves you or owes you a favor[28] without an agent. And if you have a real talent for self-publishing and self-promotion and marketing, you might even be the next Amanda Hocking or Hugh Howey.

I, however, have none of these things, as we'll get into later. Me, I need an agent to sell my work (and believe me, she knows it)—even though I did somehow manage to sell two novels without one. My agent got me much better terms on the latter deal than I would have gotten myself (and this is fact, not simply a belief),[29] and she went on to leverage that into a career that continues to surprise the laziest man alive (that is, me). But you can write and sell a novel without an agent. Whether it's wise to do so will be discussed in more detail later.

Minions. I don't much care for people, in general, or writers in particular. We writers are a whiny bunch. We sit around massaging keyboards and fondling pens, we make things up and jot down mean-

---

27 If you like to live dangerously, corner an agent at some affair, smile, and say, "I have some great ideas for a book!"

28 In fact, many so-called publishers rely on the fact that your parents, your best friends, and a few dozen other relatives and loved ones will buy a copy of your book for the entire profit margin of your novel. In other words, once you convince your whole family to buy a copy, they've made their profit.

29 If I had signed the original contract for *The Electric Church*, I'd still be required to show up at the publisher's offices once a month to sing an original song while dressed as a Doctor Who of my choosing. Why this was so important to them, I'll never know, but my agent saved me. Naturally I would have been The Fourth Doctor, as I already have the scarf.

spirited insults for later use, we drink too much and sneer at people who haven't read Proust and firmly believe in the Don Draper Nap—which commences at about eleven o'clock and ends at four in the afternoon, concluding with a loud sigh and a lengthy complaint about our busy day.

And also: All writers want to talk about is their work-in-progress (WIP). When we gather, we all sit around impatiently waiting for the story to end so we can discuss our WIP. It's madness. Madness overshadowed only by the uncomfortable silence that ensues when the bill arrives.

Now, some people believe that it takes a village to write a novel. There's the author, of course, laboring over a narrative. Then there are beta readers, which, to be honest, is a term I encountered rather late in life. Once I had published a few books and started showing up at events, people would ask me about my beta reader policy, and I was mystified. Of course, being eternally afraid of looking foolish, I pretended to know exactly what they were talking about,[30] but the fact is, I don't have beta readers—at least not regularly. I do occasionally ask The Duchess to read a manuscript to get her take, and in a sense my agent is the ultimate beta reader, as she pretty much determines if anyone else will ever read the book. But a group of people who read every manuscript and give me feedback? Never in life.

And I'll tell you why: Feedback is evil stuff, folks. Feedback should be handled while wearing a standard-issue horror movie antiplague suit. It should be handled with tongs, or preferably via some advanced virtual-reality interface wherein you never actually come into physical contact with the stuff. Feedback is powerful, like uranium-235. It can change your manuscript (and your life). Prolonged exposure can also ruin you, and your book. The problem is that the feedback loop can become self-sustaining. As noted before, in my experience when people are asked to offer feedback, by gum they will dig deep and offer some.

The other aspect of beta readers that doesn't appeal to me is how it can turn into tailoring your manuscript to suit a few narrow tastes.

---

30 Refusing to admit I don't know something is my greatest flaw. To this day I have to keep up elaborate ruses to maintain the fiction that I speak Mandarin Chinese.

There's certainly nothing wrong with listening to advice from people whose opinion you respect. It's just that sifting that advice and choosing what to pay attention to and what to ignore requires work and collaboration, and, as I may have stated, I don't like other people. Or work.

See, I started writing in part because it doesn't require collaboration. I work alone. I sit in my spectacular mind palace[31] and make up my little universes and have fun, and the fact that I don't have anyone teleporting into my brain to incept me is part of the appeal, frankly. I know plenty of writers swear by the beta reader system, and if you like getting that feedback, great. I don't. I like to sweat over my manuscripts in the dark, lonely room of my creative salon in total solitude, emerging pale and thin several years hence with six hundred manuscript pages, only to be told that it doesn't make much sense and that I've switched tenses somewhere in the middle.

Money. Writing doesn't require much money, and publishing doesn't have to cost you a dime. You might decide that hiring someone to review your manuscript, design a cover, edit and proofread, or promote you and your work is worth the money. And there's nothing wrong with that. But if anyone tells you that you *must* spend money to write or publish a book, don't believe it. You can write a book and publish it for free. Choosing to spend money on it is up to you, and anyone who tries to tell you otherwise is fairly obviously selling you something.

The too-long, didn't read version is this: All you need to write a book are ideas and something to write with. Everything else is negotiable—and unnecessary. If something helps you write or sell a book, great. If not, don't be afraid to discard it—no matter what anyone else might tell you.

---

31 My *god* you should see the bar in this place. For some reason, I have imagined it as a cash bar, likely due to my sad Catholic upbringing. But still.

WRITING WITHOUT RULES

2

BUTT-IN-CHAIR, SURE, BUT IT'S YOUR BUTT AND YOUR CHAIR

Monday, 1:30 P.M. At my desk. Implement: Desktop computer. Number of cats sitting on me: 3.

Writing is both mysterious and simple. On the one hand, it is literally the joining together of words to form sentences, then stacking sentences together to form paragraphs and paragraphs together to form *The Sound and the Fury*. Simple! On the other hand, no one can really explain how you imagine characters, see plot twists, or summon a room into being where no room has ever or will ever exist.

Yet, humans have this drive to explain everything. Instead of just sitting naked in a field enjoying the stars, early humans kept wondering *why* about everything. Now we have Netflix and craft beers. Similarly, instead of just spinning our stories and collecting our paltry royalties,[1] writers have been trying to explain the *process* of writing for centuries,

---

1 Have I ever received a royalty check for $1.35? I have. Can you purchase alcohol that won't make you blind for $1.35? No, but I am pleased to report the blindness is temporary.

in ways both clinical (e.g., *The Elements of Style*) and spiritual (e.g., *On Writing*). None of these guides actually agree on anything, of course; the idea that there's a single, one-size-fits-all "process" you can follow is kind of ludicrous. Writers come in all shapes and sizes, work in all manner of genres, and write for a wide variety of reasons ranging from personal satisfaction to contractual deadlines. And every writer develops his own personal process.

It's this variety that makes the concept of process so fascinating, of course. There are as many processes as there are novels. Still, as you dig through the mountains of writing advice out there, you find that most of the writing gurus offering their two cents share a few basic tenets: One, every writer *has* a process—an identifiable, replicable system of writing—and two, every writing process has at least one feature in common—that you write every day.

Wednesday, 2:03 A.M. In bed. Implement: Laptop. Number of cats sleeping on me: 4.

This is sometimes boiled down to the pithy advice known as "butt-in-chair." The idea is a simple one: You can't daydream your way to a novel; you have to actually log hours sitting in a chair in front of a keyboard or notebook or whatever you write on or in. All the planning, outlining, research, and character sketching doesn't mean a thing unless you get your butt in a chair and actually *write*.

And this is true! Except when it isn't. Because I don't have a process.

THE INEXORABLE
SADNESS OF PENCILS

Wednesday, 12:34 P.M. At my desk. Implement: Desktop. Number of cats sitting on me: 1.

Perhaps it's a bit more accurate to say that I have many processes, and I engage them, discard them, and bring them back from the past as circumstances dictate. And while I do write every day, or mostly every day, this is a consequence of circumstances and not a hard-and-fast rule that I stick to for fear of offending the Writing Compliance Office or my muse.[2] I'd argue that creating some sort of arbitrary process and then forcing yourself to stick to it is the opposite of how to write a book, because (my reasons follow):

Wednesday, 2:17 P.M. At the Brass Rail Bar in Hoboken, NJ.
Implement: Notebook. Number of bourbons consumed: 3.

1. **WRITING SHOULD BE FUN.** I know there are writers in the world who regard writing as a dour, serious-business art form that requires lots of grimacing at the page, silent thinking sessions, and ritualistic burning of manuscripts because they are so badly disappointing that the writer can't bear to let them exist. Me, I write about murderous husbands, magically enabled con artists, and futuristic assassins living in dystopias. I have *fun*, and the more regimented my process, the less fun it is. I want spontaneity, looseness, and unpredictability. In other words, I had a day job for eighteen years and I don't want to repeat the experience with my own creative efforts.[3]

UNCONVENTIONAL TIP

There's a simple rule of thumb I'm surprised more writers don't endorse: If you're not enjoying what you're writing, no one will enjoy reading it.

---

2 Besides, my "muse" is generally a liberal mixture of alcohol, old cartoons, and whatever I read, watched, or listened to the night before. It works like this: Get drunk, then read a book or watch a TV show that impresses you, have a dream where you re-imagine it as an old-timey cartoon, then wake up hungover and try desperately to steal every idea you can remember. The reason this works is because I remember things ... differently when sober, so nothing makes sense and the eventual manuscript is almost completely different from its inspiration. In other words, me genius.

3 It's less remarkable that I had a day job—plenty of authors need jobs to support themselves, after all, since writing books will make you realize the word *hundredaire* exists. What's more remarkable is the second part, where I held that job for eighteen years. I am not ashamed to admit I was terribly incompetent at this job but was saved via a series of mergers, managerial changes, and the fact that I turned out to be the only person capable of writing Word macros within a five-mile radius of our office.

Wednesday, 9:33 P.M. Back of police cruiser. Implement: Phone speech recognition. Pairs of pants I am wearing: 0.

2. **GRINDING GEARS IS COUNTERPRODUCTIVE.** A regimented writing process wherein you write at certain times and set certain word count[4] goals might seem like a way to ensure productivity—and if you have a natural leaning toward that sort of regimentation, it just might. For me, and for a lot of people, forcing yourself to write when the spark isn't there—when you're tired or uninspired—isn't going to produce *good* work. You might have pages when you're done, but most of it will get tossed in the trash when you reread it. That's not efficient, even if you feel efficient at the time.

UNCONVENTIONAL TIP

Sometimes having a community of writers you share work with and commiserate with is supportive and healthy. Sometimes it encourages you to pursue statistics like a daily word count goal just for the back slaps and attaboys. Always know whether a metric is helpful to you, and not just an empty achievement.

3. **YOU CAN'T CHANGE REALITY.** A firm process and schedule might make you feel professional and in control, but sometimes it's just not practical. If you're not a morning person, forcing yourself to get up and write before work won't lead to good writing. If your life is hectic and unpredictable, trying to shoehorn in a schedule is foolhardy.[5]

---

4 Word counts are the most overrated statistic in the field of fiction. Yes, it's true that almost any contract you sign regarding writing professionally—in fiction or nonfiction—will include a word count of some sort, writing toward a daily or weekly or monthly word count goal is just silly for the simple reason that a large percentage of the words you force yourself to write will be terrible.

5 Of course, you may not have a choice. For some people, finding time to write is nearly impossible, and when they do find the time sandwiched between school or jobs or other exhausting responsibilities, they're likely drained and stressed. So all this kvetching about the time to write should be taken with a grain of salt and the clear stipulation that finding that time is your chief obstacle to begin with.

WRITING WITHOUT RULES

Friday, 4:30 A.M. At my desk. Implement: Desktop. Amount of Lost Time Suffered: 18 hours.

UNCONVENTIONAL TIP

None of this means you shouldn't *make* time to write. We're all busy with life, and it's easy to let every day slip past without writing a word because you didn't have the ideal moment to dedicate to it. Sometimes that means you have to think outside that box.

Author Sean Ferrell[6] (seanferrell.com) wrote several books on his *phone* while riding the New York City subway to and from work every day. His commute was pretty lengthy, and he rarely got a seat and didn't want to carry around a laptop anyway. So he used an app on his smartphone, which he could write on even while standing up in the most crowded subway cars. Between work and his family, he didn't have a ton of unstructured free time, so he *made* time.

If you think you don't have any time in which to write, think again. No matter how busy you are, between today's technology and your own creativity, there's a way. Find it—and be flexible about it.

So, *should* you write every day? Sure, if you can. You should write in every possible moment, because you're going to die one day. The key is to maximize your time in a way that works for you, not a way that's dictated by other writers, even if they're super-successful. All those "Secrets of Successful Authors" articles on the internet are fine to gather ideas, but you can't just replicate someone else's process. You have to find one that works for *you*—or, better, an arsenal of processes that you can adapt to any situation.

MY NON-PROCESS

Friday, 5:30 P.M. On a rapidly sinking boat. Implement: Phone speech recognition. Number of hours I can tread water before passing out: 1.

---

6 Ferrell wrote *Numb* (2010) and *Man in the Empty Suit* (2013), the latter of which remains one of the greatest ideas for a novel I've ever encountered. If I ever acquire a time machine, forget killing Hitler, I'm going back to steal that idea.

For me, my writing is haphazard and opportunistic. It stems from my years in college and at an office job.

I attended a huge state university, which means most of my classes were held in ginormous lecture halls with a minimum of several dozen—sometimes as many as several hundred—other students. If you imagine I was a good student, you could not be more wrong.[7] My class attendance was spotty and linked directly to whether or not my professors took attendance, and I frequently forgot all about classes I had signed up for, leading to panicked trips to the registrar's office in order to drop classes just before the deadline for doing so struck.

I was also housed on a campus far away from the buildings where my classes were held, so I wound up taking the bus a lot. And between the bus rides and the huge, anonymous classes and my own lack of interest in things, like taking notes or relying on anything other than my immense brain and creative spirit to pass tests, I started writing all the time. I wrote on the bus. I wrote in class. I wrote in my dorm room. Basically, I wrote constantly.

When I (somehow) graduated and (somehow) got a job,[8] I carried over this attitude. I wrote on the bus into work every day, I wrote at my desk, I wrote in conference rooms during meetings if I thought I could get away with it.

Saturday, 8:31 A.M. At my desk. Implement: Desktop. Number of cats sitting on me: 1. Number of times The Duchess has asked me where I've been these last few days: 46.

---

7 You also obviously opened this book to a random page and began reading, because I've already made my lack of academic gumption pretty clear.

8 Here's your lesson in the price of incompetence: After graduating college and spending a year trying to live a minimum-wage life, I cut my hair and went looking for a better job. I thought publishing was a good choice because it was adjacent to *being* published. I thought, *I'll make connections! I'll network! I'll go to lunch with Stephen King and some literary agent will meet me and think I'm adorable and brilliant and pull a slightly damp contract out of their coat pocket and demand I sign it!* I applied my usual levels of observation and brains to this, which is to say I indiscriminately applied to every job on offer and wound up taking $17,000 a year to be an editorial assistant with a medical/science publisher. Needless to say this did nothing for my literary career, though someone did take me to lunch, once.

WRITING WITHOUT RULES

UNCONVENTIONAL TIP

If you have to work for a living, friends, and you have the space to be picky about your career to a certain extent, look for a job that involves a lot of word processing. This way you can write at your desk without fear of anyone wondering why you're always typing words. That may sound silly, but I made that work for me for eighteen years. Entire novels were half-written at work while I was supposed to, you know, be doing my job.

And thus, a non-process was born. I don't have a schedule. I don't have daily goals, or weekly goals, or, you know, *goals*. Sure, if I'm under contract I hit my dates, and if there's a word count in the contract (there usually is, because writers are a slippery bunch and none of us are above handing in 30,000 words and insisting it's a novel and that we're owed the second part of our advance), but I don't write with any sort of coherent, preplanned schedule or set of goals.

What's more, if I don't feel like writing one day, or simply don't have time, I just ... don't. I know that to a certain subset of Internet Writing Gurus this is a terrible, terrible sin, since we *must* write every day or our brains atrophy and our future dims (this somehow involves an equation that takes the number of words you've written that day and computes all of your future writing success), but I adhere to a simple rule: *If it feels like work to write it, it will feel like work to read it.*

Of course, somehow I *do* manage to write pretty much every day, mainly because I enjoy writing and it's my go-to activity when I'm bored.[9] And the reason I rarely go a day without getting some good

---

9 All right, I'll confess: I do have what could be construed as one process-oriented habit: I write a short story every month. I've been doing it for nearly three decades now. I write them longhand, with a pen, in a standard college-ruled notebook. The reason I don't consider this a "process" is that the stories aren't necessarily written for publication—it's an exercise. I like to force myself to come up with story ideas, then force myself to flesh out those ideas into working stories in order to keep my brain moving, as well as record ideas instead of letting them drift away, lost. I can always revise and expand the stories that actually turn out promising, but not many do. Writing a story in thirty days might not seem difficult considering people who participate in NaNoWriMo write entire novels in thirty days, but most of the stories written in this way are mere sketches. Whether or not this should be considered part of my writing process is, I think, debatable; it doesn't apply to novels I'm trying to write, or freelance work, and if any of the stories themselves seem viable, I have to revise them more or less completely. If we're keeping count

work done is the flexibility of my non-process: I write wherever it's convenient, whenever I have some inspiration to work with.

I think *avoiding* process should be your overall goal. Process may put words on the page in an efficiently robotic manner, but too much of that is the enemy of great writing. The trick to making a non-process work for you is to look unto your inner Boy Scout and Be Prepared.[10]

Saturday, 12:05 P.M. At dining room table. Implement: Notebook. Number of cats engaged in ninja plots to steal my lunch: 5.

IMPLEMENTS ARE YOUR FRIENDS

The key to a non-process is the ability to write anywhere, any time. Obviously your mileage will vary here; some people *need* a quiet place, or a certain routine, or specific implements in order to write.

For me—and, I suspect, a lot of other people—writing can be a more gloriously messy and unplanned activity. Without a fixed process, I manage to work every day and write a lot of material—material I'm very happy with, as a rule—by making sure I'm able to work under any conditions. Here are my tools of the trade:

- **DESKTOP COMPUTER.** I do a lot of freelance writing as my Day Job these days, so I'm sitting at a desk tapping a keyboard more or less all day. I also work on my fiction from my desk, so I have a big desktop computer to work on when I'm home. **Advantage:** My stocks of liquor are right downstairs, and there's no law against drunken writing, yet.

---

at home, I've handwritten nearly four hundred stories in these notebooks, and sold thirty-four of them. Writing is a terrible, terrible thing for your ego.

10 I actually was a Boy Scout—an Eagle Scout, no less. Most people I encounter do not believe this, partially because I am clearly a drunken, irreligious lout and partly because I can't tie a square knot to save my life and have only the vaguest recollection of the deep secrets of scouting, like the oath and what I had to do to earn my Citizenship in the Community merit badge (you don't want to know). I've had to post my Eagle credentials online a few times to counter people who loudly declare me to be a liar, because apparently Eagle Scouts can't be, well, me. I've considered writing a hilarious novel about my time in the Scouts along the lines of *M*A*S*H*, but I'm pretty sure no one would believe my stories.

WRITING WITHOUT RULES

- **LAPTOP COMPUTER.** When I travel, I bring along my Chromebook. It's lightweight, the battery lasts forever, and between a thumb drive and the Cloud, my files are always available to me. I can work in the car, on the plane or train, and in any airport lounge, hotel room, or in-law's spare bedroom.[11]

Saturday, 6:09 P.M. In living room. Implement: Laptop. Number of whiskeys consumed: 6.

- **PAPER NOTEBOOKS.** The downside to a computer, of course, is that it requires electricity and, increasingly, a network connection to truly work. Plus, even the most lightweight of laptops can be awkward if you're not seated at a surface of some sort. For those reasons, I also bring an old-school college-ruled notebook and some pens wherever I go. They're lightweight, operate under just about any conditions except perhaps underwater, and carrying one means you'll be able to work whenever the mood strikes you.[12]

Monday, 1:34 P.M. Sitting at Desk. Implement: Desktop. Number of cats sitting on me: 4 (one on head, oddly assuaging my headache). Amount of Lost Time Suffered: 13 hours.

- **SMARTPHONE.** Smartphones are amazing things. Did you know you can download word processing apps for your phone? You can! Not only that, you can actually use some pretty incredible voice recognition software so you don't have to type on those tiny, shifting software keyboards. I'm not in love with dictating a story or novel, but sometimes it's the easiest way to work when life throws you into an inconvenient situation—or if everything else has a dead battery, or if you've dropped your notebook into the bathtub. Again.

---

11 I do a fair amount of freelance writing, including memorials and obituaries when famous writers pass away. Several times now I've gotten emergency emails asking if I can quickly write an article about a writer who has died, so having a laptop is an economic necessity. It also allows me to suddenly sit up straight and shout, "Everyone be quiet! A writer just died!" as I whip open my laptop and start typing feverishly.

12 Because I am a strange, strange man, I will only write short stories in my notebooks using a specific brand of cheap blue pen. The Duchess once bought me an expensive fancy pen because I'm a writer, and the fact that I refused to use it almost caused a divorce.

Now, it's not exactly groundbreaking advice to say "carry a laptop around so you can write!" The key here is not the hardware you carry around, but rather making it possible for you to write three lines whenever you have fifteen minutes to yourself, or three thousand words when you're trapped on the tarmac when your plane is delayed for four hours.

UNCONVENTIONAL TIP

In the age of cloud storage, create a Writing Go Bag: Put all of your implements in a bag so you always have what you'll need to be able to write no matter where life takes you, or under what conditions.[13] There's nothing worse than having a brilliant idea for how to resolve a plot problem and have nothing on hand to write with.

Wednesday, 4:56 P.M. Fleeing the wrath of The Duchess in back of pickup truck heading South on N.J. Turnpike. Implement: Phone speech recognition.

MECHANICS

Okay, that covers the physical aspects of process—when, where, how—but what about the creative aspects? What's the right process for actually *creating* a novel?

As you might guess, I don't think there is one. Reflecting my approach to the other aspects of writing a novel, I've done it all. I've outlined. I've gone full-throttle pantsing.[14] I wrote a book in three months, and I've spent fifteen years working on a novel off and on. I've quit working on books for years and come back to them, and I've written them straight through. I've written novels on a mixture of notebooks, screens, and imaginary slips of paper that drop, noiselessly, into wormholes, never to be seen again. I've started short stories meant to be a few

---

13 Except, as noted, underwater. It's just impossible to write underwater.

14 If these terms aren't familiar, we'll discuss them in chapter four. If they're still not familiar after chapter four, remember that there are no refunds.

thousand words and emerged, frail and stunned, six months later with a full novel. I've written two short, terrible novels and later combined them into one brilliant novel.

What it boils down to is that every novel is its own beast, and I develop a process for it on the fly, or, more often, several processes that mutate and shift according to a long list of factors, both knowable and unknowable.[15] I've likely written a novel using whatever process you might suggest, and if there are a few processes I haven't tried, please email them to me and I will try them immediately on the two novels I'm writing when I Alt-Tab away from this screen.

Thursday, 1:49 P.M. Sitting at The Ugly Mug, Cape May, NJ. Implement: Notebook. Number of whiskeys consumed: 0, because I "look like a vagrant."

MY NON-PROCESS IN ACTION

The key to the non-process, once you're prepared to write all the time, is to *not try to write all the time.* So, how does that work—how do you get to be extremely productive if you don't have a strict process?

It's simple, really: Any given moment could be a writing moment. I write in short bursts all day long. Sitting here at my desk, I'll work on freelance assignments for a bit, then suddenly click over to a novel and write for ten minutes there, then switch back. Lunch might be spent writing in my notebook, working on that monthly short story, or getting back to my current WIP.[16]

I'll go for a walk, and if ideas strike me I'll jot them down or whisper them into my phone. Or not. Sometimes I don't write a word, or even think about my WIP.[17] And since I don't track word counts or any other stats unless I'm being paid to do so, taking a break—even a lengthy

---

15 The knowable ones include sobriety level, how confused I am by my own plot at that point in time, how hungry I am, and whether or not a song is playing within earshot that I must dance to. And if you now have the image of a paunchy middle-aged white guy dancing in your head, I just earned my advance.

16 Or napping. Don't judge me. Or, if you must judge, do so quietly.

17 There is something glorious about purposefully not working on something. The glory increases to blinding levels when you're being paid to work on it. Take that, corporate masters!

break—from actively working on a writing project doesn't bother me much. I jump back in when I feel like it.

This approach may not be possible; your schedule or time commitments may force you into a schedule not of your choosing. I get that. It's important to understand that the ideas and advice in this book are not meant as commandments hurled down from the mountain. The idea is that there *is* no Right Way. If you can pick and choose when you work on your writing, don't force yourself into a rigid process just because someone tells you that you must. On the other hand, if you *like* rigid schedules, don't let me talk you out of it. And if you have little control over when you can sit and work, don't waste any time feeling like you're doing it wrong—because there *is* no wrong here.

Saturday, 3:45 P.M. In back seat of my car, The Duchess driving me home after apprehension. Implement: Notebook.

THE TOO LONG, DIDN'T READ takeaway here is simple: Process, both in terms of creativity and the physical act of writing, is way overvalued. Not only is there no "one" unified process that serves all writers equally, there isn't a unified process that serves all *novels* equally. People who want to tell you what your process should be are likely selling something (probably, you guessed it, a process) or assuming that because they enjoyed success writing a novel in a certain way, everyone can enjoy similar success following similar rules. That logical fallacy alone has caused more terror and sadness and terrible, terrible novels than any other force in the universe, including fan fiction. Finding your own process—or non-process—is an organic evolution that will happen naturally, and there's literally no wrong way to do it.

3

FANTASTIC IDEAS AND WHERE TO FIND THEM

When I give my presentation "Take Off Your Pants and Write!" at the Writer's Digest Annual Conference in New York,[1] I usually quote George R.R. Martin at some point: "Ideas are cheap," he once said. "I have more ideas now than I could ever write up. To my mind, it's the execution that is all-important."[2] My presentation is all about plotting a novel, so the quote is a great way to kick off the discussion, but every time I use it a few people in the audience frown. They're thinking that ideas are certainly *not* cheap, that they haven't had a good idea for a book in ages, that the ideas they do come up with have already been done, and how dare I imply thinking up novel ideas is easy? And, yes, they would like their money back, thank you.

---

[1] When people meet me in person for the first time, they almost always ask me the same three questions: *Are you really wearing pants? Where is The Duchess? We'd rather meet her. Do you know where the bathrooms are?*

[2] From The Rolling Stone Interview, 2014 (www.rollingstone.com/tv/news/george-r-r-martin-the-rolling-stone-interview-20140423)

The question "where do you get your ideas?" is one every writer is familiar with, and plenty of writers do struggle with inspiration quite a bit. Sometimes all the worry over where to write, what to write with, and how to find time to write leads you to staring at a blank page or screen with the dawning realization that you have absolutely no idea what your book should be about.

The flip side of this is just as horrifying: Having an idea, getting very excited about it, and then literally feeling that idea die as you work on it—every line strangling it, every new page burying it—until the whole novel just collapses and you're left wondering how you went from the best idea ever to a steaming pile of words.

It can seem almost magical the way other writers seem to effortlessly come up with idea after idea, all of them brilliant, all of them filled with great twists and meaty ideas—all of them *complete*. Staring at that blank page and then glancing at the best-seller lists can make coming up with ideas for a book seem like the most difficult thing in the world.

It's not. It's easy. I know it's easy because I do it all the time, and believe me, the list of things I am *incapable* of doing is very, very long.

The problem many writers have when it comes to ideas is they think it's more complicated than it is, because, let's face it, writing often seems like a superpower. Anytime I hear a writer discussing their inspiration for a story, I always imagine a lot of SCENE MISSING frames interrupting the story, because a lot of writing a book is pretty unknowable.

From what I can tell, though, the biggest obstruction most aspiring novelists have when it comes to ideas is that they are somehow under the impression that their idea for a novel has to be *original*. Let me put it plainly: It doesn't. In fact, it probably shouldn't be.

NOTHING NEW UNDER THE SUN

Literary scientists—which is a thing I assume exists—are not in agreement concerning how many plots there actually are. In Christopher Booker's seminal book *The Seven Basic Plots*, he argues there are, you guessed it, seven fundamental stories that can be told: Overcoming the Monster, Rags to Riches, The Quest, Voyage and Return, Comedy, Tragedy, and Rebirth.[3] An academic study in 2016[4] fed more than 1,700 stories into computers for analysis and concluded there were only six. And in 1959 William Foster-Harris declared there were just *three* basic plots in *The Basic Patterns of Plot*. About the only thing anyone seems able to agree on regarding plots is that there is some limited number of them.

In fact, everything's been done before, if you break a story down to the bare metal. A novel like Gillian Flynn's *Gone Girl* seems pretty in-

---

3 How crazy is Booker? Well, his system leads him to declare that *Terminator 2* is a more successful story than anything written by Kafka or James Joyce. So, you know, pretty crazy.

4 Read it here and try to stay awake: https://arxiv.org/pdf/1606.07772v2.pdf

novative until you start describing it as simply as possible: The unreliable narrator, a woman scorned, a faked death or disappearance, the false diary—none of these things are *new*. It isn't the idea that makes *Gone Girl* a great book, it's the *execution*: the specific way Flynn combined these elements, and the style in which she wrote.[5]

In fact, you can take any book and describe it in such basic terms that it loses all sizzle—this of course makes you realize that the *sizzle* is the important part.[6] You can take any work of fiction and reduce it to a story you've heard before. *Romeo and Juliet* is about two teenagers from rival families who fall in love but are forbidden to date. *The Great Gatsby* is about a war veteran who amasses a vast criminal fortune in an effort to impress a girl. *Ulysses* is about a guy walking around Dublin in June. If none of those ideas seem particularly original or mindblowing, it's because they aren't, even if the final product is.

And that strange alchemy is the unknowable part, of course. You can take any standard story—bank robbers planning a heist, man and mistress plotting wife's murder, lowly kitchen boy is secretly the scion of a powerful wizard—and work it into something incredible, something *original*. It's not the *idea*—as our friend George R.R. Martin[7] said earlier, ideas are cheap—it's the execution of the idea. Which makes banging your head against the wall in an effort to come up with an idea that seems original a fool's errand. Forget about original. Just grab an idea that you find interesting, and *work* on it in an original way.

---

5 If I have just spoiled *Gone Girl* in some way for you, I apologize—and welcome you to the future. I hope your lengthy coma was restful.

6 A few years ago there was a game on the internet challenging people to describe books badly—accurately, but badly. One of my favorites was about the Harry Potter books: "Noseless man has an unhealthy obsession with a teenage boy." If you think about it, it's not wrong.

7 Not really our friend, as we've never met the man. I don't even think I've been in the same room as George R.R. Martin. Most famous writer I've met? Lee Child. He never remembers having met me, but is always super classy and gracious. He was filmed by CBS News while at Bourchercon in 2010, and if you ever watch that footage you'll get to see The Duchess herself, fangirling all over him (watch here, cued up at 1:50: https://youtu.be/ZUVHZcQgTxY?t=1m50s).

WRITING WITHOUT RULES

IDEAS ARE EVERYWHERE

Easier said than done, you might say. Even if you embrace the fact that your idea for a book doesn't need to be particularly original, you might find yourself unable to come up with an idea that you can write 80,000 words about. Which is ridiculous, because I am here to tell you that you can write 80,000 words about anything. Good words? Words people will want to pay good money to read? Well, *that's* the real trick, isn't it? But ideas? Easy. Here are the ways I've generated ideas for my own novels, both published and unpublished.

STEAL LITTLE, STEAL BIG

Writers don't *really* steal ideas. At least once a month I'm contacted by yet another young writer who wants to know how I protect my precious ideas from thieves, imagining a world where black hat authors hang around local bars eavesdropping on my workshop conversations, then rush home to gleefully type up a version of my novel and get it published before I can. Believe me, if the literary world worked like that, it would be loads more exciting.[8]

Since we've established, via my foolproof method of simply saying things and then walking away, that no idea is wholly original these days, no one can really steal your idea. Even if they write a similar story—you must trust me on this—similar stories are being written right now by *sheer coincidence*. There's no need to worry about rogue authors stealing your books.

However, all authors "steal" in the sense of building on the work of others. And one of my favorite techniques for generating story ideas is to contemplate the "Road Less Traveled" in other stories.[9] It's simple; in just about any story you read, watch, or listen to, there will be details that get glossed over, "Noodle Incidents" that are never explained, or fascinating character moments that catch your imagination but are

---

8 If you are now imagining your favorite authors engaging in musical gang warfare like *West Side Story*, battling over stolen plot ideas, then you are my people.

9 I wrote a longer examination of this technique for *Writer's Digest* in their September 2016 issue: www.writersdigestshop.com/writers-digest-september-2016.

not pursued. So, you pursue them. You take a small and overlooked aspect of someone else's story and focus on it, blow it up, and explore it.

What's a Noodle Incident? It's a past event that characters refer to but never explain. In the film *Hot Tub Time Machine*, for example, the characters repeatedly reference something that happened in Cincinnati—but never actually explain what happened. That's a Noodle Incident, and it can be a powerful writing tool, because you let the reader's imagination run away with them, making the Noodle Incident infinitely cooler and more interesting than anything you might have actually come up with.[10]

That's how I wrote what became my second published novel, *The Electric Church*. I read a book by Douglas Adams in college called *Dirk Gently's Holistic Detective Agency*. Adams was a writer who crammed a nonstop barrage of ideas into his books, and one of the ideas in this one was The Electric Monk, which was an appliance invented to believe things for you. A brilliant idea! And while The Electric Monk did factor into the plot in subtle and complex ways, it was also never fully explored or explained, and so I started thinking about it. And I ran it through my own brain, and I began work on a dystopian science fiction novel. What emerged were the Monks of the Electric Church, a religion that believed a normal human lifespan wasn't enough to achieve salvation— you needed eternity, immortality. This was achieved by transplanting your brain into a cyborg body so you could live forever as a Monk and contemplate your sins.

A bit darker, sure, but it's an idea I got by flipping over Douglas Adams's couch cushions and searching for his discarded ideas.

CHANGE THE CONVERSATION

Another approach to coming up with ideas for a book is to take some shopworn premise—a story that's been told endlessly, over and over— and apply a Crazy Ivan to it. "Crazy Ivan" comes from Tom Clancy's *The Hunt for Red October* and describes a tactic used by Russian sub-

---

10 Did I just reference *Hot Tub Time Machine* in the context of writing craft advice? I did. And I have only minimal regrets.

WRITING WITHOUT RULES

marine captains in which they suddenly, unexpectedly stop dead and turn the sub at a right angle to see what's sneaking up behind them.

Apply that to a story—figure out where the story's going, and then do something different. Think about *Gone Girl* again. It starts off as a story about a man who comes home to find his wife apparently abducted, alternating with his wife's increasingly depressed diary entries. Everyone who read the book thought they knew where it was all headed—and then came the big twist, at which point Flynn orders a Crazy Ivan and her novel almost breaks in two as it throws the engines into reverse. It's brilliant.

It's also something *you* can do. Every story has an *obvious* ending, a well-worn rut that other writers have cut into the pages through repeated use. All you need to do is figure out what that rut is and climb out of it, strike off in an unexpected direction. It won't always work; sometimes you'll just get lost in your own writing, and sometimes the Crazy Ivan will be a little *too* crazy. But you'll have something unique, that's for sure.

THE EXTRAPOLATION

Your own life can be a rich source of ideas, of course. Not in the sense that far too many people think—not simply transcribing your existence into a narrative and squinting until it looks like compelling fiction. Rather, you can observe your own life and simply wonder how it might be different. What might happen at your job that would change your life forever? What might happen tonight, while you're watching TV? How would you react?

The power of this technique should be obvious: There's no research required, because you've lived all the backstory. And you can use your own reactions to fuel your story, just by imagining that your protagonist behaves more or less exactly as you would.[11] In fact, you can keep applying the latter technique every time you get stuck in your plotting—just ask yourself what would you do.

---

11 Of course, if you're being honest with yourself, you'll come to the same conclusion I do when I wonder what would happen if I got into a *Die Hard* situation: Die, quickly, painfully, and very likely nearly immediately. Pro tip: Don't write those books.

I used this one when I wrote my first published novel, *Lifers*,[12] which is about a bunch of unhappy twentysomethings who decide to rob their place of employment. I was an unhappy twentysomething when I wrote the novel, and imagining a heist at my job took only the minimal amount of revision to my standard fantasy of burning the place down. Once I'd established the premise, deciding how my characters might react required little more than imagining myself in the situation. Yes, including the sex scene my publisher asked that I add to the book prior to buying it.[13]

THE ELEVATOR PITCH APPROACH

Another technique I've used to gin up inspiration for novels is to imagine the One Big Difference, something that can be explained in a pithy elevator pitch. An elevator pitch is the super-succinct summary of your idea's compelling point, short enough to spit out in the duration of an elevator ride. The idea is that you should always be ready to pitch your idea in under a minute if you have a sudden opportunity, and so you have to reduce your story concept to the bare minimum that sells the premise.

Now, I don't wander around muttering elevator pitches all day—I have much more important things to mutter.[14] But I do use the concept in a nonobvious way: I imagine a fictional universe or setting, then try to come up with something "different" about it that can be expressed in an elevator pitch. A simple example would be the imagined elevator pitch for Franz Kafka's *The Metamorphosis*: The world is exactly like ours, except one man wakes up having been transformed into a giant cockroach overnight. It takes less than ten seconds to say, and yet even if it weren't already famous you would buy that book on sight.

---

12 I have thousands of copies of *Lifers* at home. When I'm bored I like to pull out the boxes and build elaborate forts with them.

13 See chapter thirteen in this book for the full story about *Lifers* and the infamous sex scene.

14 Like threats against other authors, declarations of sovereign citizenship, schemes to make the Michigan Bottle Return scheme from *Seinfeld* work, nonsense songs sung to the tune of Joey Purp's "Girls @," erotic Christmas carols, and the word "*Pontypool*."

That kind of elegant, powerful, high-concept premise is pretty easy and fun to spin up, but out of every hundred elevator pitch-style premises, about one *might* be truly viable over the course of 80,000 words. Still, it's a great exercise to play with, and when it *does* inspire a novel, it's a great moment. I used this when working on my novel *We Are Not Good People*. The elevator pitch was something like this: The main characters are low-level con men who have been initiated into the domain of blood magic, which has been kept secret throughout man's history—and now they have to save the world.

UNCONVENTIONAL TIP

Not only are there more techniques for generating ideas for books than the ones I've listed here (an infinite number), but you're not restricted to using just one. Use one to get started, then switch over to another when you're stuck. Maybe you started off imagining an epic fantasy that pivots on the elderly, senile old king *not* dying and *not* causing a succession crisis, but then you get a little stuck—why not try a little extrapolation and ask yourself what *you* would do if you were that old king?

FRANKENSTEINING

There's a very simple solution to a lack of ideas in the present: Go back to the glorious failures of your past. This can work in two ways: One, obviously, if you have an old idea that you were never able to successfully turn into a finished novel (or a *good* finished novel), then simply return to it. Just because you've tried a dozen times to write that novel based on your experiences as an interpretive jazz dancer doesn't mean the idea is dead—maybe it just needs one more try. In other words, sometimes the best idea is an old idea walked through a warm room. After all, I tried several versions of *The Electric Church* between the immature first draft written in 1993 and the draft that sold to a publisher in 2005; I walked that book through a warm room so many times it had sweat stains.

Finally, there's a scenario that isn't as common as the other two but can yield incredible results. All it requires is not *one* failed novel to go back to when you're struggling but *two* failed novels. Two failed novels that share something[15] that can be Frankensteined together.

It's no secret that many writers have certain themes they return to over and over again, certain tone poems they employ repeatedly. Whether you realize it or not you've probably written books or stories from the same inspiration several times, albeit with different characters, plots, and sensibilities. We all do this, and it's easy to find such patterns in the works of published writers.

Look at John Updike. A wonderful writer, a master of language, and a man who wrote endlessly about sex, religion, and Rabbit Angstrom. To say that everything Updike wrote shared common themes is an understatement; in some ways everything by Updike from "A&P" to *Terrorist* is about religion and sex. That's not a criticism—you have to write about *something*, and if you do it as well as Updike, who's complaining?—it's just an observation. In my non-science fiction and fantasy work (and in my science fiction and fantasy work, just less noticeably) I have a tendency to write about men and their fathers, death and funerals, and potential insanity.

Not every writer has a huge inventory of failed and half-finished novels to fall back on, of course; for one thing, if your whole problem, as we've been discussing, is a lack of viable ideas (or lack of faith in those ideas), then you likely don't have a bunch of broken manuscripts to work with. But if you do have a number of old failed novels, go through them and see if there are two that explore the same thematic territory, the same premise or plot devices. If so, why not combine them? Take what's working in each and meld them together into a wholly new novel.

It might sound a little crazy, but I've actually done this. Years ago I wrote a novella about a man who'd died but was still hanging around as a ghost—haunting his own life. He doesn't remember everything, and slowly comes to realize he'd been murdered. The story had a through-line,

---

15 Aside from, you know, failure.

a skeleton of a plot, but not a lot of meat on the bones.[16] A few years later, I wrote a story about a man going home for his mother's funeral and dealing with the emotional baggage of a horrific childhood event—and literally being haunted. It was finished, but it lacked a plot, a purpose, and was more of a character study.

UNCONVENTIONAL TIP

Some writers believe you can't have a dead narrator, because it violates some rule of good writing. This is, to use a scientific term, bosh. You can try anything you like in your novel—the only question is whether you can pull it off with your writing. You can safely ignore anything else these people tell you.

And one day, uncertain what to work on next, I reread those two works and realized they shared a tone, a setting, and a supernatural element. A light bulb went off.

Combining the two wasn't all that difficult. Characters were blended,[17] tweaks were made, and a thorough revision implemented. And when I was finished, it was a damn good story—a story I'd been telling for years in different ways, without realizing it was all the *same* story. My agent agreed and while we haven't sold it yet, we will. Because it's a good book I Frankensteined out of two failed books.

Now, there's some luck involved with Frankensteining. Even if you do return to the same themes, tropes, and character types repeatedly, you can't take, say, two Beautiful Failures and mash them together—they're too *finished*, too close to being complete. Frankensteining is a strategy that requires two rough and unfinished stories that have complementary flaws—you're not going to find that very often. But the po-

---

16 It also has a character named Candace, which has become a joke between my agent and me: I seem to always have a character named Candace. Why this is remains a mystery; I've never known a Candace in my life. This is problematic also because my wife is convinced that every female character in my novels—including zombies, space aliens, and female unicorns—are modeled on ex-girlfriends.

17 For no reason at all I offer this advice: Never get really inebriated and then think you can just search-and-replace your way through combining two novels into one.

tential it offers means it's worth your time to look back through failed efforts to see if you have two—or more—that might be combined in the laboratory to produce a new form of life.

JUST DO IT

In the end, waiting for the perfect idea to hit you is a fool's game. Novels—stories—are journeys. Sometimes the most important part isn't where you begin, but where you end up. Great stories can be told using some seriously shopworn materials, so if you find yourself paralyzed because the "perfect" idea or the "original" idea hasn't come to you, forget about perfect and original and *just tell a story.*

Of course, something else people often don't tell you is the percentage of *completed* novels that will be utter crap. It's close to 100 percent. Not *exactly* 100 percent, which is what gives us all hope, but pretty close. You're going to get a lot of enthusiastic support and encouragement when you tell people your mad plan to write a novel, and that's a good thing. But never forget: 99.9 percent of your attempts to write anything will end in failure and drunkenness. You have to finish novels, or you'll never have a novel to sell. But most of the ones you finish will stink. Which is helpful (in a perspective sort of way) to keep in mind when you're struggling over a failed novel: Sure, the book you're fighting to finish isn't very good, but then, so few of them *are.*

4

PLOTTING, PANTSING, PLANTSING, AND GOING HAM ON ENDING IT ALL

I used to think that the old cliché of people telling you their ideas for books and then suggesting a fifty-fifty split of the "profits" if you write it up for them was just that—an old cliché, something that couldn't possibly actually happen.

Then I became a moderately well-known author.

I'm certainly no household name, but word gets around that instead of the chronically unemployed indigent your old friends and extended family expected you to become, you're actually making money as a writer. Cousins and old school pals do a double take in the local Barnes & Noble when they see your name on the spine of a book. Old co-workers email you Amazon links with the subject line "Is this really you?" I try very hard not to be hurt by the obvious disbelief. I mean, I'm no genius or anything but I *am* the guy most of these people cheated off in English class. That should count for something.[1]

---

1 SPOILER ALERT: It does not.

People who don't write for a living also have a very outsize, Hollywoodish concept of what your lifestyle is. Put plainly: A lot of people assume that if you've published a book, you received something like eleventy billion dollars for it and now have a standing lunch appointment with Leonardo DiCaprio.[2] They also think that since you (or your agent) were able to sell one novel, now you can basically write anything you want.[3] And so they totally, absolutely, 100 percent *do* suggest their great idea for a novel, which they believe is worth 50 percent of any money you get for it because they are terrible people and have no idea how much work goes into actually *writing* a book—as in, researching, typing, revising, and *plotting* a novel.

Now, I just spent a whole chapter discussing how you can come up with ideas for books, so if I'm about to suggest that those ideas are worth, at best, less than 1 percent of the profits[4] from any book, it's going to be awkward. But, you know, life is hard. And awkward. And while having an idea for a book is an essential part of the process,[5] it's also the *least valuable* part of a book once you start writing. The premise that any idea, no matter how clever, is worth half a book's value is ridiculous and will get you nothing but sneering contempt from working writers—unless you're buying drinks, in which case we will nod and shine you on for hours. But I digress. Again.

Plot is what makes a book a book and not, you know, a collection of semirandom words. And *plot*, unlike ideas, is hard. If you've ever sat around with some friends spit balling and brainstorming ideas, you know how easy it can be to rattle off a dozen concepts in a half hour. That's because concepts and ideas don't require any architecture or sup-

---

2 Or, failing that, at the very least, Tobey Maguire.

3 Imagined scenarios go something like this: **Jeff to his Agent:** My next book will be about a pair of Converse Chuck Taylors hanging over a power line in Jersey City who dream of being on the ground again. It's about racism and how that's bad. **Agent to Jeff:** That's gonna be a tough sell. I can only offer you a hundred billion-billion dollars for it. **Jeff to His Agent:** I also have this spy novel I thought of in the bathroom this morning. **Agent to Jeff:** I'll buy both for infinite monies.

4 You get that I'm using the term *profits* here ironically, right? Because I think I actually owe money on my last few novels.

5 Unless you're Karl Ove Knausgaard, in which case you just start writing about what you had for breakfast and keep writing down everything that happens to you until you collapse, and that's a book.

　　　　　　　　　　　WRITING WITHOUT RULES

port. They exist as flimsy things that float and flutter, divorced from any need to earn their existence.

> **UNCONVENTIONAL TIP**
>
> When you have a great idea for a story, don't just write down a word or two, certain you will remember it later—do something with it. Expand it; sketch it into a rough story. Write a summary, outline a possible plot. Flipping through a notebook or scanning an app on your smartphone with dozens of mysterious phrases and obscure references to ideas you had six months ago will be more or less useless. A notebook or document on your computer that actually contains a *developed* concept that can be refined and expanded is pure gold.

Like pure ideas, many of the aspects of book writing come to people naturally—world-building, individual scenes, the initial concept—often in flashes of exciting inspiration.[6] In contrast, figuring out how to make all of those things fit together into something satisfying and meaningful is where the work comes in.

Is there a secret to plotting a novel? There is.[7] Contrary to what a lot of young writers believe, however, the secret isn't a specific approach or technique. There is no "one way" of doing it that you can memorize and practice like dance steps. The secret lies in knowing your Writer DNA—whether you are, at heart, a Plotter or a Pantser—and training yourself to recognize when each approach is your best way forward in a story.

PLOTTING AND PANTSING

We all have skills as writers. Just as a professional athlete has strengths and weaknesses, every writer has certain aspects of the craft they're

---

6 A good way to know your novel will never work is to ask yourself a simple question: Have you spent hundreds of hours imagining the legal system of your fantasy world, the technological evolution of your space aliens, or the specific emotional abuse your serial killer endured in the orphanage, but you have no idea what happens in your story? If so, your novel is already doomed.

7 I resist the temptation to demand $1,000 and a nondisclosure agreement form in exchange for the secret only because I am a very good person who also fears jail very much.

naturally good at, and others that require more conscious effort and work. Maybe you're a writer who finds it easy to come up with ideas, but difficult to organize those ideas into coherent 80,000-word narratives. Or you spin up amazing opening scenes—the sort of first chapters that make people desperate to keep reading—but then lose all your excitement and never write chapter two. Or you're great at dialogue but awful at character development. Whatever it is, we all have certain skills that come more naturally then others.

This applies to how we plot, as well. We all have a natural inclination to be either a Plotter or a Pantser. If you're not familiar with one or both of those terms, hold onto your butts, because we're going on a magical 300-word ride.[8]

LET'S PLANTS

Plot is, in its simplest form, a series of events that your characters experience. You can come up with plot in a lot of different ways, but when you boil plot down to the basics, you're left with two approaches:

Pantsing means you write "by the seat of your pants." You start off with some characters or an image and you sort of make it up as you go along. Every time you plot yourself into a corner, you cast about for inspiration and work your way out of it.

Plotting means you map out your plot before you start writing. This might mean an old-fashioned outline, a spreadsheet, six million pieces of paper, or a complicated software package. Whatever you use, you know what's going to happen before you write a single word.

If you've never thought about it before, take a moment, and you'll find you probably slot into one of those categories pretty naturally. For Plotters, the idea of writing a novel without some sort of outline is insanity. For Pantsers, writing with the plot already figured out is like keyboarding someone else's novel. At writers conferences, dance battles frequently break out between the two groups.[9]

---

8 If you are familiar with those terms and are now questioning your relationship to me and to this book I have (somehow) convinced you to buy, let me restate that there are no refunds.

9 That was only 199 words. Which is, of course, the fundamental problem with word counts as writing tools: They cause more problems than they solve. The moment you decide that a project or

WRITING WITHOUT RULES

The terrible secret no one will tell you, of course, is that both approaches work just fine depending on any number of factors. Each one has advantages and disadvantages: Plotters, for example, know the whole story—that's powerful. They can shade in all sorts of details that will increase the impact of their plot twists and character development. But that also means there will be fewer opportunities for sudden brilliancies—and more opportunities to become bored with their own story. Pantsers get the thrill of feeling *creative*; when a Pantser is firing on all cylinders, their plot can seem to erupt out of a gushing font of imagination, and they often amaze themselves with sudden inspiration. On the other hand, brilliancies often turn out to be ... less than brilliant in the cold light of day. Sometimes making it up as you go along results in a hot mess.

UNCONVENTIONAL TIP

Don't worry if you can't explain how you came up with a novel, or if you are sometimes haunted by the sense that you're not really writing these stories but are instead simply a conduit for some supernatural force.[10] Many writers experience the strange sense that they can't really explain how they came up with something, or how they pulled off a specific literary trick.

Remarkably, a lot of writers just accept broken, failed plots as a sort of cost of doing business—an unavoidable fact of life. And yes, anyone who has tried to write more than one novel has more than one *failed*

---

a section within a project must be a certain number of words, you're either made a liar or you have to fill in all those words with empty flourishes that waste everyone's time. In a perfect world, everything written would be exactly how long it was supposed to be in the sense that it would accomplish its artistic or economic goals and then stop. *Now* it's 300 words.

10 I actually can't even remember writing several novels I have lingering on my hard drive and wouldn't be able to tell you what they're about in even the vaguest sense. This surprises no one who has ever spent time with me, as I am a man whose memory is theoretical, at best, and whose relationship with time makes him basically the Frosty the Snowman of the literary world, in the sense that every day I wake up, shout *Happy Birthday!* and have to read through several dozen *Memento*-esque tattoos on my body to even remember my own name. My wife, The Duchess, is not amused. My agent, friends, and fellow writers abuse this fact in order to get me to buy multiple rounds of drinks.

novel on their hard drive, and usually that failure has to do with a plot that just never cohered or had holes in it big enough to fall through into a frightening two-dimensional otherworld. Did I mention that plot is hard?

Broken plots may be common, but they don't have to be. All you need is flexibility. All you need is **plantsing**.

UNCONVENTIONAL TIP

Some writers are natural Plantsers, of course, and have been using this hybrid approach more or less instinctively their whole lives. When it comes to creativity, you don't have to place yourself in a box. Advice like the kind you'll find in this book is useful, especially if you're struggling with your writing, but any so-called expert who tells you how you *must* approach your work is either lying or shilling confirmation bias.

PLANTSING!

When I first gave my presentation "Take Your Pants Off and Write! The Benefits and Pitfalls of Pantsing vs. Plotting a Novel" at the 2014 Writer's Digest Annual Conference, no one in the audience had heard of the term *plantsing*, and I felt like a genius.[11] In recent years, everyone seems to be using the term, which is either because I invented it and failed to trademark it, and thus lost a fortune in licensing, or because I didn't really invent it in the first place.

Plantsing is a hybrid approach to plot that recognizes that plotting and pantsing each have their strengths and viability as approaches, and involves switching from one to the other as needed. The basic approach is to start with your natural inclination—your writing DNA—and work

---

11 If you couldn't attend those conferences to hear (and see!) me in all my paunchy glory, you can buy the audio of the presentation online (www.writersdigestshop.com/take-your-pants-off -and-write-audio-download), or you can read the article I wrote summarizing the presentation for *Writer's Digest* magazine (www.writersdigestshop.com/writers-digest-magazine-may-june -2016-digital-edition). Or you could offer me a fifth of bourbon and some Doritos, and I'll happily come to your house and give the presentation in person. If you're smart, though, you won't give me the bourbon until after I'm finished. That won't stop me from being slightly drunk during the presentation, but it might stop me from passing out in your rec room.

that way for as long as it's successful. When you get into trouble, instead of just pounding away at a process that's stalled, switch to a different process.

UNCONVENTIONAL TIP

The simple concept of sticking to something *as long as it's working* is probably the greatest lesson you can internalize. If you're producing material you like, there's no reason to try exotic approaches and new theories of literary productivity. On the other hand, if you just built a bonfire using all five thousand drafts of your struggling novel, that might be a hint that the time has come to shake up your process.

For example, say you're a Plotter and you've mapped out a shiny, intricate plot that fits together like an elegant puzzle. You set to work, and everything goes swimmingly ... up to a point. Slowly you feel the excitement draining from your story. The plot that seemed perfect in outline form is stiff and nonreactive when put into motion, and you're not excited to keep working on it. A Plantser slaps a "Stop Work" order on the process and backs up to the last moment in their story that felt alive, that felt like it was working. Then they lob a creativity grenade into it— they make something up and pull a literary Crazy Ivan. They put their careful notes aside and just take a left turn off the road they've built for their novel, and see what happens.

Sometimes this works wonders. It injects a jolt of energy into the story and paves a new way. Sometimes it doesn't work so well in terms of getting around blockages,[12] but it provides an interesting diversion for your brain and shows you the wilderness around your story that you didn't know was there, which gets the creativity flowing again. It also

---

12 Does writer's block exist? Yes and no. Are there moments in every writer's life when a way forward isn't obvious, when the will to sit down and type out your thoughts or organize those thoughts just isn't there? Of course there are. Is it as life destroying as movies and some extremely dramatic folks like to make it out to be? Of course not. Getting stalled in a story happens, and there are plenty of strategies for getting the story going again. Most of my solutions involve alcohol, but your mileage may vary. We'll be discussing writer's block in more detail in chapter ten.

gives you a fresh perspective on your plot, making it easier to see the knots and missing bits that are causing all the trouble in the first place.

Then—and this is really the secret—when you feel like you're back on the right path, *go back to plotting*. Then repeat the process as necessary. Writing in your natural mode (plotting vs. pantsing) and switching to a different approach when things get stalled—then switching *back* once you're back on track, that's the key.

If, on the other hand, you're a Pantser like me[13], you start off with some small kernel of inspiration. This can be anything from a visual, a character, a few lines of dialogue, or even a plot fragment—sometimes it's even the climax or a key scene from near the end. You take that kernel and just start writing, surprising yourself as you go.

Of course, that sort of *where-we're-going-we-don't-need-roads* approach can often lead you astray, as I can personally attest. And when the Pantser wakes up one day and realizes they have 345,000 words in their latest novel and no idea what the plot is, they will often despair and just delete the whole thing, certain there's no way to salvage the muddled pile of forgotten secondary characters, unresolved subplots, and that entire chapter apparently written while in the desert trying peyote for the first time.

But a *Plantser* would say, *wait!* Just because you pantsed the heck out of that novel and got lost in your own words doesn't mean you have to just keep pantsing. Instead, apply some liberal plotting to salvage your disaster. Go back to the beginning and reread your unfinished failure, outlining the plot as you go. Reverse engineer your own novel, in other words, and slowly the muddled mess will become clearer and ways forward will present themselves. And, just as with the Plotters who pants for a bit, once you've figured out your problem, follow whatever plan your plotting adventures generated until you once again run out

---

13 I'm a Pantser because Plotting seems suspiciously similar to work. I prefer to get day drunk, saddle up the ol' creativity horse, and go galloping around until I run smack into a tree limb or something. The fact that I "pants" leads to a lot of jokes because I am also famous for not wearing any pants. I am so pants-adverse, someone once set up a Twitter account for my pants, and it remains up to this day (https://twitter.com/JeffsPants). I now regret writing that here as I wonder if that disturbance in the Force I just felt is several thousand people marching back to the store to get a refund on this book.

of road. Then go back to pantsing away without a plan in sight—until the next time you get into trouble.

CHUM AND MY PANTSING SHAME

This switching back and forth between plot techniques isn't mere theory for me. I've done it several times—most notably for my novel *Chum*, which was published in 2013 by Tyrus Books.

I began *Chum* way back in 2001—and it landed me an agent in 2002. It's also the novel I've spent the most time on; after my agent took it on in 2002, she sent me some notes, which I dutifully worked up into a revision. Then in 2005, we sold *The Electric Church* through a series of events discussed elsewhere, and for a long time *Chum* was back-burnered as I worked on five novels in the Avery Cates series for Orbit Books.[14] Over the next eight years, Janet would occasionally send me notes on *Chum*, and I would revise a little here and there, and slowly but surely I lost track of the plot.

UNCONVENTIONAL TIP

There is no such thing as a dead project. Just because a novel has been shopped for a while and revised several times without a sale doesn't mean it won't sell eventually. If you like the book, keep working at it, keep submitting it, and keep workshopping (if that's your thing) and revising it. Yes, your worst-case scenario is that it never gets published—but if you give up on it because some arbitrary number of years or submissions has gone by without success, you're *guaranteeing* it will never be published.

You see, *Chum* jumps around in time and tells the story from multiple points of view, sometimes repeating scenes from someone else's perspective. After years and years of on-again, off-again revision, I'd completely lost the through-line and had no idea if my sequence of events made sense or if there were plot holes (a character knowing something

---

14 I will always remember saying to Janet just after signing the contract for *The Electric Church*, "Don't forget about *Chum*!" I really love that book.

they couldn't possibly have known, for example). I'd pantsed my way through the original story and the revisions, but the time had come for some plotting. So I took my own advice and went back to the beginning, reread the manuscript, and started a chart to outline the plot.

And it worked. I regained control of my narrative, identified the places where everything had slipped, and figured out scenes that could be cut, moved, or enhanced. A decade's worth of pantsing was clarified and tamed, and a tighter, more streamlined novel emerged. All it took was the willingness to switch up my plotting approach when things were clearly not working. Flexibility is the key—not adherence to a specific ritual[15] or process, not doggedly grinding the gears of your creative engine when it's clearly stalled out.

FINISH HIM

Now, once you've solved your plot problems, only one thing remains: Finish the damn book.

That might seem facetious. Of *course* you have to finish the book, right? I mean, that's the point. Except ... I'm willing to bet that you—yes, *you*—have a lot of unfinished novels on your hard drive right now. Books with 10-, 20-, even 30,000 words that have been quietly rotting for a long time.

Because inspiration is one thing, and a plot outline—if you're a plotter—is another. And 20,000 hot words tapped out in a fit of inspiration is yet another. But there are many more steps to actually being able to say you wrote a novel—and the most crucial one of all is to actually finish it. Actually ending a story is the most powerful thing you can do, in fact, and a skill that is well worth developing. And it *is* a skill. Writ-

---

15 Which is actually hilarious because I am the King of Rituals—or, more accurately, the King of Ruts. I like a good behavioral rut. I like to find a way of doing things and just wallow in it, repeating the same actions every day. It drives The Duchess crazy, because I am that crazy character on a TV show who gets upset and depressed if he has to vary his daily routine in any way. For example, I wake up and I have coffee at 8 A.M. every day. Not 7:45, not 8:05, 8 A.M. When The Duchess offers to go get us coffee in the morning, she knows better than to bring it later than 8 A.M. (Weird? Yes, but I am so charming it doesn't matter.) And yet I firmly believe that the secret to writing for money successfully is to be flexible and change up your approach at the slightest hint of a problem.

ers often wax poetic about inspiration, about that flash of exciting brilliance, but all that does is get you started. Writers often want to discuss process, their specific strategies for writing a novel, but process only gets you to the finish line, not over it. If you're not typing THE END, did you really write a book?[16]

You might wonder how many unfinished manuscripts I have littering my hard drive. At the moment, the answer is *three*. And they won't be unfinished for long. Let's not misunderstand each other: These are not necessarily *good* novels that I expect to sell to a publisher someday—in fact, a great many of the books I finish aren't ever going to be published. But they *could* be, because they are almost all in finished, coherent shape—perhaps not brilliant, but as soon as I attain Kanye West levels of famous I'll be able to release about fifty-seven books all at once, because they are all *finished novels.*

All joking aside, being able to end a novel is just as important as the inspiration to begin, or butt-in-chair discipline, or the ability to jump between plotting and pantsing. It's a skill you can work on, and it's a skill that will serve you well, for three very important reasons:

1. 100 percent of the stories that lack an ending fail to get published (or, you know, 99.9 percent, once you consider the occasional oddball like *Ulysses*).
2. Sometimes the only difference between an unsellable manuscript and a contract is an ending.
3. The difference between an unfinished manuscript and a story that just needs revision is an ending.

That last one is the most important, because the difference between some jumble of words you never got around to finishing and a manuscript you can go back to and work on is often whether or not it has an ending. The ending doesn't have to be perfect. It doesn't even have to be particularly good—that can be fixed in revision. It just has to exist.

---

16 Someday, when I am hugely famous, I will host a conference presentation where I bound on stage to a cool rock song, then wait for absolute silence, ask this koan-like question, and proceed to stand there for two hours while the audience contemplates it. Then I will collect everyone's money and go have a drink.

But as anyone who's tried writing a novel knows, the reason we have so many unfinished manuscripts is because endings are hard. A lot of plot problems can be dealt with via a liberal dose of plantsing—and sometimes you can even get past a plot knot by simply throwing caution to the wind and taking the craziest Crazy Ivan you can imagine. Some problems can be papered over with a "Later Note" like *Write death scene later* or *Insert reasons for this massive coincidence later*.[17] But an ending? You can't end your novel with a "Later Note," or, god help me, XXXX. There has to be *something*. And that something transforms your hot mess of words into a hot mess of a *novel*, and that's powerful.

And that makes being able to end your book a crucial skill. It's something you can learn to do just like you learned to stop using *affect* when you meant *effect*, or when you finally realized that your main character should *not* be a slightly taller, richer, and funnier version of yourself. Assuming you have a book that's more or less finished, creating an ending for it—and thus moving it into the Needs Revision category—can be very easy, if you know how. And lucky you, you're reading an entire book about how to write novels. Here are a few simple ways you can generate endings for your stories—whether you're a Pantser who needs to complete a project you've been working on for years or a Plotter whose novel currently exists on six hundred and forty-three index cards.

The Plane Crash. Sometimes you just can't come up with something elegant and subtle. Sometimes your characters just won't learn any lessons, and the bread crumbs of solemn profundity that you've been dropping everywhere, hinting at some sort of life-changing denouement, resist coalescing into anything that makes any sense. Sometimes your house is literally on fire and you need to type THE END and

---

17 I have to search every single document I write for a string of four Xs ("XXXX") because that's what I routinely use as, a) a mark to remind me where I am when re-reading a manuscript, and b) a generic placeholder for things like brilliant dialogue I can't think of at the moment. I have to do this no matter what stage the manuscript is in, because there have been times when I've sent my agent a manuscript I swear is clean, and she sends it back saying I have XXXXs in it. Someday, when I am rich and powerful, I'm going to name a character XXXX just to drive everyone crazy. Also, I just realized that most of these footnotes involve fantasies about what I'll do when I'm rich and famous or revenge plots against imagined enemies. This book is going to be evidence in a murder trial someday, isn't it?

upload your novel to the cloud within the next thirty seconds or you and your book will be char.

In those cases (and that last one happens more often than you might imagine), just take a deep breath and set off a bomb. Kill everyone, tear down the town, invent a serial killer—go 100 percent soap opera on that story. This method is messy, but sometimes it's brilliant, and more often it produces a huge revision looming in the future. But in the meantime, you've got a finished novel, and if it needs a thoroughly new ending, so what? So do a lot of *published* novels.

The Quantum Leap. Sometimes the reason you can't end the book is because you're fighting against the current—just because you plotted out a series of events doesn't mean they will work on the page. If you've been writing chapter forty-five for seventeen months, with four more chapters to go—undoubtedly just as much work—it's time to cut to the chase.

Maybe—just maybe—you're bored? Sometimes a plot you devised seems brilliant and exciting, right up until you have to write that final act that suddenly seems about as interesting as a pile of dirty socks. So, do what you would do if you walked into your living room and found a pile of dirty socks on the floor. Step over or around it—just leap over those boring chapters you don't want to write. A time shift, a perspective shift—heck, even a *Five Thousand Years Later*[18] title card will work. Sure, you might have to go back in revisions and fill in that missing info. You might even have to redo the ending entirely. But in the meantime, you have a finished novel.

18 This is a real thing: In Neal Stephenson's 2016 novel *Seveneves* (it's excellent, you should read it) there is this whole story about the end of the world, and then—and I am not making this up— the chapter heading *Five Thousand Years Later.* You read that and you look around for a hidden camera, because you can't believe he just did that. But he did, and it works.

> words, the more you have to work writing that chapter/section/
> entire godforsaken novel, the less willing people will be to read it.
> In other other words, if writing that chapter feels like you're lifting
> the Parthenon with your bare hands, reconsider. Writing is one of
> the few labors where more effort does *not* always equal better work.

Lord Kincaid's Farewell Address.[19] Maybe your novel has a point. Personally, I deprecate having a point in general, and especially in novels—but to each their own. If you're making a point with your fiction, chances are you've designed your plot accordingly, or you're pantsing with a purpose. Either way, if you just can't seem to pull together the energy or the organized thinking to make it across the finish line of your book, why not simply get to the point? Think of crazy, old Ayn Rand and *Atlas Shrugged* and just have one of your characters step away from the set and address the reader directly. Have them simply outline the point, make the argument, and then walk away from the camera. It's inelegant, crude, and kind of annoying[20]—but goddammit, it ends the book.

There are probably a dozen other ways to end a novel that doesn't come gracefully to an ending. It doesn't matter *how* you end your book, only that you do actually end it. Much as I am about to end this chapter: with a smoke bomb and an evil laugh.

---

19 This heading comes from a note my brother Yan made on a novel I wrote when I was twenty years old. The last chapter was a lengthy stream-of-consciousness speech from the main character, named Bill Kincaid, where he ranted on a variety of subjects. It was awful. My brother put a comment in the margin that noted the insufferableness of this technique and suggested I rename the chapter Lord Kincaid's Farewell Address. It was meant as criticism, but I am immune to criticism, so I did just that: renamed the chapter just to spite my brother. The novel remains unsold. I wonder why.

20 Very much like Ayn Rand herself.

SETTING

NO ONE CARES
WHAT THE ROOM SMELLS LIKE

Since you spent money on this book[1] and in some vague sense I have a moral duty to provide entertainment and information to you, I'll let you in on a little secret: In one of many, many hilarious details about my writing process, every time one of my characters lives alone in an apartment, it's an apartment I lived in from 1996 through 2001 in Jersey City, New Jersey.

I mean this literally. In every story or novel written since 1996, when one of my characters is wandering through his or her apartment, it's Apartment No. 9 in that old apartment building. I obviously have the imagination of a cat, whose brain is typically the size of a racquetball,[2] but that old one-bedroom apartment with the floors painted brown and

---

1 Uh, you did, right? I mean I suppose you might have found this book discarded in the trash somewhere after someone obviously tried to burn it, or perhaps in a library, or sitting on a friend or acquaintance's desk or bookshelf just waiting to be stolen. Then again, maybe you shoplifted it, or downloaded it from www.RussiaRuinsOurEconomy.ru for free. Which would make me very sad. To underscore how sad it makes me, here is a Sad Face emoticon: :-(

2 This is deceptive, of course; my own cats have essentially turned me into their butler, thus proving their intellectual superiority.

the gas-on-gas heat[3] remains in my head for some reason probably having to do with my youth and the number of times I descended into a *Heart of Darkness*-style madness within those rooms.[4] So, if you take a few sections from various novels and compare them, you'd more or less be able to plot out the layout and approximate the size of that old place, and even figure out the places where I hid fifths of bourbon from guests.

You've likely heard the term *world building*. You probably think of it as something that only science fiction and fantasy writers have to worry about, but you're wrong. Personally, I believe strongly in an economy of detail when it comes to setting because creating the setting for your novel is enough work as it is. Some younger writers are under the impression that you have to craft every single detail, from your main character's shoe size to the precise way each and every room they enter smells, when you're creating a setting—which is, frankly, why they don't finish too many novels. Setting is the hardest work you'll ever do when writing a book because creating the setting for your story *is* world building, and you're almost certainly doing too much of it.

UNCONVENTIONAL TIP

Elmore Leonard once said, "If it sounds like writing, I rewrite it." Sometimes in our rush to pour details into our setting, we end up with characters engaging in internal monologues that sound nothing like what people actually think or observe. When you walk into a room, you do not, I'm willing to bet, stand stock-still for whole minutes, cataloging every detail of the visual, auditory, and olfactory presentation of the space. Neither should your characters. Setting should be treated in the same gentle, subtle fashion as backstory,

---

3 A feature (?) of many old Northeastern apartments, this means that the only heat source in the place was literally part of the gas stove in the kitchen. This meant that in the winters, the kitchen was heated to a temperature that melted my glasses off my face, while the bedroom, on the other side of the apartment, was cold enough to serve as an ersatz fridge. Good times.

4 I once barricaded myself into my apartment with nothing but a box of Cheez-Its and a few bottles of liquor, and vowed to establish a sovereign nation and to resist all attempts to arrest me. No one noticed. Three days later I went back to work, claiming I'd been sick. Which wasn't exactly a lie.

necessary exposition, and any other show-don't-tell aspect of writing, which is of course all of them.

THE WORLD PROBABLY IS ENOUGH

Every piece of fiction exists in its own alternate universe. No matter how much it's *based* on the real world, it's *not* the real world because it's being filtered through your throbbing brain. My old apartment never appears on the pages of my novels precisely the same way twice; I forget little things, reimagine them in different ways, or sometimes consciously alter the facts for the purposes of awesomeness. No matter how closely you want your setting to hew towards reality, it *isn't* reality. It's just a simulacrum of it, and that means you're building a world.

Now, world building is big stuff. Like, really big. Whether your novel is set in an alternate universe where people have personal flying carpets and ray guns, or in Los Angeles just this morning, part of your job as the writer is to dress those sets and enforce the rules of physics, whatever they may be. This is both easier and harder than it looks.

It's **easier** because no one cares what the room smells like:[5] In other words, a lot of writers think they have to imagine every tiny detail, but this isn't true. All you need to do is sketch the setting and the world. You can't possibly describe every grain of sand, so just describe the beach.

It's **harder** because your cheats have to be load bearing. You can't waste the time and energy describing every grain of sand, but you have to somehow convey the sense that there's an infinite number of them between the toes of your character.

LESS IS MORE

The real trick in creating a setting for your novel is to know what you can safely leave out. A good place to start is to remember something

---

5 If it isn't obvious, I am desperately trying to make "No one cares what the room smells like" a thing. Please print it on T-shirts and join the struggle.

else Elmore Leonard said:[6] "Try to leave out the part that readers tend to skip." I sometimes rephrase that to be: *Don't write the boring parts.*

One of the biggest mistakes writers make when dealing with setting is how specific they get. They drill down to the molecular structure of everything in every room, offering up drowning waves of detail for one of two reasons: Either they think it adds to the verisimilitude, or they can't think of what to write and are stalling.

The verisimilitude argument doesn't work because, as mentioned, all that detail isn't just suffocating and boring, it's unnatural. People don't notice details. We *think* we do, but we actually don't. Consider how disturbingly unreliable eyewitness testimony is in court cases; there is plenty of evidence that not only do people remember things 100 percent incorrectly in many cases, but it's frighteningly easy to "create" memories in people, more or less convincing them that they saw something they absolutely did not see.[7]

So, the suggestion that the only way to convince people that your setting is rock solid is to smother them in details is sketchy. People just can't process details like that. We carry with us impressions of things we've seen, events we've witnessed, and we fill in the details later, when we need to. And we more or less make up those details on the spot, even if we're convinced we actually saw them. So instead of pouring 5,000 words into how the room smelled, just say you're in a room, mention a few salient details, and rely on your reader to fill in the rest.

Now, if you're just writing about the many, many unsavory ways the room smells because you're stuck, well, you're actually on to something. Writing through problems—blocks, plot problems, the sudden realization that you're writing a really terrible novel—can often be a solution. We'll discuss that in more depth later.

---

6 Hey, if you're going to write a chapter that is essentially 90 percent quotes from another writer, you could do much worse than Elmore Leonard.

7 My favorite example of this is the film *Shazaam*, starring the comedian Sinbad. This movie does not exist. It was never made. And yet thousands of people on the internet not only claim the movie exists, but also claim to have seen it. And they get hilariously upset when they're told it never happened. This is how I plan to handle my juvenilia: simply deny it exists, and call everyone liars when challenged. Smoke bombs and lawsuits may also be involved, but let's be real here: Smoke bombs and lawsuits are involved in just about everything I do.

WRITING WITHOUT RULES

UNCONVENTIONAL TIP

Zero[8] and first drafts don't have to be perfect, or even in the same ballpark as perfect ... or even in the *parking lot* adjacent to perfect. If you can't write the second sentence of your story until the first sentence is perfect, you're playing a losing game, because all the sentences wind up interrelated. You can spend weeks making that first line perfect, but line seventeen might undermine that perfection, and before you know it, you're caught in an endless loop of going back to "fix" your previous work. Leave revisions until you've finished the draft.

Instead of trying to note every mote of dust in the air when world-building and establishing your setting, take a step back and try a higher-altitude approach, trusting your readers to fill in many of the infinite details that true verisimilitude requires.

THE WHITE ROOM

I start my world building with a White Room, a technique that will work for anyone. Start at the very beginning, the first day of creation in your fictional universe. Whether you envision a complex fantasy world with its own culture, history, and laws of physics, or the present-day situation in your hometown, start with a White Room, a blank cube. The cube could be room sized, or planet sized, as long as it's white and empty. Then, drop your characters into it.

Don't have characters? Okay, just place some people in it. At this stage it doesn't matter if they're important or even people who will survive revisions of your novel, as long as you have recognizable beings in your White Room. Then, ask yourself: What do these people need? What do they interact with? What would they touch, what would they notice? You don't notice 99.9 percent of the information around you on a daily basis. You don't wonder at every tactile sensation and flicker of movement around as you make your way through your busy day. Neither should your characters.

---

8 A "Zero Draft" is essentially that hot mess that you can't call a novel with a straight face. Whereas a first draft implies at least a minimum of structure and character arc, a Zero Draft is a lot more chaotic and speculative. Whether you use this term and concept in your own writing is up to you.

Instead, walk your characters through some scenarios. Just imagining your characters working their way through your White Room will tell you pretty quickly what *needs* to be in that room. And to start with, that's all you want: the absolute necessities. Don't get caught up in what kind of oil is in the lamps of your medieval-lite fantasy universe, or the kind of shag on the rug in your stockbroker's apartment—unless those details are necessary for your story.

Keeping your narrative lean in terms of setting and world building will not only move you through your first draft faster, it will also help you focus on what really matters, allowing you to emphasize (or, if you're me, discover) your themes, lay the foundation for your twists and reveals, and tell your story. Writers sometimes put too much pressure on the first draft—or even the Zero Draft that is the New Coke of drafting[9]—and feel like they have to have a fully-formed novel by the end of it, which, well, sometimes happens! But not often, not always, and it's not required. All that's required of a first draft is a story. You go back, you smooth the edges. You buff out the blemishes. And, if need be, you pour in details, you firm up your setting, and fill in the blank spaces that will be obvious when you reread. And if they're not obvious, then consider the possibility that they don't need to be there at all.

UNCONVENTIONAL TIP

Revision is some powerful stuff. Ian Fleming, author of the original James Bond novels, wrote first drafts very quickly because he left out most of the details, and concentrated on the plot and the characters. Then he went back and added in the sumptuous details of the dangerous, luxurious world Bond inhabited. When you go back to reread your first draft, you will instinctively notice what's *missing* in terms of detail, and you can add it in. But if there's already too much detail, that's much more difficult to notice, aside from the fatigue of reading it.

---

9 Fun fact: Most of the sentences in your Zero Draft are perfectly fine sentences.

In fact, we can extend the concept of the White Room even further.

I used to play a lot of text adventure computer games—sometimes referred to as interactive fiction. These games were often incredibly complex, well written, and expansive, very much like novels that had been transformed into pick-your-own adventures[10]—often longer than most novels, as the stories had to have scenarios written up for the large number of possible outcomes the player might experience. Playing these games was great fun, and in fact I think they were a useful exercise in plotting. Thinking 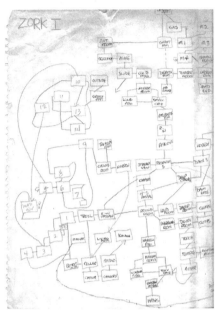 about your story as a game someone is playing is a way of seeing plot pathways you might otherwise miss because of confirmation bias or other blind spots.[11]

When I played these games I would make maps, by hand, in order to orient myself and be able to see, at a glance, where I'd been and how locations related to each other. Above is one of the maps I made as a kid, for the classic game *Zork*.

10 In fact, Douglas Adams, author of the *Hitchhiker's Guide to the Galaxy* series, wrote several, including an adaptation of Hitchhiker's which turned out to be one of the most difficult of these games ever devised. It included a brilliant puzzle involving the inventory that you carried; in these games you were able to carry items from room to room and could see what you were carrying at any time by typing the instruction "inventory" (or the abbreviation "i"). In Adams's game, your inventory always included the item "no tea," because one of your goals in the game was to get a real cup of tea, a goal you hilariously failed at several times. The brilliance was the revelation that in order to prove to a computer that you were, in fact, intelligent, you had to figure out how to simultaneously have tea and no tea, a puzzle imbued with such philosophical depth I passed out when I was thirteen trying to solve it and only recently emerged from the coma.

11 I created a short interactive fiction as part of the promotion for the third Avery Cates book, *The Eternal Prison*. It used to live on the book's official web page, which has since been taken down. It wasn't very long, but it took a *long* time to set up, because anticipating people's decisions isn't easy.

As you can see, these maps are basically a bunch of White Rooms linked together. And each of these White Rooms has a description—a setting—that is poured into it. These interactive fiction games offer a model for creating your world, your universe, and your setting: Boxes inside boxes. You start with the universe, and into that box you place all the other boxes. Each box is a setting, or a part of the larger whole of your setting. Each box has a description that might change depending on what your characters do. They're linked together. And all the white space represents the places you *don't* bother to go to, the places that don't require any descriptions because you don't go there in your story. And if you decide to go to one of those places? You just drop in a new box and fill it up with the necessary details.

WRITING AS CODE

Of course, no matter how you slice it, creating a universe—even one more or less based on the one you see every day—can be a daunting task. Which brings us back to my old apartment.[12]

The whole reason I reuse the same floor plan and general mental image when setting scenes in an apartment is so I don't have to imagine every single detail from scratch. Unless the character and the story require a custom-built apartment setting that somehow weaves into the theme or drops hints of the character's real identity (or something like that), then recycling my old apartment[13] gives me that setting quickly, with all the verisimilitude I could ask for. I don't have to invent it from scratch, and I can always go back in revision and alter it or fix it as needed.

In computer programming, there is a concept of code libraries: You don't want to re-code something like a button animation every single time you place one in your interface, so you just take a snippet of generic code, tweak it as needed, and replicate as often as necessary. This

---

12 Just in case you were losing faith that I had a coherent point to make here. Which happens to me all the time, because people are hurtful.

13 Please don't go to Jersey City and look for my old apartment so you can set up a little shrine to me. If you're that sort of person, for god sake's come to Hoboken and find me in person and I will initiate you into the cult and set you to cleaning the house without pay.

is a powerful concept you can use with background elements like settings—don't reinvent the wheel each time you have your character get in a car. Just insert an existing memory or mental image of a car and tweak it later. I treat a lot of setting components like those code libraries, and the apartment is a perfect example: When I need a small, slightly seedy apartment for a character, I just put them into No. 9 and rely on my memories of the place to fill in the details.

I should note that this doesn't mean you should literally copy and paste *actual words* into your story. This is a mental exercise, not an encouragement to self-plagiarize. The key concept here is that when I use my old apartment as a stand-in for all the apartments in my current work-in-progress, it's a mental image I use as I write 100 percent, absolutely original words.[14] Having that reusable mental image speeds things up because I don't have to ponder the unnecessary question of what some character's apartment is like—unless it *is* important, in which case I do—I just load the memories and start writing.

This can be applied to any aspect of setting—in fact, if you've ever written a story set in the "modern world," you've already done this, because you're just loading up your own experiences living in this world and interpreting them, fictionalizing them, using them as a template for your literary madness. It's exactly the same thing—instead of spending several years re-creating *this* world from scratch, you're using the actual world as is. So it is with my old apartment: Lacking a reason to create something bespoke for a scene, I just imagine the old place and *keep writing* without getting lost in minutiae.

IN CLOUD CITY, WE LIVE IN YURTS

Of course, if you're writing in a speculative genre, you may not be able to apply my old apartment,[15] because your imaginary people might not live in apartments, or even spaces that are apartment-like in the rough

---

14 If any of my fiction publishers are reading this, I swear this is true and there is no need to perform some sort of CSI-level comparison of text files. No need. Excuse me, by complete coincidence there is a car waiting to take me to the airport where I have plane tickets for a nonextradition country. *Throws smoke bomb. Runs for exit. Pants fall down. Trips, and bursts into tears.*

15 Actually, I hope you can *never* apply *my* old apartment, for what I think are obvious reasons. Unless you actually lived in my old apartment after I moved out, in which case we are Dwell-

outlines. I mean, maybe they are—if you look back at how ancient Romans lived, it wasn't *that* different, in the sense that people lived in what were essentially apartments with various rooms meant for various purposes. You could conceivably take the layout of *your* old apartment and apply it to the dwellings your superintelligent lizards inhabit. And the technique can be adjusted and applied: Once you've created a salty tavern where Paladins and Blackguards rub shoulders, you can use it as a template for all future taverns in the same way. Creating these sorts of "code libraries" for your setting and world building doesn't have to draw from real life, and it doesn't have to involve places you've actually been. These libraries of settings that can be plugged into your stories can be built over time.

It's also important to remember that, of course, you don't have to use these libraries. This technique is designed for speed and simplicity— if you have a clear image in your head of what a setting looks like, you don't need to load up something previously sketched out. But if you're stuck, or if you're bogged down by the sort of detail mania that tells the reader what the room smells like when that information isn't at all necessary to your story, pulling up something you've already fleshed out in your head is a time-saving verisimilitude machine.

The great part about writing is that nothing is ever a mistake. If you take my advice a little too literally and your novel's setting ends up being a series of white rooms, you can always claim it's your new minimalist style, launch a literary movement, and spend the rest of your days regretting the day you bought this book.

---

ing Mates, and I only wonder if you ever found the fifth of Early Times I hid in the drop ceiling. Call me.

WRITING WITHOUT RULES

6

CHARACTERS
LOVE MEANS NEVER HAVING YOUR PROTAGONISTS LOOK AT THEMSELVES IN THE MIRROR

If you're wondering about my lazy and incompetent bona fides (ah, for those halcyon days when people weren't 100 percent *certain* of my laziness and incompetence![1]), here's a good example: I attended college mainly because I knew my parents would not allow me to lounge around the house, eating chips and playing video games, if I chose not to. I knew that college wouldn't require much effort; like Mark Zuckerberg in *The Social Network*, I knew college would require the *minimum amount* of my attention, whereas a job of some sort would likely require considerably more. And, since I was seventeen at the time, a job would likely require some sort of uniform.[2]

---

1 I assure you such days did exist.

2 My years and years in the Boy Scouts of America have soured me on uniforms. My scout uniforms used to fit me like they'd all been designed for a middle-aged man with a potbelly. I spent six years hiking up my pants while trying to recite the Scout Oath. The fact that I became an Eagle Scout is so improbable that I now wonder if there's another Jeff Somers out there ruined by a paperwork mix-up.

As I've said, at college, I knew I would be an English major. Not because of my great love of literature or my love for and need to write—although both of those things are absolutely significant in my life—but rather because I knew getting a bachelor's degree in English would, again, require minimum attention. I'd read the books and I am a very good writer. I figured (accurately) that I would just muddle through. I'd get passing grades, and in four years I'd have a degree that theoretically could be cashed in for a job like a coupon.[3]

Which means that over the next four years of my college life I had probably the most unsupervised free time of my entire life.[4] And so I wrote—a lot. One of the great things about college is that when you do have to attend a class because circumstances force the issue, you look like the most attentive student ever because you're madly typing or scratching into a notebook. You appear to be taking some serious notes, when in fact you're hungover and drafting a kickass fight scene.

Add to that a steady diet of being introduced to classic literature, new ideas, and different sorts of people, and naturally the writing went really well during school. In fact, I wrote the original draft of my novel *The Electric Church* under those circumstances, barreling through the story in about three months of feverish writing. The draft was far from great, of course; first of all, I was about nineteen years old, so the chances of it being anything other than juvenilia were slim, and second of all, I made the mistake of populating much of the book with my friends.

UNCONVENTIONAL TIP

The best writing advice you'll ever receive (and which you've no doubt already received several times) is to *read*. If any supposed

---

3 If you're at an age where you're considering a college career, let's just say it: A bachelor's degree in the liberal arts is not exactly a gateway to riches. The first real job I got out of school paid me $17,000 a year, which would be about $27,000 in today's dollars; this was largely because my four-year degree had prepared me to do absolutely nothing useful, unless composing witty emails counts, which it does not. I ate a lot of Ramen, drank a lot of cheap liquor, and had a television so small I needed one of those magnifying screens from the film *Brazil* to watch anything.

4 If you're wondering how I survived ... so am I.

Literally. In that storied first draft, a clean version of which was typed onto that manual typewriter I stole from my sainted mother, several of the secondary characters were named after my buddies and were, in fact, imagined *as* my buddies, as if they had been beamed directly into the plot.

At the time, this seemed kind of genius, a literary act of revolution. Of course, even though I was writing a science fiction thriller about murderous cyborgs, I thought I was writing the book that would trans-form literature as we knew it—as noted elsewhere, I entered college with a signed book contract, and even if it turned out to be worthless, I was still under the impression that my literary celebrity was imminent. If I thought putting my friend Jeof into the book and making him say hi-larious inside jokes no one else would ever understand was a great, dis-ruptive idea, who was going to argue?[5]

Well, as it turned out, every single person who read that draft, but that's a whole other issue. In subsequent revisions of *The Electric Church*, I didn't exactly remove all of my old college friends—because one of the key ways to create great characters is to base them on real people you know. You just have to put in the work to ensure they're characters on the page as well as in your head.

---

5 I lived with Jeof and my other friend Ken for several years during and just after college. At one point we acquired a video camera (in the days before smartphones) and spent some time try-ing to make a horror movie about insanity and cannibalism, culminating in a climax scored to "Dance of the Sugarplum Fairy" where we each emerge from our rooms with a weapon, intent on murdering each other. If this video is ever discovered, our lives as we know them are over.

record; if an idea inspires fifty terrible books but the fifty-first is great, that's all that matters.

YOUR FRIENDS AND NEIGHBORS

I'm always a bit surprised when writers ask me for the secrets of creating great characters—a pretty common question.[6] The main reason people seem to be confused, as far as I can tell, is because many writers simply place *themselves* into the story, because that's the only person they feel comfortable approximating.

UNCONVENTIONAL TIP

Writing the Other can be intimidating—how can you write characters that come from different backgrounds and cultures, or a different gender? Research helps—conversations with people can give you plenty of material to work with. For non-POV characters—whose heads you don't have to get inside—you can base descriptions and reactions on observation alone. In other words, if you're not sure how to handle the Other, the simplest solution is to leave them as the Other.

Not only is making yourself the main character of your story a dubious proposition, making *every* character a version of yourself is like one of those weird off-off-off-Broadway vanity projects your actor friend puts on, where he plays every character in a *Game of Thrones* adaptation—not something anyone wants to pay for. Unless you are *literally* the Most Interesting Person in the World, a character based on you *will* make the worst character in your book.[7] First, there's the ever-present

---

6 And yet I am surprised, every time. Which gives you an idea of the intellectual capacity of Jeff Somers, Super Genius.

7 Things get subtle here: Earlier I encouraged you to plot a novel by imagining yourself in the story and gauging your reactions and responses to fictional events. Here I'm telling you not to make yourself a character. These are two very different propositions, but they are very easy to conflate, and doing so can get you into trouble. The key is to use the first technique to evaluate re-

danger of making a Mary (or Marty) Sue, which is a term describing a "perfect" character who is always clever, always right, and typically a thinly veiled stand in for the author. Mary Sues are the worst. Don't be a Mary Sue (or a Marty Sue). Second, since you're a writer, you obviously think you're clever and hilarious, so you will think your character is clever and hilarious and resist all criticism stating otherwise. You'll have a blind spot. Always be on guard against casting yourself as a character, my friends.

So if basing your characters on yourself is bad, how can you come up with characters who feel real, hold interest, and surprise the reader? It's very simple, actually: Don't base characters on yourself, base them on *people you know*: family, friends, neighbors, co-workers, weirdos who accost you on the subway,[8] strange high school classmates who can't seem to take a hint. The easiest way to create believable, multi-dimensional characters is to start with people you actually know and tweak them.

The word "know" doesn't mean you have to be *intimate* with them. They just need to be observable in your life—in fact, the more of a stranger they are, the better, as it means you're burdened with less Actual Knowledge. Trust me—the less Actual Knowledge you possess about things, the better writer you'll be.[9]

Here's why this works: The kind of people we're talking about—people you see and interact with, but don't know well—are more or less characters in your own story. Most of us imagine ourselves (consciously or unconsciously) as the hero of that story; we generally think all it needs is some editing and postproduction work and our life would be an Oscar-winning film. You might exchange a few words with the guy living down the hall or your regular bus driver, but you don't really *know* them. You have a superficial concept of them: their general look,

---

alistic reactions that can yield plot turns you might not otherwise see—but that's not the end of it. After that you have the second job of mapping those reactions to characters that are recognizably not you.

8 For various dull legal reasons I must pause here to stress that in this sentence I am not referring either specifically or obliquely to my agent.

9 By this measure, of course, I am the Greatest Writer Who Ever Lived.

the way they talk, a smattering of preferences and opinions. That vast unknowable space behind the surface is where you get to play author—why do they use a certain phrase? What does that tattoo mean? If you had to describe them to someone else, what would you start with? How would they react if you were trapped in a hostage situation together? What if one day they asked you to help them rob a bank?

By the time you're done with this process, you'll have something more than a sketch of a real person—you'll have a character. A character who can have any thoughts, beliefs, and background you want, because you're using their surface traits as a jumping-off point, you're not literally putting a real person into your story. They'll just *seem* real.

THE REALITY ANCHOR

A big mistake a lot of writers make is trying to make their characters—especially, but not exclusively, villains—extreme and "memorable." The general thinking seems to be that since most people are kind of boring, your characters had best be anything but. The end result is usually a pretty terrible character that isn't like a person at all, but rather a collection of tics and bizarre, over the top catchphrases and supposedly fascinating psychology—plus, usually, some interesting fashion choices. In case this isn't clear, the equation a lot of writers have in their heads goes something like this:

PERSONALITY TICS + ODD CLOTHES + INSANITY = AWESOME.[10]

It doesn't matter if your work-in-progress is set in a galaxy far, far away or deals with a serial killer who likes to make his victims into dioramas matching the ones his mean-spirited teachers made him craft back in grammar school,[11] going extreme with your characters is a fool's errand. It's distracting, and it siphons away some of that precious Sus-

---

10 For the record, this equation works for me in my personal life, but then I am a real, actual person. A real, actual person who is right now wearing a purple robe of velvet, a stovepipe hat, and bunny slippers as he wanders his abandoned mansion muttering to himself.

11 Note to self: Totally write that last book. It's gold, Jerry!

pension of Disbelief (SOD) that every reader generously donates to every story they read. There's only a finite supply of SOD, however, and if you choose to waste some on a ridiculous character that no one can possibly take seriously, the end result is a reader who starts to give your entire novel the stink eye.

The problem's easy to see: Characters are just a collection of traits and actions. Giving your character something that differentiates them is necessary. Giving them a few traits that differentiate them is probably advisable. And thus the temptation to give them every single cool trait you can think of is sometimes irresistible. So why not the constant stream of witty one-liners, the tattoos of mysterious symbols, the Old West duster, the dark glasses, the limp, the psychic powers, the dashing handsomeness, the tendency to sing old show tunes ironically, the tendency toward John Galt-like speeches that go on for pages and pages? If each one of those traits is awesome in isolation, surely they combine to form a formidable force of awesomeness no reader can resist!

Except, yeah: They *will* resist.

Think of the people you know in real life—there may be people who have a couple of interesting traits, but generally speaking the people capable of functioning in society are not insane balls of interesting tics. Or, if they are, they have learned how to hide it well. In order for your characters to work, you have to resist the urge to dump a whole box of awesome on top of them. And modeling them on real people is an excellent way to know when you're going too far, because the character won't fit inside the model anymore. That's why starting off with a template based on people you've already observed works: If you're judicious in the details and traits you apply to them, you're guaranteed to wind up with a character your readers will believe.

A CHARACTER'S PURPOSE

Knowing how easy it can be to create great characters, however, leads us to the existential question of *why*. Why create a character? Well, sure, it can be fun—more on that below—but it's also necessary. Unless you're writing "There Will Come Soft Rains"[12] or something similar, you're going to need some characters to move your story along. The trick is, the characters you do create should have a purpose in the story.

Some of these are easy: protagonist and antagonist; hero and villain. Every story has to be about someone, and every someone has to struggle against something—or someone. After that it gets a bit more complicated: Every character you introduce beyond that basic dichotomy should have a purpose. That purpose doesn't have to be terribly complex, or even unexpected. It just needs to exist.

That means you can justify characters who exist for comic relief. You can justify characters to create stakes for the protagonist or antagonist. You can justify characters who represent aspects of your hero's past life, or who serve as obstructions, temptations, or love interests. The only thing you shouldn't do, really, is insert a character into your story who doesn't have a purpose. Your character's purpose is the skeleton you hang everything else on top of—how they look, what they do, their dialogue.

That said, I'll be the first to admit that I don't always think about purpose when I'm drafting. I'm a Pantser—I'm making up my stories as I go. That means I often create characters on the spur of the moment, without any larger plan. But when I hit the end of that Draft Zero, hungover and shivering from malnutrition, I go back and ask myself what the point of each character is—what purpose I've managed to carve out for them. If there isn't any, I can delete that character, combine them with another, or find another purpose for them. This doesn't always work, because I am incompetent (more on that later), but it *almost* always works. All you have to do is read your manuscript. When a new character is introduced, ask yourself what his role is, what pur-

---

12 Haven't read this short story by Ray Bradbury? *My God.* Stop reading this drivel immediately and spend your time more profitably reading that story. It's genius.

WRITING WITHOUT RULES

pose he serves in the story. If you can't answer, it's time to think about deleting him.

OVERPOPULATION

In an article published in *Writer's Digest* magazine not too long ago,[13] I discussed one of the easiest mistakes writers make: inserting too many characters into their novel. Now, the phrase "too many characters" is subjective. There is no formula that will tell you that your crime thriller should have fifteen characters total or that one hundred point-of-view characters is far too few for your million-word epic fantasy.

That doesn't mean your book can't have too many characters, though, and an excessive number of characters actually is a pretty common problem—in fact, when authors complain that their work-in-progress isn't jelling or is somehow dysfunctional for mysterious reasons, there's a pretty good chance the underlying cause is too many fictional people crowding the universe.

One reason this happens is simple: World building is fun, and populating your universe is part of that. Inventing people and giving them funny lines or awesome action moments is *fun*. And once you've created a character you enjoy, you start to have affection for that character, and you want desperately to keep them around—so you do, inventing chores for them, coming up with excuses for them to loiter about scenes. And if you lard a character up with enough business, you can convince yourself that they're necessary, that they're crucial to the whole story, even if they're not.

Another reason you can wind up with too many characters in your story is because characters are useful problem-solving devices. If your story needs something—a rescue mission, a computer hacker, an expert to wander around explaining things—it's very easy to invent a character to fill that role. The problem here should be pretty obvious: Once your newly minted character has explained the eldritch horror, defused the bomb, or provided the poignant backstory your main character has been heroically hiding for 200 pages, they've served their purpose and

---

13 You can read it in the July/August 2017 issue (www.writersdigestshop.com/writers-digest-july-august-2017-wd0817).

they either fade away with a sad smile or they hang around, acting as guests in your story. And we all know what they say about guests in stories: They begin to stink after about thirty pages.

How can you tell if your novel's problems stem from a crowd of useless characters? There are a couple of simple tests you can apply:

- Examine each of your characters and ask yourself what they've done for you. Characters who don't have an active role, or whose active role was brief, are usually not very useful.
- If a character does little more than offer up sparkling commentary and epic one-liners, they're not particularly useful. That great dialogue can be assigned to another character.
- Ask yourself if you can describe your character—do you know what they look like? How they dress? If *you* can't offer up a description, your readers certainly won't be able to—and that's a clear signal the character can be removed.

Sometimes a character isn't a real person at all, but rather a Plot Device—in other words, they were brought into existence to pull a specific Plot Lever because you couldn't think of a more elegant way to do it. Go back and reconsider that scene to see if you can't eliminate the character.

Is your character a clone? Sometimes we love a character so much we unconsciously start duplicating them. If you have characters who look, sound, and act the same, you might do better to consolidate them into one person.

Sometimes writers will fight this, citing some doorstopper of a novel that teems with characters—perhaps even characters that violate some of these "rules" I've just laid out. Hey, it's your book, kid. There are certainly very successful novels that have a huge cast of characters, many of whom could be classified as useless—*The Lord of the Rings* is a perfect example, as it has several examples of fundamentally useless characters (every Hobbit not named Frodo or Sam) and duplicated characters (Glorfindel, your pointy ears are burning). But—and here's the difference—*The Lord of the Rings* is a successful novel in just about every other way. The fact that Tolkien never saw a reason to cull those

WRITING WITHOUT RULES

characters is due to two things: One, the man worked on that novel for decades and *did*, in fact, remove dozens of characters over the years as he refined both his story and his mythology; and two, while it's amusing to note that a character like Tom Bombadil is basically an excuse for Tolkien to slip in some poetry, the fact of the matter is the story is so strong otherwise it doesn't really matter.

UNCONVENTIONAL TIP

Be aware of your ability to fool yourself. You're a writer. You spin lies for a living. Lying to yourself is pretty easy, and when someone offers up a steaming mug of acidic criticism about your novel it's very easy to convince yourself that your decisions are right. You very well may *be* right, and you shouldn't accept critiques of your story blindly. On the other hand, ask yourself if you're being defensive and coming up with justifications for bonkers plot twists, useless characters, info dumps, or other writing sins. Probably the best skill you can develop as a writer is the ability to step back and be objective.

Ask yourself: Is your story that strong? If you're struggling enough to consider doing a character head count, the answer's obviously *no*.

I've struggled with this myself, actually. I worked on my novel *Chum* for more than a decade. I worked on the original version for a few years before my agent took it on, and then I revised it several times over the next eight years as we kept refining it. We finally sold it in 2013.

I introduced a character named Mike in the very first draft. Mike was a bit square—in a novel that sports a large cast of nasty, unhappy people doing terrible, terrible things, his role was to be the constantly outraged Voice of Reason. Mike did a lot of handwringing and warning the other characters about social norms and legal ramifications. He was there almost as a calibration character, to ensure that the amoral and distasteful behavior on the part of all the other characters stood out.

Over time, I reduced Mike's role, because I realized I didn't need him;[14] I was hedging my bets, but I'd created great characters who stood out and made sense on their own. Without consciously thinking about it, I made Mike's role smaller and smaller. He's still there in the final version of the novel, but when I reread it now, Mike lacks a good reason for being present. I could easily delete him from a revision and the book wouldn't be any worse—and might be better, because there would be that much less wasted text. On the other hand, Mike's not doing any active harm—which is why he survived approximately one million revisions.

Of course, sometimes writers wonder whether it's okay to have a character just because they're entertaining. Of course it is. There are no rules, really; the things I bloviate about in this book are meant as helpful guidelines and tools, and you can—and should—ignore them if you think it's wise. Novels with characters who do no work for the story get published all the time, and these characters sometimes are the most popular in the book because they're the most entertaining.

What it boils down to is this: If your story is *working*, if it's cranking along and taking the twists and turns like a sports car hugging the road, defects can be ignored. If your story is lumbering about like a drunk bear, *that's* when you need to start thinking about stuff like how many characters you've stuffed in there and whether they're all necessary. Which, if you think about it, is also life advice of a profound sort, but sadly we're out of time.

---

14 To be honest, I also realized I didn't like him. As a handwringing worrywart, Mike is precisely the sort of guy I would never want to hang out with in real life, and so all the other characters in the book were constantly mean to him.

DIALOGUE
ME TALK PRETTY ONE DAY

"Writing is trickery."

"Why do you say that?"

"Well, we have to say *something*. This is the seventh chapter of the book. They aren't going to wait forever. Also: Writing *is* trickery. It's all about fooling the reader. At least, fiction is."

"*Who's* not going to wait? And what book?"

"I mean the trick of writing fiction is that you're creating the simulacrum of reality, but it isn't anything like reality at all. Take dialogue: Do you know how people *really* talk?"

"Of course I do! We're doing it right now!"

"No—uh-huh. We're *book talking* here. In real life, you sound like this: Of course—of course I do! Uh, see, we're, uh, we're doing it right, you know, now!"

"I do not."

"You do."

"You, sir, are no gentleman."

"No, but I'm right. In real life we stammer and stall for time, we backtrack and repeat ourselves, we use empty place-keeper sounds, we ramble, we're incoherent. When writing, the one thing you *don't* want to do is replicate what dialogue actually sounds like in real life."

"Yes, but everyone knows that, and that's not the only key to writing great dialogue. How do you ... make good ... with the ... words your characters say?"

"Easiest thing in the world. You just have to remember that dialogue is character. Then do some method acting. And finally, when all else fails—or, you know, right away if you're lazy—just steal someone's rhythm."

And ... *scene.*

Dialogue is probably the most challenging aspect of writing fiction for some writers. Not me, though, for one very simple reason: I talk to myself. A lot.

Okay, so do crazy people. And so do a lot of totally noncrazy non-writers. I've always done it, all the way back into childhood.[1] In fact, when I was a kid I would often more or less conduct one-man shows—imagining long conversations between different folks, to the point where I'd get lost in the narrative and literally wake up fifteen minutes later, a little confused about what I came to know as Lost Time.[2]

Sometimes I still mutter to myself for no specific reason, but I just as often do it as an exercise. Because, put simply, the best way to understand dialogue is to think while you talk—to actually pay attention—and if you do that while actually having a conversation with someone, you're going to come off a little weird. So I pretend to have conversations, and make mental notes about how people speak and how those tics and quirks can be *implied* without forcing people to read the *ums* and *ahs*. I like to call this The Method Method.[3] But, because I am in-

---

1 To answer the obvious questions: No, I was not the Weird Kid in the Neighborhood who had no friends and thus invented them, although I was the Weird Kid whose mother made him wear his church clothes anytime he was invited to a birthday party, which led to a distinct lack of birthday party invitations. Yes, talking to myself does sometimes get me into trouble, like when The Duchess walks into the house, hears me talking, and races upstairs with a baseball bat to "beat the floozies." Yes, sometimes I am actually talking to my cats, and no, I am not sure which is better.

2 Yes, when I was a kid. This definitely does not happen today, when I am a grown man and supposedly normal. Nope. Doesn't happen.

3 I'm a card. I must be dealt with. *Wait! Come back!* I promise I won't do that again.

WRITING WITHOUT RULES

competent in all things except the actual writing of stories and essays, before we discuss the Method Method, we're going to have to talk about how dialogue is character, and *vice versa*.

YES, VIRGINIA; DIALOGUE IS CHARACTER

Writers sometimes underestimate how important dialogue is because they view it as mundane—a mere tool used to convey information. Every now and then, they concede that your characters will have to walk into a room and open their mouths to tell the reader, or another character, something. The result is uninspired dialogue that is ironically often overdone—pages and pages of characters just asking and answering questions, or repeating themselves.

What those writers are missing is that dialogue is actually *characterization.*

When you try to envision a fictional character, you tend to do so in visual terms. That's natural, and it leads to those endless debates about what actor would play the character in a film version.[4] In reality, no matter how much effort you put into describing your characters physically, it's the dialogue you put in their mouths that will define them for readers.

UNCONVENTIONAL TIP

When it comes to describing your characters, less is more. A few physical details will help the reader form a mental image. More than a few details will start to sound like you're trying to sell them something.

Every line of dialogue should be considered from the point of view of the character speaking it. Who is this person? How do they talk? Do they have an accent? What's their education? Who are they emu-

---

4 Trick question. The answer is obviously always Gary Busey.

lating—an old teacher, their parents, a celebrity? Are they smart or stupid? Do they *know* whether they're smart or stupid?

You can probably see where this is going: Your characters' dialogue should be shaped by their personalities, their backstory, and that deep iceberg of data about them that probably never sees the light of day on the page. In order to figure out how your characters talk, you're going to have to know your characters really, really well. If you think about it, your own speech is shaped by an infinite number of data points. You probably freely quote TV shows and movies you saw twenty years ago, pepper your speech with creatively constructed profanity, and adhere to rules of conversation you were taught as a kid. Every word you utter is a hint of your personality, and so it should be with your characters. Which means you need to *know* your characters pretty well—better than your readers ever will. And that brings us to the Method Method.

THE METHOD METHOD

I get the term *method* from acting—you've probably heard of method actors. On a basic level, method acting means the performer tries to get inside the head of their character. They want to know where they grew up, what their favorite food is, who their best friend was in seventh grade. The idea is, even if those details aren't in the script and the audience will never be aware of them, knowing the character that well will inform the performance in infinite ways, making it more realistic and more powerful.

That's what you need to do with *your* characters for *your* dialogue.

UNCONVENTIONAL TIP

One of the reasons the phrase "show, don't tell" is often such awful advice is how easy it is to misunderstand the point of it. The point isn't to make everything visual; the point is to foster a sense that your story is taking place in a real, lived-in universe where people don't feel the need to point at everything and put a button on it.[5] With dialogue, that involves the tricky balance between things you need your reader to know and understand, and things that your characters would naturally leave unsaid. The point isn't always that your reader should pick up on those details. The point is that *you* know those details.

This is where we get back to me talking to myself.[6] Getting into the head of your characters isn't just sitting in a quiet room tapping at a keyboard. It can involve several strategies:

- Writing short stories, or even flash pieces, about them.
- Writing diaries or school reports they might have had to create.
- Scouting locations, as you would for a movie, where your character's backstory happened.
- And, yes, imagining you are having a conversation with them as you talk to yourself.

The goal here is to know your characters, even the relatively minor ones, so well that when you imagine yourself having a conversation with them, you know how they would speak. The turns of phrase, the accent, the vocabulary level—it should all be obvious to you.

---

5 I like to call this the Moron Line. Imagine a world where everyone picks up their phone and then says, "I'm going to call him on my *phone!*" and you know what I mean.

6 Once again, your lack of faith that I have a point to all this is disturbing. And hurtful.

Now, maybe you're not willing to go scout locations, or are unable to, or you don't relish the idea of talking to yourself because clearly that's what insane people do, probably before they do something crazy like write a novel even though no one has ever indicated that they would ever pay them for a novel, not in a million years.

When you use the Method Method, your dialogue choices stop being arbitrary Rule of Cool choices or flat imitations of yourself; they become specific beats tailored to your character. You may not include those details in your narrative, so your reader may not actually find out why that character has a lisp, or why they always uses the phrase *bless your heart*—but you will. And knowing these things will affect every other decision you make for that character.

As an added bonus, you'll have the perfect excuse for wandering the house talking to yourself.[7]

WE DIDN'T NEED DIALOGUE. WE HAD FACES.

Of course, knowing what your characters should say and writing dialogue that reads well are two different things. There are two easy traps to fall into:

TRAP ONE: Everyone Is You. Whether you realize it or not, you have a distinct way of speaking. From the accent (and, yes, you have an accent, although you may not be aware of it if you're surrounded by other people who have the same accent) to the vocabulary, your speak-

---

7 The bottles of your own urine and the tissue boxes on your feet as "shoes"? Those may require a bit more creativity.

ing style is like a fingerprint. It's very easy to end up with a novel where every single character speaks like you do, resulting in characters who have very little distinction even if you've used the Method Method to inform each line of dialogue.

UNCONVENTIONAL TIP

You are not nearly as cool or interesting as you think you are. Keep that in mind when you have the urge to make one of your characters a stand-in for you.

TRAP TWO: Everyone Is the Same. Similarly, even if your dialogue doesn't just replicate your own way of speaking, it's easy to write everyone's dialogue the same way. Your dialogue might be very good, but if every single character's speech uses the same rhythms and the same idioms, it will have a flat effect, and it'll be harmful to your book overall. A quick test for this is easy enough: Ask someone to read some dialogue with all the tags[8] removed, so it's just lines of discourse, and ask them to identify how many different people are speaking and which lines are theirs. If they can't, you've got some work to do.

The key to dialogue is rhythm. We all speak in a specific rhythm, the words tumbling out in a pattern that can be as unique as any other aspect of our personality. The same phrases will turn up in predictable spots, as will the same stall words[9]. We tend to use the same sentence structures and stock phrases.

The easy way to ensure that your characters' dialogue is not only tied to their personality and backstory but always *sounds* like them is to model their dialogue on someone. This could be someone famous, like an actor (think of the way William Shatner reads his lines as Captain

---

8 An example of a dialogue tag is "he said." These can become pretty tedious if every single sentence in an exchange ends with "he said" or "she said" or "the pink lute-playing dragon said." Still, resist the urge to get creative with dialogue tags. Play with rhythm to reduce that tedium instead of googling "100 ways to say 'said.'" In fact, don't ever make the mistake of assuming that finding new and unusual words or phrases for common parts of speech is ever a good idea.

9 Stall words are the noises you make when you're stalling for time to think—*uh*, *ah*, and *er* are all stall words, as are real, actual words like *so*, *anyway*, and, if you're me, a variety of profanity.

Kirk—now *that's* a rhythm), or someone you know from your own life. Listen to them—really *listen*—and take notes on their rhythms. Now take the great, character-illuminating dialogue you created and cast it to match that rhythm, to mimic those speech patterns. So, in the case of the Shatner example, we'd have something like this:[10]

"Writing ... is *trickery*."

"Why do you say that?"

"Well, we ... have to say *something*. This is the seventh ... chapter of the book. They aren't going to wait forever! And writing *is* trickery. It's all about ... fooling the reader. Fiction. Fiction is about fooling the reader."

Now, no one reading those lines in isolation will know that I was hearing Captain Kirk when I wrote them—but the rhythm I'm matching, when used consistently throughout that character's dialogue—will mark those words as *theirs*. The reader will be able to identify those lines even if you decide to go full Cormac McCarthy[11] and eschew all dialogue tags and most punctuation.

You don't need to model your dialogue rhythms on famous people, though it's an easy avenue to explore. You can model those rhythms on real people—but keep in mind if you've already modeled your character on them physically and in other details, making your character *sound* like them too might be a little weird. Just something to consider—the goal here isn't to simply steal someone's outer life for your fiction, but rather to find a sturdy frame on which to hang your words.

UNCONVENTIONAL TIP

In fact, if you're looking for someone to model your dialogue on, look to some of the great writers and steal the rhythms of *their* char-

---

10 I feel compelled by all that is good and holy to urge you to never model your dialogue on Bill Shatner—or Christopher Walken, or any performer whose delivery is so oddball that it's become iconic. Just because everyone at a party can bust out a Shatner impression doesn't mean those rhythms are the best ones to model your dialogue on.

11 Serious note: Never go full Cormac McCarthy, unless you are Cormac McCarthy. You'll just hurt yourself.

WRITING WITHOUT RULES

acters. And if you're thinking, *gosh, this guy just keeps telling me to think of something famous and copy it, that can't possibly be the sum total of his bankrupt writing advice,* you're wrong. It *is* the sum total of my bankrupt writing advice, because that's what writing *is*; that's what *art* is. You build on what people have done before you. There are so many writers throughout history who are so good at writing dialogue, trying to internalize those rhythms and patterns, tricks and brilliancies can only improve your own work. If you need a few suggestions of writers whose dialogue would make great models, read some Dashiell Hammett, Ernest Hemingway, Elmore Leonard, Toni Morrison, and Stephen King—they're all different, and just the tip of the iceberg, but you could do worse than starting with those five.

AN OPEN DIALOGUE

Writers usually put way too much pressure on themselves to get every aspect of their novel "right" on the first try. I prefer a more rambling, shambolic approach, which involves writing a lot and then going back later to see if any of it is any good, or makes sense.[12]

That "write first, revise later" approach may not work for you. Maybe you're a Plotter and prefer to at least start off with a plan. Or maybe you're a Pantser but still prefer to pause before each scene to ensure what you write is at least somewhat coherent. Whatever your reasons, that's fine—but I suggest you still try a little bit of a ramble when it comes to writing dialogue. Specifically, I suggest you let your characters talk to each other.

I mean that literally. Forget about advancing the plot for a moment, and find moments in your story when two or more characters are in the same space. Then just have them chat. It doesn't matter what they talk about. Simply imagine a conversation and try to keep in mind who your characters are—their points of view and speaking style.

---

12 Then getting drunk and burning everything, which used to be all rock star and badass but has become kind of expensive in the digital age when you have to burn laptops.

This might seem like an exercise,[13] but it's an exercise that can actually enrich not just your characterization, but your dialogue and even your plot. What it really does is force you to imagine your characters as real people, people with varied opinions, disagreements, and speaking styles. It will let you practice managing several different voices at once, and it will kick-start a lot of ideas about where your plot can go. In other words, the worst-case scenario is some pretty kick-ass character work, plus polished dialogue-writing skills that you'll be able to employ on everything you write. The best-case scenario is the sort of plot epiphany that temporarily blinds you. You simply can't lose.

Dialogue is a tool, but it's a tool with a multitude of purposes, and a tool capable of doing a lot of damage (no matter how cool your plot is, if your characters sound like a bunch of morons your novel is dead on arrival). It's also a tool you mastered a long time ago, if you've ever had a conversation. All you need to do is get comfortable talking to yourself.

---

13 Possibly because it is an exercise.

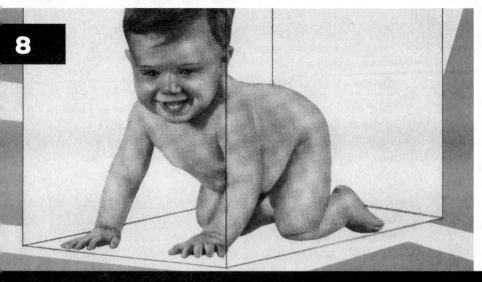

REVISION
NAKED CAME THE STRANGER

I know a writer who has been working on the same book since he was about thirteen years old. One novel. It's been through so many iterations, revisions, and reinventions at this point that it's quite a different novel than what he started out with,[1] but it's still one novel that has taken thirty years and counting to write.

Revision is an essential tool for any writer, of course, and there are plenty of famous examples of authors who really, *really* like to revise. Ernest Hemingway's first draft of *The Sun Also Rises* is remarkably different from the final version, for example. Henry James liked to go back and basically rewrite his earlier novels and then republish them with scathing notes about how awful the original was. Stephen King woke up one day and realized he was Stephen King, Most Powerful Writer in All of History, and decided that all the edits he was forced to make to *The Stand* back in the day could be reversed, so he released a version of the novel that is so large it comes with its own gravity field. And no one knows if we'll *ever* have a final, 100 percent correct version of James Joyce's *Ulysses*.

---

1 And since he was thirteen when he started it, you can imagine what he started with: a lot of boobs.

UNCONVENTIONAL TIP

Don't Kill Your Darlings. This piece of advice, originally offered by Arthur Quiller-Couch in the early twentieth century, is one of the most-quoted and least-understood old saws passed around by writers of every generation. The phrase gets trotted out a *lot* to justify all sorts of crazy theories, but all it means is that you should never keep a sentence, paragraph, or chapter in your novel *just because* it's beautifully written. It *doesn't* mean that you should delete your favorite bits or characters. It means that every single line in your story should be doing some work beyond being pretty.

And it's also not unusual for an author to dedicate huge amounts of time to a single novel; Ralph Ellison is famous for his one novel, *Invisible Man*, but he worked on his follow-up, *Juneteenth*, for four decades, passing away before he was satisfied enough to publish it. I mean, if Ralph Ellison can't finish a book, why shame my author friend?

UNCONVENTIONAL TIP

The most important piece of advice you can ever internalize is this: Just because someone famous does something does *not* make it a good idea.[2]

Which leads us, of course, to the whole point of this chapter: How often do *I* revise manuscripts before I deem them ready to submit? Am I like Raymond Carver, who once admitted he revised his stories forty or fifty times before publishing them? I am not. I *usually* revise my books exactly *once*, and that's mainly to fix spelling errors and other typos.

Note the weasel word *usually* in that sentence; there are exceptions. I'm not averse to revision if there's a point to it,[3] it's just that I actually

---

2 Thank goodness I am not famous, so you can safely do everything I tell you to.

3 Or if an editor says something like, "We'll pay $5,000 for this book but you have to revise it"—in which case I begin revising immediately, right there in their office, using whatever writing ma-

very rarely *see* that point. And let's make another distinction, because this is my book and I can ramble on about whatever I want: There's a distinction between *revisions* and *drafts*, at least in my mind. A draft is a whole new effort. A draft is where I set my hard drive on fire and begin fresh on an idea I've been trying to bang into shape. A revision is when I decide one of those drafts is worth shaping. Another way of thinking about this is that a draft, to me, is a major new effort. A revision is when I'm pretty happy, and I'm just trying to make the manuscript look like it was written by an adult with a mastery of basic English.[4]

UNCONVENTIONAL TIP

Version control is your friend. In the old days, everything I wrote was on paper, and I stuffed drafts into a folder. The only way they could get mixed up was if I got drunk one night and started throwing paper into the air. These days it's very easy to quickly amass one hundred beginnings of an idea, all in files named "Unnamed_Manu_2016.docx." Keeping track of your efforts (by using a coherent file naming convention) will make it easier to take bits and pieces of books that *do* work and paste them into a fresh draft.[5]

Revision is, to put it bluntly, overdone. It's overemphasized, and its importance to your work is overstated. The reasons for this are pretty easy to pinpoint; it all comes down to the infinite supply of opinions, the

---

terials are available to me, all while muttering, *"Five grand! Hoo-boy, that's a lot of pudding!"*

4 Both harder and easier than it sounds. I'm like that drunk old actor who mostly mutters unintelligibly but then every now and then shouts out crystal-clear Shakespearean phrases. Plus, I have a bad habit of allowing bad habits to become part of my "house style"; for a long time I consistently misspelled the word *monkeys* as *monkies* in every single thing I wrote. It drove one proofreader friend of mine insane. Even after I realized what I was doing, I continued to misspell the word out of a stubborn belief that I could influence the entire English-speaking world.

5 While this is perfectly sound advice that I fully endorse and hope you follow, my hard drive is littered with similarly named files that contain single paragraphs as I tried—and failed—to start a novel.

diminishing returns of wordsmithing, and the uncanny valley between writing a novel and addressing a marketing questionnaire.

EVERYBODY HAS ONE

Back in the dark days when I had a Day Job in an office, I had to attend meetings fairly frequently because that's pretty much society's conception of "work": constant soul-sucking meetings. As detailed elsewhere in this book, I used a lot of that wasted time to write, scribbling in a notebook and hoping that it looked like I was the most interested person in the room. But still, meetings become intolerable pretty quickly, and there's a magic moment when you can tell that everything's finally wrapping up and you'll be free to head back to your desk, where some semblance of freedom awaits you—an electric buzz in the air, the scent of release. And then the boss or whoever was leading the meeting would say, "Any questions?" and there was one co-worker, let's call him Earnest, who always—always!—had at least three questions.[6]

To be clear, Earnest didn't actually need answers to his questions. Earnest had read somewhere that you should always ask questions at meetings so your boss remembers your name, so Earnest *always* had questions. And we'd all groan and sink back down into our chairs as Earnest gave our boss an excuse to bloviate for another ten minutes.

There's an Earnest in every meeting, because people are predictable creatures. You may think free will is a Thing and that we all exercise it, but the fact is, we're all easily manipulated and suggestion is a powerful force—if you speak the magic words "Does anyone have any questions?" an Earnest in your audience will, in fact, have questions.

A similar dynamic exists with beta readers and getting opinions on your novel drafts. We touched on this earlier: Put simply, if you ask people to critique your novel, by gum they will come up with critiques, no matter how much effort is required. This is human nature—it's the

---

6 A special place in Hell is reserved for people who ask questions at the end of afternoon meetings. In this place, such people are shot out of a cannon every time they ask any question, at any time, under any circumstances.

WRITING WITHOUT RULES

Challenge: Accepted! Syndrome. When you ask someone for advice, or a critique, they see it as a challenge—if they fail to come up with a response, then they will feel that they've, well, failed.

Consider this: Every few years some delightful rogue decides it would be a truly epic prank to take some famous, classic novel, slap a new title and author on it, and send it off to publishers. When the rejections come in, they expose the prank, and a lot of hot takes are written about how the literary gatekeepers wouldn't know good writing if it hit them over the head.[7] What it also demonstrates is that what makes great writing is often very subjective, and your novel might get wildly different reactions from different people, which brings into question the value of all that feedback in the first place. To be fair, the retitled classics prank doesn't take into account the changing marketplace, taste in literature, and evolving writing style—the fact that *Pride and Prejudice* might not suit the current book-buying public shouldn't surprise anyone—but the fact remains if Austen's classic can't get praise, you have to give the whole concept of feedback the yellow eye.

UNCONVENTIONAL TIP

Don't get hung up on what's getting published. Yes, there are bad books being published—and they sell well. Keep in mind that everyone's idea of a "bad book" is different,[8] and people read for different reasons—sometimes just to pass the time. Dwelling on a perceived unfairness in the book publishing business won't get you anywhere.

---

7 Probably the most famous recent stunt in this vein involved David Lassman, who runs a Jane Austen festival in England. He sent off three of Austen's novels (including *Pride and Prejudice*) to publishers with new titles and search-and-replaced character names, and got seventeen rejections, with only one publisher catching on. It's hard to believe that no one in the publishing industry recognized the iconic opening line of that novel, which is among the most perfect openings in fiction history. If you do not know the line I am referring to you, I am afraid we will never be friends.

8 The Duchess wrote a note here: "Goodreads proves this all the time. I get sucked into these highly rated books that suck ass."

Part of the dynamic at work there is Challenge: Accepted! Syndrome; publishers and agents prove they are discriminating because they reject manuscripts. Thus, they have to reject manuscripts in order to prove themselves discriminating. Your beta readers or other sources of feedback have to offer criticism in order to prove they're *really* reading and thinking about your manuscript. Thus they *will* come up with criticism.

I'm not arguing that feedback and criticism of your manuscript is bad, or useless. I'm arguing that you have to keep a lid on how much of it you engage in. Because you *will* get feedback on every single iteration of your novel. Your beta readers *will* tell what they don't like about each and every draft, and if you keep trying to write something that everybody loves, you'll be like my friend from the first paragraph who's still writing the same novel thirty years later. The trick is to stop taking feedback and stop revising at some point. For some people, that's twenty or thirty revision cycles. For others, it's two or three. For me, it's pretty much one. I get a lot of work done that way.

THE INEXORABLE SADNESS OF COMMAS

I'm pretty certain 93 percent of all the wasted time in the universe revolves around commas in fiction. Some pretty famous authors have agonized over the sentences, punctuation, and other minutiae of their novels, struggling to figure out if they have attained the perfect word order and clause structure of every single line. They tear at their clothes over the placement of commas; they invent neologisms because the words they've been supplied with after centuries of human evolution are insufficient.

I do sometimes think many writers worry a bit about how, you know, *easy* writing can be,[9] so they embrace the idea that you have to agonize

---

9 I'm not talking about me. Writing this book was hard. *Hard.* Very difficult. Most difficult thing I've done in my life. I deserve every penny of the advance, and more. Much more. I've got blisters on me fingers!

WRITING WITHOUT RULES

over every word, sweat dripping from your brow as you tremble from the strain of it.

The truth is, most of the sentences you write are fine. *Fine*. 100 percent perfectly good sentences. Can they be improved? Sure. And some sentences—maybe, for you, *many* sentences—are in dire need of some tough love. I'm not arguing that you shouldn't *revise*; I'm arguing that you very quickly—much more quickly than you realize—hit a point where you are spinning your wheels and trying to improve sentences that are just fine as they are. In other words, the diminishing returns graph for wordsmithing is pretty steep.

My wordsmithing is pretty minimal; I tend to be happy with my words more or less the first time through. I won't pretend to be some insane purist—I do in fact revise, and sometimes I even tinker with word choice or punctuation. But in general I regard finished drafts of novels as, you know, finished. Maybe they're imperfect, maybe they're in need of a light review, but I don't lose sleep pondering whether a particular sentence is the best matrix of words ever produced. Whether this makes me a lazy hack or a genius is up to you,[10] but I am absolutely certain that you could take most drafts of a novel and polish them for typos and they'll be generally as good—or better—than future revisions.

---

10 Definitely a lazy hack, but to be certain you'll need to do some research, so please purchase all of my books and read them before making any determinations.

There will be exceptions; my writing style is very naturalistic and instinctive, but some writers achieve their style through conscious effort. As mentioned earlier, Hemingway's early drafts of his novel *The Sun Also Rises* were vastly different; his signature terse style wasn't present. It was only after numerous revisions that he honed the style and achieved the effect he wanted—it was absolutely an act of will, and if I time traveled to a place I could buy young Hemingway cocktails and explain my theory of No Revision Necessary, Ernest would have ended his days as an alcoholic journalist who'd published some nice, unremarkable books.[11]

Ask yourself, though: Do you build your style through revision, by meticulously choosing words, deleting phrases, and weighing every sentence on a mental scale? Or are you just revising because you're supposed to, just reacting to the feedback you got yesterday? There's a difference. We talked a little about your Writer DNA earlier in this book; part of your DNA is how you achieve your style—and if you're naturalistic and instinctive like me—a Pantser—then it's possible that even a little revision is wasted effort. In short, different words, fewer words, shifted words are not necessarily *better* words.

BETA READERS

I don't use beta readers, which surprises a lot of folks because apparently you're *supposed* to use beta readers. I've always been sort of antisocial and misanthropic, so I am always finding out about stuff decades after it hits big, and I'd never even heard the term *beta reader* until I'd published about five novels. Suddenly it was all anyone could talk about, and I began to wonder if I was crazy and doing it wrong, despite having published pretty well without them.

I do occasionally send a manuscript to a trusted friend who is also an author, and I often show material to my wife The Duchess to get her

---

11 Completely undermining my premise is part of my genius, double-secret strategy for success. This is why all of my strategies for success are double-secret. It's also why I carry smoke bombs in my pockets for quick escapes.

seal of approval.[12] But I don't have a regular team of beta readers, and I don't plan to set one up. If you are in trouble with a novel and need feedback desperately, then by all means get some readers together. But for me it's not something I want or feel like I need, because I'd rather write a book that *I* like, flaws and all, rather than a book that is walked through a committee.

UNCONVENTIONAL TIP

If you do decide to use beta readers, consider the fact that just because someone is generally smart—or is maybe an accomplished writer—doesn't mean they have what it takes to be your beta reader. Ideally beta readers should have some qualifications:

- Be well versed in the specific genre of your book
- Be widely read in general
- Be willing to commit to turnaround dates; busy folks often *want* to be of service to their friends, but if you're waiting sixteen months to get their notes, it's not going to work
- Be someone who scares you a little. Ideally, if you're looking for feedback, find someone you're terrified to show your writing to.

As with all things in this book, your mileage will vary. If you work well using regular beta readers, don't let me stop you. Just remind yourself that even smart, well-intentioned readers will be wrong sometimes.[13]

---

12 This isn't just out of affection (or fear); my wife is convinced she has The Sight when it comes to which of my novels will sell. This dates back to our Early Days, before marriage, when she wasn't 100 percent certain a boozy incompetent who "wrote novels" was an ideal match. She remained dubious about my ability to monetize the rambling imagination in my head until I showed her *The Electric Church*. At first she was reluctant to read a stupid science fiction novel that opened with a monologue about removing brains from people's heads, but then she got hooked and came home that night to tell me very excitedly that THIS was the book that would sell. And it did, and ever since she has been insufferably certain that she has The Sight.

13 Unlike smart, well-intentioned authors, who are always right and damn your eyes if you think otherwise.

THE EVENT HORIZON

One of the most difficult things for a writer to navigate is the gulf between writing purely for yourself and writing for a market—for readers. For some lucky folks, these two countries aren't that far apart; the things they write for themselves also appeal to a wide audience. But even if that's the case with you, part of the struggle with the feedback you'll get and the urge to revise your work is the perceived gap between the two—in other words, if your goal is to sell your work, sometimes you start thinking in terms of whether or not readers will like what you're writing. And the bigger the audience you desire, the more you might feel the need to revise with that audience in mind.

It works in two ways: the Carrot and the Stick. When you think about writing to please an audience, you think mostly about The Stick, which is the negative comments you get on your revisions— what they didn't like, what they felt was forced or unbelievable. So you revise to "fix" those issues. This can be maddening because it's almost like stamping out bugs in a computer program—every change you make to "solve" a problem raised by a beta reader or other critic often introduces whole new issues on the next round of feedback. Getting into a pattern of trying to "solve" problems raised by a limited number of feedback sources—no matter how trusted— can quickly turn into an infinite loop.

The Carrot hurts too, although we often overlook it. The Carrot is when our beta readers *love* something. They read a chapter written in a specific style or using a specific technique, and they come back filled with praise—it was great! They loved it!

And so you repeat the trick. You start using the technique a lot more. If it worked once, it will work every single time!

Of course, sometimes it doesn't, and you can waste a lot of time chasing that Carrot.

In the end, you have to write for yourself. Every time I've ever tried to write with a marketing goal in mind, it's been a failure. In fact, many of the novels and stories I've sold to publishers and had success with weren't the ones I *thought* I'd do well with. *The Electric Church* languished on my hard drive for years, and ultimately saw publication through a series of near accidents, because it never occurred to me at the time that it was a manuscript I could sell. In fact, I've come to realize that my own sense of what's marketable in my body of work is very, very borked.[14] This is one big reason I need my agent. I can't tell you how many times I've sent her a novel with a breathless note referencing the gold toilets I will purchase with the advance and option monies, only to have her send back notes on the first 50 pages that strongly imply I start looking into regular old porcelain toilets, and possibly secondhand ones at that.[15]

Feedback and revision can help you shape your novel, of course. If smart people tell you something isn't working, there's reason to think about their comments and possibly revise your book. But you have to avoid Carrot and Stick Syndrome—every piece of advice has to be filtered through your own sensibilities, and the easiest way to do that is to simply ask yourself one simple question: Is the book you're writing one *you* would want to read?

BE SELFISH

Writing a book you'd *want to read* sounds like such simple advice it can't possibly be correct. Writing a novel has to involve alcoholism and blood leaking from your eyes, right? It can't possibly be all about entertaining and indulging *yourself*?

Of course it is. Now, granted, if you're seeking to write the next breakthrough in experimental fiction, this advice may not apply—but if your goal is to write a novel without using the word *and* or a novel without a plot just to see if you can, you're not really writing a novel

---

14 This is a real, actual word and one of my favorite words of all time, mainly because it allows me to do my famous Swedish Chef impression.

15 The "golden toilets" thing has been a running joke with my agent for so long, it's evolved into a sophisticated code: When she sells something, she emails me a picture of a golden toilet like the one Pablo Escobar had. Would I ever actually buy a golden toilet? The things I would do if I became rich enough is long and includes not only golden toilets but also a private island where I would hunt the Most Dangerous Game and pay people to dance for me at all times. I am not a good person, I am merely a poor person.

that's meant to be read and enjoyed. You're cooking up an experiment like a mad scientist.[16]

My novel *Chum* is one of the few exceptions to my usual practice of barely revising; I worked on that book on and off for a decade, tweaking and freshening it. I'm not sure the final version is *remarkably* better than the first version my agent took on, but the final version is the one that sold, so let it drift.[17]

My agent would occasionally get feedback from an editor or someone else and pass it on to me. At one point, she asked a colleague of hers who worked in young adult books to read it and send me notes. The notes were *awesome*. They were smart and detailed, offering a way that I could revise the novel as a YA book and try to sell it to that market—this was smart; this was my agent trying to think outside the box. At that point she'd had the novel for eight years or so, and a little fresh thinking was certainly welcome.

But—and here's the thing—I didn't want to make *Chum* into a YA novel. I don't read a lot of YA, so it's not my scene. In other words, I didn't want to make *Chum* into a book I wouldn't read. It was really that simple; the notes I got were gold, and if I'd wanted to, sure, I could have pulled it off. But I chose not to, because I wanted to write a book I'd want to read.

I can't say that my resolve to keep *Chum* adult is why we sold it a few years later, but I *can* say that choosing to ignore feedback and advice—even compelling feedback and advice—was the right decision. Before parsing any feedback from any source, you have to first know exactly the kind of book you want to write, and then stick to your guns.

On a final note, I should point out that when I am contractually obligated to a publisher or editor and they send me notes, I don't casually reply that I don't like to revise and so won't be paying any attention. I am lazy and disorganized, not stupid. I write books I want to read, and

---

16 And if science fiction has taught us anything, it's that the number one life goal of such creations is to murder their creator. Good luck with that.

17 I am also not 100 percent certain I sent the most recent draft to my publisher after we signed the contract. Don't tell anyone.

publishers publish books they think can sell, and when you've accepted the advance money you've entered into an adult partnership wherein you've agreed to certain parameters, accepting editorial guidance being one of them. That doesn't mean you just meekly do as you're told, or that you don't push back, argue against, and interpret notes and feedback as you see fit. It just means that even if I think some revision is just gilding a lily, I do it, because I signed the contract. And most editors are smarter than me, so they're usually right.

Revision is a) a tool and b) a personal decision. My advice: Don't force yourself into revision cycles or feedback loops that don't come naturally. And whatever you do, don't spend thirty years on one novel.

TRUNK NOVELS, BEAUTIFUL FAILURES, AND THE STRANGE ATTRACTORS

MAKING NOVELS OUT OF NOTHING AT ALL

Here's the secret, the *real* secret: I finish everything.

I'm leery of the modern tendency to transform various negative personality traits—up to and including mild mental disorders—into virtues. And yet, I'm about to do it, because this is my book and I can do as I please: I hate to leave things unfinished. Oh, a story that's basically a sentence fragment I walk away from. A few lumpy paragraphs I can forget. But once I cross a pretty shallow Event Horizon of words, I must—and will—finish every project I begin.[1]

---

1 Does this disorder extend into other areas of my life, such as cleaning the house, various maintenance projects, a bottle of whiskey—which, once opened, must be finished or I will lie in bed at night staring at the ceiling and contemplating the possibility that I will die in my sleep and never get to finish that whiskey? Of course not. That would be crazy.

This leads me down some grim paths, of course: meandering novels that should be put out of their misery, hapless short stories that flame out rather spectacularly, gruesome novella-like ... things ... that are neither novel nor short story. I won't claim that everything I finish is fantastic, or even advisable. But I am definitely *not* one of those writers with a lot of unfinished manuscripts littering his hard drive. Whether that's a good or bad thing is up to you, but please don't tell me.

Why is this humblebragging about my awesome ability to finish books important? It's simple, really: As I pointed out when I discussed ending novels back in chapter four, you sell exactly 0 percent of the novels you don't finish.

DEARTH VADER[2]

Probably the number one complaint struggling writers make concerns a dearth of ideas.[3] That's not the same as writer's block, which we'll discuss in the next chapter; I'm talking about that horrible moment when you stare at a blank page or screen and just have no idea what to write *about*. Writer's block is something that happens in the midst of a book.[4]

This can happen to any writer, at any point in his career. Some folks have only one moment of inspiration in an entire lifetime; others seem to effortlessly come up with new ideas all the time. Most of us, however, are in the middle: We have ideas on a regular basis, but sometimes struggle. And when you struggle to come up with inspiration for your next project, it can seem like something deep inside your brain has shut off; that can lead to a real sense of existential panic. For many of us, our creativity is hardwired into our sense of self. If that sense suddenly seems to have stopped working, it's like a light has gone out, and we're left in the dark, and that can lead to panic.[5]

---

2 This pun is like the Heisenberg Uncertainty Principle of puns. I keep changing my mind on whether it's hilarious or the opposite of hilarious. If you look at it straight on, it's terrible. Catch it out of the corner of your eye, it's playful and funny.

3 Number two: Society's insistence on pants. Number three: Having to write synopses of your novels for heartless agents.

4 One of the joys of writing your own book is that you can make up your own definitions of what words mean, like the President.

5 Also: Memoirs.

UNCONVENTIONAL TIP

If you're feeling panic because you haven't had a good idea for a book in a very long time, here's what *not* to do:

- **DON'T** write a memoir. Memoirs are for people who have led interesting lives, not authors who are out of ideas.
- **DON'T** chase a trend. Any trends you're aware of stopped being a thing two years ago behind the scenes. Publishing schedules have long tails.
- **DON'T** complain. Your friends barely tolerate your writerly stuff as it is. Whining about the lack of a creative spark will only make them avoid you *more*.

There are a lot of strategies you can pursue when you can't get excited about any of your ideas, but most of them are dreamy mental exercises. And those can totally work, but I'm not one for dreamy mental exercises—I like to keep my hands moving.[6] That being said, you need to be careful not to grind gears[7]—typing just to type. If you don't have any ideas, forcing yourself to grind on something[8] will not only waste your time, it will add to your frustration when you go back to read the horror that you've created.[9]

The point about "keeping my hands moving" isn't to just blindly work your way through a lack of ideas, it's about finding an idea you *can* get excited about even when you don't *have* any ideas. The easiest and most effective way to do that is to go back to an idea that you *were* once excited about but couldn't make work: Your **Trunk Novels** and **Beautiful Failures**.

---

6 You have a dirty mind.

7 You still have a dirty mind.

8 Ibid.

9 A related anecdote involves a novel The Duchess insisted I write; I'd shown her two shorter works and she thought they would make a great novel if mashed together. I disagreed, but The Duchess does not brook refusals, so she kept bringing it up. Finally I gave in and wrote the damn novel, and, as expected, it was a glorious, dull-edged mess. The Duchess accused me of muffing it on purpose, but she hasn't insisted I write anything since.

The trick here is to admit when you're beat: If you can't come up with a *new* idea you're excited about, then go back to an *old* idea you were once excited about and try to spin gold out of that dusty fail.

TRUNK NOVELS

You very well may be familiar with the term *Trunk Novel*, which is a novel you've finished but have been unable to sell, or are otherwise dissatisfied with. The idea is that this novel stays in your trunk, like an old stuffed animal, and you haul it out every now and then, dust it off, and try to make it sing and dance.

The defining characteristic of a Trunk Novel is that you refuse to give up on it; yet many writers fail to think about their Trunk Novels when they lack inspiration. This is a novel you've actually finished! Well, sort of; it's written, but by definition, you're either unhappy with it or haven't been able to get anyone else interested in it. If you're frustrated by a lack of ideas, dig out one of those older books and read it again. Trunk Novels tend to fall into one of three categories:

Juvenilia. A novel you wrote when you were a kid might have incredible ideas but be immature in execution.[10] A complete rewrite might bring those brilliant ideas back to life.

A Pretty Mess.[11] These books contain great ideas and some truly fine writing, but never "gelled" into a coherent style. Some ruthless cutting and papering-over of gaps in the narrative might be all you need.

Insanity Bombs. Hey, we all have our experiments. Sometimes you finish a book and it's just bonkers. Absolutely bonkers. So bonkers you quietly put it in a plastic bag and bury it in your backyard. Well, if you're unable to see your way through a dearth of ideas, an Insanity Bomb usually contains more ideas than should be in a single novel, so

---

10 For example, you can likely pinpoint exactly where I was in my pursuit of an English Degree by reading some of the novels I wrote in college. Did I just learn about stream-of-consciousness? There's a novel written entirely using that technique. Was I taking a class on noir detective fiction? There's a novel narrated by a world-weary operative. At the time, I thought I was brilliant. These days I frequently look down to discover I am wearing milk cartons as shoes.

11 Coincidentally, this is my wife's nickname for me, usually uttered with a gentle pat on the head and followed by a request for a sandwich.

instead of trying to make a crazy book work, just go tear it apart for spare inspiration.

BEAUTIFUL FAILURES

Sometimes a Trunk Novel is something else entirely—a Beautiful Failure. Beautiful Failures are usually really good novels in many ways. They have a great premise, or at least a promising one. They contain great writing. The plot works nicely. And yet ... there's something missing. It resembles a successful novel in just about every way, but it *fails* in some mysterious, impossible-to-define aspect.

Beautiful Failures are the most frustrating kind of failed novel because they're so deceptively good-looking.[12] Sometimes it's even difficult to figure out *where* they go wrong, because when you reread it you think, *damn, this is actually really good.* Then, after another seven months of reworking scenes and cutting ruthlessly, you still can't quite put your finger on it, but it's still only an amazing simulation of a novel.

---

12 No, this is definitely 100 percent not a metaphor about me. I am deceptively good-looking, but I'm not frustrating; I'm delightful.

WRITING WITHOUT RULES

A Beautiful Failure can become an elusive unicorn that eats all your time and slowly drives you insane. But, if you're dealing with a lack of ideas, why not return to one of your Beautiful Failures and give it another go-round? Performing an autopsy on one and creating a plan to rework it into a real, live novel is a time-consuming task, so the perfect time to go for it is when you've spent the last few weeks not sleeping as your brain races around the empty space that is your current level of inspiration.

There are a couple of strategies you can use to transform a Beautiful Failure into a working novel:

The Do-Over. Of course, one extreme option is to just trash what you have and start over with the same premise. The upside is that you know at least *one* approach that didn't work.[13]

The POV Switch. Often a Beautiful Failure is a great *idea* for a novel done the wrong way—and changing the character who tells the story might be all you need.

The Serial. We tend to think in monumental terms when it comes to novels. If you have a Beautiful Failure, why not rework it as if you were publishing each chapter like a soap opera—you need a "hook" at the end of every chapter. This shifts your narrative in small ways and opens up unexpected new directions.

While it was not a conscious decision at the time, I used this technique when I revised *The Electric Church* in 2004. I wrote the original draft in 1993 and returned to it several times, never quite certain how to make it sing. One day I literally googled the phrase "get paid for fiction," and found the website Another Chapter, which was looking for serial fiction pitches. Their idea was to mail people one chapter of a story every week, like a literary soap opera. They preferred open-ended stories but would consider anything novel length. So I followed their very involved guidelines and pitched *The Electric Church*; they accepted it.

Revising the novel for Another Chapter meant every chapter of the book had to end on a beat—a hook—in order to (hopefully) entice subscribers to keep coming back. While the publisher didn't last very

---

13 If you're like me, this quickly turns into about sixty-seven ways that didn't work.

long and went out of business[14] before half the book went online, that serial style kicked my revision into high gear, and the draft I produced there eventually sold to Warner Books (and then moved to Orbit with my editor).

The Road Not Taken. You've got a great premise, maybe great characters, so your problem is the ending. Back it up, delete the final third (fourth? eighth?) of your story and send it careening down a dark mine shaft.

Beautiful Failures can be tough to crack because they're, well, *beautiful*. It's easy to tear apart your homely, 100 percent Fail novels. It's much more difficult to take something that's *almost* great and perform surgery on it.

UNCONVENTIONAL TIP

This is where the advice to "kill your darlings" might actually come in handy. If you have a novel stuffed with great writing that still doesn't work, you're going to have to start deleting bits that you think are—and might actually be—brilliant.

Finally, consider the **strange attractors** you might have lying around, and see if you can Frankenstein two failed novels together, as discussed in chapter three.

GETTING TO THE FINISH LINE

Of course, whether you're dealing with several older manuscripts that have the potential to taste great together or a fresh idea that has you excited, the key is to finish that book. While we've just looked at how unfinished novels can provide material for the next time you're struggling for ideas, if you *have* an idea, your next step is to *finish* that idea.

---

14 I didn't have access to a Super Mainframe Computer to calculate my royalties from Another Chapter at the time, but I believe they were in the $2.70 range. Thanks to the joys of Amazon's self-publishing services, that is not the smallest amount of money I've ever earned on a book.

To put it simply, writers often give up on novels too soon. And anytime you stop working on a book before you've typed *the end* is too soon.

As a final thought, consider this: Not finishing projects and struggling to come up with ideas for your writing are *directly related*. It's so easy to undermine your own confidence, and having a pile of unfinished manuscripts does the job about as well as anything else. Over time, it's very easy to blame unfinished projects not on your process or discipline, but on the *ideas* you started with. You can get some crazy ideas *about* ideas, like the following:

- Ideas must come to you fully formed, with a clear plotline and an ending, or they're not worth pursuing.
- If you can't finish the story, the idea is somehow "poisoned" and can't be picked up, dusted off, and used again.

Finishing the stories you begin builds confidence and flexes a lot of writing muscles. Staying productive when your muse doesn't want to cooperate flexes those muscles even more. Do both consistently and you'll have more material to publish, and more skill at producing it. Plus, saying "I've written three novels" reads better than "I've written sixteen lumps of words that ramble and trail off." Trust me on that one.

10

WRITER'S BLOCK
YOU'RE FOOLING YOURSELF,
YOU DON'T BELIEVE IT

If you watch TV shows or movies, you might be forgiven for thinking that writer's block is one of the most deadly disorders known to man. Writers afflicted with this terrible syndrome day drink constantly, devolve into some sort of protohuman evolutionary stage, contemplate suicide, and eat a lot of fast food. Consider what Hollywood thinks happens when writers get blocked:

- Murder, like Johnny Depp in *Secret Window*.
- Career immolation, like Michael Douglas in *Wonder Boys*.
- Total alcoholic life breakdown, like Ray Milland in *Lost Weekend*.
- Attempted murder of entire family, like Jack Nicholson in *The Shining*.
- Split personality and emotional breakdown, like Charlie Kaufman in *Adaptation*.[1]

---

1 The Duchess, who has established that the film *Love Actually* is a generic holiday film appropriate for any special occasion (including but not limited to Christmas, Easter, Groundhog Day, National Secretary's Day, Monday, and today), notes another possibility: "Or they find love like Colin Firth in *Love Actually*!"

Basically, not being able to see where your story goes next more or less snaps the writer's delicate mind like a dry twig, and moments later we're drinking directly from a $2 bottle of liquor and screaming as we stab someone.[2]

Now, every writer has experienced that awful moment when you can't think of what happens next. Those times when every sentence you write seems leaden and uninspired; those moments when you wonder if that thirteenth Tequila Fanny Banger the night before might have—maybe, the science isn't settled—burned some part of your brain to ash, and you'll never have a good idea again.

It's terrible. But here's the thing: There is no such thing as writer's block.

Half of you just threw this book across the room in disgust or threw it in the trash, then fished it out just to hate-read the rest.[3] Because writer's block can be a touchy subject for writers, in my experience. It's *our* syndrome. *Our* struggle. Plus it's the only time we get to complain, really, because writing isn't particularly hard work. Mentally challenging, sure. And when you're cobbling together fiction and freelance contracts to make a living, it can be stressful and time-consuming, yes. But you're not working in a mine, lifting bales all day, or col- lecting garbage. You're *typing.*

UNCONVENTIONAL TIP

Nonwriters do not—I repeat, *do not*—take writer's block or any other writerly complaint seriously. People really do believe that writing is easy; this is why everyone assumes they will someday write a book themselves, when they have the time. At the same time, some writers use writer's block to define their entire careers, explaining how it's possible their expensive business cards have said *Writer* for the last twenty years, but they have written exactly nothing. Don't be that writer.

---

2 Or, as I like to call it, Monday.

3 If you did this only to remember you're reading a digital copy on your tablet, that is unfortunate. And likely expensive.

So writer's block has become a Thing, but it's really just a collective label for a bunch of writerly problems—writerly problems that *are* 100 percent real and *are* 100 percent debilitating to your creative efforts. Things like a lack of ideas, mental fatigue, or simply a manuscript that's not working can conspire to slow down your work and cripple your confidence. But here's the thing: Using a catch-all term like *writer's block* simultaneously trivializes those problems while also obscuring them. Mental fatigue, a confused plot, a steaming pile of spirit-crushing negative feedback? Those things you can deal with. You know what they are and you can come up with a solution for them. *Writer's block* is a meaningless term that seems monumental, monolithic, impenetrable— and thus incurable, ultimately leading to the aforementioned mental breakdown, day drinking, and possibly public weeping.[4]

That's not a useful way to look at writing and creativity challenges. Think of it this way: If you're told you're simply "sick" or "ill," you'll be alarmed, frightened, confused—you don't have any information, and the blanket term *sick* isn't useful. But if someone says, "You have a stomach virus. It'll go away in two days; remember to drink a lot of fluids,"[5] now you have information and can focus on dealing with the problem.

It's the same way with writing: Telling yourself that you have writer's block is a scary, meaningless term that might mean anything from a momentary lapse of creativity to a brain tumor that causes you to only be able to write the word *salad*. Instead of wandering around, wrapped in a sad, vague cloud of misery, get specific. Diagnose your specific problem and take steps to work through it effectively.

WRITER'S BLOCK, HUH, WHAT IS IT GOOD FOR?

Come on people, we're writers.[6] The term *writer's block* is lazy language. What do we mean when we say we have writer's block? It's composed

---

4 Or, as I like to call it, Tuesday.

5 I know what you're thinking, but alcohol apparently doesn't count as fluids, despite being composed of fluids. The universe is a crazy place.

6 If you purchased this book and you're not a writer, you have made a terrible mistake.

WRITING WITHOUT RULES

of five specific problems that you might suffer from individually or in a group:

1. **LACK OF IDEAS.** We discussed this in detail in chapter nine.
2. **INABILITY TO SEE THE WAY FORWARD IN YOUR STORY.** This is probably the most common thing people think of when it comes to writer's block: an unfinished novel and no idea how to get moving.
3. **PROBLEMS WITH THE TELEMETRY.** You have an idea you're passionate about, but you can't figure out how to make all the plot points fit together, and you're frozen.
4. **A LACK OF CONFIDENCE.** You're writing, but you're dissatisfied with everything and convinced it's terrible.
5. **BEING OVERWHELMED.** Either you have too many things going on or a lack of time; the end result is you're not writing.

See? Instead of the scary and uninformative term *writer's block*, we've got five distinct problems that, either in combination or on their own, prevent you from getting work done. And we've already dealt with one of them![7] So now instead of retreating into a bottle and feeling sorry for ourselves, we can talk about how to deal with each of the four remaining problems that constitute writer's block.

No Way Forward. Sometimes you get into the weeds of a story and paint yourself into a plot corner or simply realize you're just not excited about your story anymore. You have no idea how to finish, no clue what happens next. Your first step should be to consider whether this is something you could solve with some judicious (or wild and uninhibited) **plantsing**; simply changing up your approach can often solve plot problems. If that doesn't work, your next step is simple enough: Stop writing, step away from your desk or coffee shop table, and read a book. Seriously: *Read a book*. This isn't goofing off.[8] It's research. It's

---

7 Since I signed a contract with a minimum word count specified, I briefly contemplated copy-and-pasting most of chapter nine here, duplicating a technique I used to get through most of my schooling by simply reusing my English papers from freshman year of high school. As it turns out, book editors are much smarter than high school English teachers, and I was punished for this. If there are more typos in this chapter than usual, blame it on my broken fingers.

8 One reason I love the TV show *Mad Men* is because it shows Don Draper, creative genius, frequently napping in his office and going to the movies in the afternoon, which is basically how the

work related. It doesn't matter what you read, actually; any genre or form of writing will engage your brain with unexpected ideas and weird inspirations, which is what you need when your characters have been milling about in a single scene for months, uncertain of the way out.

UNCONVENTIONAL TIP

Actually, any engagement with art or someone else's creativity will work. Absorbing other people's ideas is essential to the creative act, so it makes sense that if you're having trouble writing, one solution might be taking a break to engage with art. Other people's ideas are the fuel to your creative engine, after all.

Frozen by Plot. You had a flash of inspiration—say, you want to write a novel about a dashing, whiskey-loving, pants-hating rapscallion of a writer—and your brain kicks into overdrive, fleshing out the character, envisioning the plot points—but *not* the connective tissue. You can see the shocking twist in chapter forty, but the previous thirty-nine chapters are murky. Or you have the perfect chapter one more or less complete in your head, but the rest of it is just fog. Once again, stopping to read is a good idea—it takes the pressure off you and pours someone else's ideas into your head. Failing that, you can also try this one weird trick: Just start writing, and *keep* writing. You have a character? A basic setting? Just start telling your audience *anything* about them. Start with them getting up in the morning and taking a shower and just sort of follow them around. It's boring, it's not good writing—but as you do this, you'll be subconsciously filling in blanks and seeing possibilities, until suddenly you'll look up from the keyboard and just *know* how to get started.

---

creative process works—it looks a lot like goofing off. This is why everyone hates Creatives. You may not think they hate us, but they do, which is why we get paid pennies per word even though literally no book, series, or film would exist without us. Of course, if I take a nap in my office, I wake up smothered under five cats, screaming, from a dream of being … smothered by five cats.

WRITING WITHOUT RULES

UNCONVENTIONAL TIP

You will often be advised to "write through" writer's block. While not terrible advice, unless you know precisely what's afflicting your writing, it could turn into infinite word salad. The key is knowing *what* you're fighting. Otherwise, you're just typing.

Every Sentence Stinks.[9] This is a subtle problem, because, ostensibly, you're still working. We all have bad days, or even bad weeks, where every word we put down in pixels, ink, or graphite is disappointing. I write short stories longhand in notebooks,[10] and I can't tell you how many of those stories suddenly end with a frighteningly Manson-like scrawl of *this is terrible* or something similar[11]—and usually there are several of them in a row. In my experience, this usually happens when I'm thinking too hard about my work. Even if you're normally the sort of writer who worries over every word choice and comma placement,[12] taking a vacation from worrying about form and format is often the best way to counteract this sense of doom and failure. Just write—write fast and without thinking. *Don't* go back and edit; *don't* think about anything. Use clichés, use other writers' ideas and techniques, replicate your favorite scenes and dialogue from your favorite books. A few hours or days of just having some fun writing will cure you.

---

9 No, this is not a direct quote from a review of my last novel, though I do have affection for bad reviews. I used to publish a zine titled *The Inner Swine*, and I would publish every bad review of the zine *in* the zine, which was great fun. My favorite bad review came from another zine, *Flesh-mouth* (now defunct), which spent a good 300 words detailing all my flaws as a writer and then finished with the self-aware, classic line "What does this all mean? *It means it's wank.*" I have since adopted *it means it's wank* as my *Game of Thrones*-style House Words.

10 Because I hate my future self—so smug in his Jetsons-like outfit, motoring around in his flying car, wearing supercool shades as he teleports and time travels—I write longhand and laugh as I imagine Future Jeff forced to keyboard all those notebooks, squinting at awful handwriting, back aching, carpal tunnel kicking in. And then, of course, I become Future Jeff and everything is terrible.

11 Except, you know, substitute a more ... interesting word for *terrible*.

12 That is not me at all. I often have to fabricate positions on style questions on the spot, because I just haven't thought about it. Oxford comma? Sure, why not.

UNCONVENTIONAL TIP

Another reason word count is a terrible metric to use in terms of productivity: The words have to be *good* words to count toward anything. If you're proud of writing 5,000 words today, but delete 4,900 of them in six months, what did it matter?

Fighting the Clock. Very few writers are full-time in the sense of being able to work solely on their own projects and still pay rent. I myself worked a day job for eighteen years before I could write full-time—and even now I do a lot of freelance writing to cover the bills, so, yes, *technically* I am a full-time writer, but believe me when I say this isn't what I imagined when I was fifteen.[13] The point is, we all have stuff that crowds in and takes away the time, energy, and thought we'd rather focus on our writing. Sometimes that just becomes overwhelming, with day after day slipping by without any chance to really sit down and think clearly about that book. This is part of writer's block, whether you're aware of it or not, because it sticks with you even after the time crunch passes. You know how science![14] says we make up the sleep we miss very slowly?[15] It's a similar phenomenon in reverse: It takes a long time to get past that feeling of simple overwhelming time panic. It can cripple your writing for weeks, months—years, even. The answer isn't easy: You *must* make time to write. And it can't be a hectic half hour at lunch,[16] it has to be a serious, planned excursion. You need to decompress, then work a bit, then ramp up to return to the other aspects of

---

13 I'm not complaining—in fact, every day I have at least one out-of-body experience centered on the sheer amazement that I have earned some pretty good money with words I write. Of course, those experiences might also have something to do with the shots of whiskey I sneak from the bottle I keep in the toilet tank.

14 Science! is amazing and should always be paired with an exclamation point to underscore that fact. I love science! the way I love ballroom dancing: From a vast distance.

15 This and other amazing things are discussed over at Sleep.org, which I didn't know existed until just now when I thought I might need a link to support the statement I just made. Declare first, research later is more or less how I roll, kids. It's amazing I'm still married.

16 Don't get me wrong: A hectic half hour at lunch can be incredible for your productivity—but only when you're in a good place otherwise. If you're feeling like your life is an ocean sitting on top of you, suddenly surfacing for thirty measly minutes to feel the sun on your face just means you explode from the sudden pressure change.

your life. That isn't easy—not everyone can simply declare they're taking a personal day to work on their writing. But it's the only way to get moving again when you've been crushed, so whether it takes one day of planning or one year, you have no choice but to arrange some time to write.

UNCONVENTIONAL TIP

Making time to write is the biggest challenge that most writers face. I've already discussed my habit of having multiple writing vectors so I can write under a variety of circumstances—on the bus, in a meeting, on a plane, while being dragged away by riot police—but this assumes you have options to begin with. The best advice I can offer is this: Typing or hand-writing fiction is the *last* step. The real writing happens in your mind, and no matter what else you're doing you can always be writing in your head.

THE MESSAGE

Most of us view writer's block, or its component afflictions, as a challenge. As writers, we're like the bull who spots the bullfighter (the idea), so we charge. But sometimes an inability to make progress in a novel is a message from your muse, your subconscious, or the tiny floating green man who dictates all your stories to you.[17] And that message just might be: Change direction.

That doesn't mean give up (we've already established that I finish everything, so giving up is impossible). It means that sometimes writer's block is the universe telling you that you've taken a wrong turn in your story, started the wrong story, or otherwise lost your way. The gut reaction to this is usually to push past it, fight, triumph, which is where a lot of the "write through it" advice comes from—don't give in, common wisdom says. Attack the problem until you finish the darn book. Instead, why not tunnel under it or go around it? A lack of ideas, a pessimism about your writing, a panicked sense of being overwhelmed—

---

17 We all have those guys, right? Asking for a friend.

all of these symptoms stem from the same problem: a fundamental lack of excitement about what you're doing. That just might be your muse or subconscious trying to tell you something, and changing direction might be the answer.

Of course, you could also deploy the patented Jeff Somers Writer's Block Cure, which involves several different liquors utilized similarly to how Daffy Duck used gasoline, nitroglycerine, gunpowder, and uranium-238 in the classic Bugs Bunny cartoon *Show Biz Bugs*.[18] It doesn't help me write, but when I wake up a week later, I have no recollection of what I was working on and can start fresh.

---

18 Which, in case you are not as ancient as I am and have no idea what I'm talking about, you can watch here: www.dailymotion.com/video/xtwd4_show-biz-bugs-7_fun.

PART 2

SELLING A NOVEL

HOW TO MAKE A DIME (SADLY, PROBABLY LITERALLY)

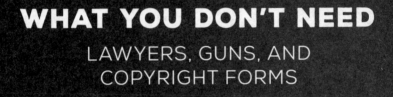

11

WHAT YOU DON'T NEED
LAWYERS, GUNS, AND COPYRIGHT FORMS

When you get invited to conferences, conventions, and literary events, it's natural for people to assume you have achieved a sort of competence as a professional writer. I've given presentations at the Writer's Digest Annual Conference; I've spoken on panels and signings at New York Comic Con.[1] And every time writers come up to me afterwards with questions—about the creative process, my work, and the legal and business aspect of writing. Which, to this day, I remember how much I know alarmingly little about.

These are stressful moments, because I can almost see my stature shrinking as the conversation goes on. When a writer first approaches me, I am a Published Author Who Knows the Secret. By the end of the conversation, I am the Incoherent Moron Who Isn't Wearing Pants, but I Could Swear He Was Wearing Pants Just a Moment Ago … My God, How

---

1 My first year at NYCC, my signing lane was right next to Lou Ferrigno, The Incredible Hulk himself. Lou was incredibly protective of his space; at one point The Duchess wandered over to get a better view of me and my adoring fans, and The Hulk got irritated and told her to stay in her lane. I don't blame the guy—that's his livelihood. But I missed an opportunity for free publicity via "Unknown Author Put in Coma by Hulk" stories, didn't I?

Did He Remove His Pants Without My Noticing? In other words, people have certain assumptions about what it takes to acquire the "professional" part of Professional Writer, and I must sadly inform them that I know and practice almost none of it.

UNCONVENTIONAL TIP

I do suggest you join an appropriate organization like the Mystery Writers of America (www.mysterywriters.org), the Horror Writers Association (www.horror.org), or the Science Fiction Writers of America (www.sfwa.org) if you qualify (they all have publication requirements for full membership, though most offer a lower level of membership if you don't meet that criteria). They offer some nice benefits in terms of legal advice, contract review, promotional opportunities, networking, and even some limited group healthcare options for freelancers. Then, once you have joined, I suggest you stay far away from them, because such organizations are almost always hotbeds of local politics, personal grudges, and the sort of outlandish personalities who find a writer's union a nice, small pond in which to be a big fish. In other words, pay your dues, take advantage of things that benefit you, give back where you can (say, in offering to mentor younger writers or something), but don't actually go to the meetings.

The fact is, people who haven't published or written a lot think it's more complicated than it really is. They worry about copyright, about people stealing their work or ideas. They worry about contracts and rights long before they've even published anything, and they assume someone who has published nine novels and dozens of stories and optioned film rights must have a phalanx of lawyers and tons of sage advice for protecting yourself against Capitalist Overlords and Anarchists who all want to steal your precious intellectual property.[2]

I don't. I don't do much to protect my work, and, frankly, neither should you.

---

2 For the purposes of this chapter, whenever I use the phrase "intellectual property," you should imagine Brigadier General Jack Ripper from *Dr. Strangelove* saying "precious bodily fluids."

CYNICISM FOR THE WIN!

Negativity is always a good bet if you want to seem smart. In any scenario, if you're positive and optimistic, people will generally assume you're either not very smart, not very experienced, or privileged in some fundamental way. If you predict horror and catastrophe, it doesn't matter whether your predictions come true—if they don't, the assumption will be that you got lucky. As a result, people who tell you everything is ruined and you're going to die never get called out for being wrong, because everyone just assumes that the ruin and death will come *tomorrow*, possibly next Thursday.[3]

Disasters that don't come are just disasters that haven't come *yet*.

So, when someone wants to establish themselves as a guru of sorts about writing and the business of publishing, an easy way to seem authoritative is to tell everyone how bad everything is or could be. And, as I know from personal experience, an easy way to establish yourself as an unreliable boozehound is to say the opposite, which is that you don't really need to worry much about anything beyond writing great stories and partnering with smart people to help you sell and market those stories—i.e., a good literary agent. What *don't* you need? Pretty much everything else.

WHAT YOU DON'T NEED

Writing, unlike some other artistic professions, doesn't have much of an amateur infrastructure. Most of us are just writing on our own, and many of us spend a significant number of years in isolation, without much input from other writers. When we start to move into a professional category, it's either through individual sales of stories or longer pieces—often done on our own through submissions—or by landing an agent who can guide us to publishers and other opportunities. It can also be a combination of both.

---

3 Consider doomsday cults, which frequently predict the end of the world, giving very specific dates ... and just revise their calculations when the dates come and go without much happening. My favorite is Harold Camping, who predicted the Rapture no fewer than three times until he finally admitted, shortly before his death, that he, you know, might have been wrong about it all.

That means many of us start making deals without any sort of experience—and that can be a little frightening. Throw in a guru or two telling us how dangerous it all is, how easily we can be ripped off or cheated, and many writers start to form an impression that if you're a successful writer, you have an army of lawyers and a safe-deposit box filled with copyright forms, and you spend half your time in a helicopter chasing down pirates who are fleeing with a bag stuffed full of your unpublished ideas.[4]

I am reminded of the time I bought a new car.

The Duchess just accepted a new job that would require a commute. We didn't own a car for two reasons: One, we live near New York City, so about 90 percent of the jobs are within a twenty-minute bus ride; and two, we'd lost our previous car in Hurricane Sandy, which helpfully flooded our street and our house, showing us that you can indeed throw away half of what you own and still survive—but I digress. The new job meant she needed to drive, so we needed to buy a car.

We did a lot of research, and we formed a plan to get the best deal possible on that car. We read countless advice articles and real-world stories, and we printed out tons of information and discussed our strategy. One day we walked into a dealership and promptly discovered that no one cared much about our research, our strategies meant nothing, and while I think we got a pretty good deal on that car, none of it was in any way what we expected based on our research. Not a single thing. Half the stuff we thought was important wasn't.

So it is with the writing business. Half the stuff people tell you that you need, you don't.

Copyright. This is probably the number-one concern of unpublished writers, the one I get the most questions about: how to protect your work. There's an idea that only the richest and most successful authors are safe, and then only because they have an army of lawyers at their fingertips. The rest of us are prey for pirates who steal our books, other authors who steal our ideas, and unfeeling corporations who will *also* steal our ideas.

---

4 Note to self: Ask agent about getting helicopter and private army, becoming Bond Villain.

First and foremost: Get over yourself. The chances that your idea is so amazing that anyone would put effort into stealing it is essentially zero—not *quite* absolute zero, but as close as science! can get. You see, the whole point of this writing and storytelling business is the added value the author brings to the idea, because all the ideas have been had. *All* the ideas. Your idea for a spy thriller has been had. Your idea for an epic fantasy—had. It's all been done before. What makes it interesting to other people—and potentially worth a few of their dollars and some of their time—is how you execute that idea.

Trust me: No one is stealing your ideas. If you think someone has, it's much more likely y'all just had the same idea at the same time.

So, do you need to file every story with the U.S. Copyright Office to get formal copyright? No, you do not. I have actually never formally filed for copyright. Not once. When my novels are published, my publisher files for copyright in my name, which is nice, and at that point it's a worthwhile formality because a published novel potentially has value beyond the actual book—in terms of film rights, audio rights, and other subsidiary rights. But prior to that, it's simply not necessary. Actually, your work is protected by copyright the moment you create it.

The big fear here is that someone will steal your words and profit from them, and while this isn't technically impossible, it's extremely unlikely. First of all, as stated, your ideas aren't nearly as special as you seem to imagine; the effort put into stealing them is simply not worth it. The most common problem any author has to deal with is piracy—stealing your works and selling them through unofficial channels, or just giving them away on file sharing networks—and all the copyright forms in the world won't save you from that, for the simple reason that pirates don't care about your copyright. Because they're *pirates*.

UNCONVENTIONAL TIP

Book piracy does happen. Whether you self-publish or get your e-books to market through a traditional publisher, chances are you'll see your work show up all over the place within a few weeks. Don't be flattered; pirates just scoop up as many files as they can and toss them out there—there's no overhead, really.

I don't worry about book piracy. Some authors *do* worry about it, and worry about it a lot, and they have very good reasons, beginning and ending with the belief that if people can illegally download your books for free they will, of course, never pay for them. If you're an author who relies on book sales for the income that feeds your family, book piracy is obviously going to be a worry.

Personally, I also believe that there is no way to effectively fight piracy. There is an economic incentive behind it, and all the vigilance in the world won't stop it, in my opinion. Now, to be clear, I don't approve of piracy and I'd much rather have the one dollar a legit copy would net me—I just don't think the effort put into trying to stop it is worth it. Would I feel differently if I was, say, James Patterson? Maybe. But I don't think so.

In fact, there are almost zero examples of someone literally taking an author's work, repackaging it, and selling it for immense profits. One reason for this is sadly obvious: A vanishingly small number of books earn enough sales to make this worth anyone's time. I mean, if you're a criminal, you're looking for high-margin crimes, not crimes that basically involve your creation of a shadow publishing company.

The other reason some new writers think they have to file for official copyright protection is the dreaded public domain, which some authors imagine is an amorphous cloud of legalities that follow you around, waiting to siphon away your work and make it free to everyone. Just as official copyright is granted to you the moment you write something, that copyright remains in place as long as you live, plus *seventy years afterwards*.[5] It's simply not something you need to worry about.[6]

Lawyers. Look, contracts are tricky things. I can't read them. I mean, I *can* read them, but I don't, and even if I did, I don't have an eye for the details, so it doesn't do me much good. Back in the day, I could sell quite a bit of fiction without a contract—magazines would just inform you of the rights they were buying (usually First North American Serial Rights) and send you a check. Today, you can't sell a piece of flash fiction without signing a contract, and those contracts often come in three distinct flavors:

Normal contracts my agent tells me to sign, maybe with a comment here and there about a specific clause that's mostly an FYI (freelance contracts always ensure you have zero rights to the material you're writing for hire, and my agent, bless her heart, points this out to me every single time).

Insane contracts written by people who imagine themselves to be towering intellects of copyright law, and who seek to own every single subsidiary right to your story, including ones that won't even be invented for a few centuries. My agent usually gets a little drunk after reading these and then emails me specific instructions about never signing anything from those people ever. She then mails me a dead rat in retaliation.

Boilerplate contracts downloaded from www.everycontractever .fake and run through a warm room of search-and-replace, chock-full of language that's alternatively inapplicable, unenforceable, or outdated. My agent usually has a stiff drink, then sends me clear instructions as to what has to change in that contract before I can sign it.

---

5 For this, blame the Disney corporation. Every time Mickey Mouse even gets into the same time zone as the public domain, the United States Congress miraculously decides to extend copyright protections. It's a mystery as to why this happens. A mystery.

6 Whether you need to worry about lousy layabout descendants of yours living in luxury off of profits from your copyright is entirely up to you. If it inspires you to build a time machine in order to check on your grandchildren and how your writing's generated wealth might ruin them, please also take the time to visit me when I'm eighty-five and buy me a drink.

UNCONVENTIONAL TIP

If you receive a contract from someone (for a story, a novel, the rights to your life, your internal organs), don't assume they know what they're doing. Boilerplate contracts abound—free for download—and people are constantly changing a few fields and sending them off; then people sign them and the end result is that *both parties* don't really understand the contract.

If you get a contract as a Word document, grab a few snippets of the language and google it. There is zero chance you won't discover where they downloaded it from, and then you can compare the documents and see exactly what they changed. It's fun and exciting!

The Author's Guild (www.authorsguild.org), the National Writer's Union (www.nwu.org), and other organizations will review a publishing contract for you. It's worth it.

If you notice, nowhere in those bullet points does the word *lawyer* appear, because I don't have one. My literary agency has a relationship with an entertainment lawyer, and I can hire them if I wish to. But I generally don't. In fact, I'll go one step further: Anytime I *have* hired a lawyer, it's made things worse, not better.

TV shows make it seem like lawyers are these superintelligent and superdedicated folks who tirelessly defend their clients' interests. While I am sure this is actually the case, the simple fact is anytime I've involved a lawyer in my publishing career, they have made things more *complicated* but not necessarily better. Your mileage may vary, of course, and the key to my disdain for lawyers is my trust in my agent—who is *not* a lawyer, but who has seen so many publishing contracts at this point that she can tell me at a glance whether something's worth signing. Plus, my agent is smart enough to know when hiring a lawyer is the right move—and those times are exceedingly rare.[7]

If you don't have an agent and you get a contract, is getting a lawyer a good idea *then*? Maybe. If you can't find an agent and you can't get a

---

7 Which is good, because I am not smart. At all. Which brings into question the wisdom of you taking any of the advice in this book, to which I can only repeat: There are no refunds.

writer's organization to assist you, getting a lawyer to review the contract is probably a good idea. You could also go the middle route and find what's called a contract review specialist—these folks aren't lawyers or agents, but have experience with contracts in a specific sector, and can use their experience to help you (for a fee, of course). *But*, I'd start off by trying to find an agent. A reputable agent will help you figure stuff like this out, because it will be in their best interests to do so.[8]

If you do decide a lawyer is a good idea, then for the love of all that's holy get a publishing lawyer with experience with similar contracts.[9] It's worth the trouble of digging around to find one, because lawyers specialize. Your uncle's brother-in-law's best friend who happens to be a lawyer may not be the best choice, and even world-class attorneys may be stymied by some of the quirks of your standard publishing contract. For example, we were once offered a two-book contract that specified what's called *joint accounting*, wherein you don't get paid any royalties until *both* books earn out their advances. My agent knew this was a new trend in contracts as publishers sought to limit their exposure, and she advised we say no, and in the end we got a revised contract with traditional accounting that treated each book as a separate entity. I would never have known to object to this clause, and because my agent *did* know, I received my money much more quickly than I otherwise would have—simple as that.

---

8 This is what some people miss about the writer-agent relationship: When your agent signs you, they're hitching their caboose to your engine. When you do well, they do well. That relationship almost always works in your favor.

9 When I sold my first novel, *Lifers*, I did so without an agent, and I didn't hire a lawyer because I was broke. When I got my agent, she asked to see the contract and nearly passed out when she saw it. The best way to put this is that I was very relieved when that publisher went out of business shortly afterwards. In other words, don't sign contracts unless someone with some knowledge reviews it.

On the other hand, without going into detail, I can say that the one time I hired a lawyer to review a contract for me—because my agent couldn't review it (long story)—it was a disaster. The lawyer was an entertainment lawyer at a very successful, big firm. And they sent voluminous notes on how the contract should be altered, and the response from the other party was, basically, *uh, no.* In the end, it cost me money and I ended up signing the contract as is, and, frankly, it all turned out perfectly fine and I regretted bothering with the lawyers at all.

That's one anecdote, of course. I can't promise your experience will be the same, and I can't prove that I would have been worse off if I'd insisted on the changes the lawyer suggested. But my experience—for which you've paid by buying this book—is that, in general, lawyers are needless complications in the specific milieu of publishing. Getting a good agent is much more important and useful.

Blogs. You will, at some point in your career, be advised to start a blog. This is not bad advice *per se*, and if you want to have a blog, by all means do so. I have a blog! Most writers do, and having a blog is a fine way to engage with fans and other writers and to have some fun, post samples of your work, and promote yourself.

Just don't imagine anyone will actually read it.

UNCONVENTIONAL TIP

You won't make money from your blog. The amount of traffic you have to generate on a *daily* basis to make a dime from your blog is prohibitive, and if your sole selling point for the blog is your sparkling personality, you're doomed. Even if you have a very tight niche subject, someone else is probably already running a blog about it.

Consider this: John Scalzi, a great writer and delightful internet personality, runs one of the last holdovers from the Golden Age of Blogs over at *Whatever* (whatever.scalzi.com). In 2015, he reported nearly six million visits to his blog for the year, which is about 16,000 visits a day. Impressive, until you consider that the Huffington Post gets about 110,000,000—*one hundred and ten million*—visits per month, according to www.ebizmba.com.

> The blog gold rush is over and has moved to YouTube, where Millennials are vlogging for dollars at a furious pace. By the time you figure out how to launch your own YouTube channel, that gold rush will be over, too. And so it goes.

Oh, they might—some folks are good at it. I'm not. I mean, I think my blog posts are entertaining and well written, but in this busy world, very few people regard my blog posts as essential reading. You might have a knack for blogging and do much better, so if a blog seems like fun, by all means, launch one.

The age when blogs could lead to book deals is, however, pretty much done. Of course there will always be exceptions,[10] and if you manage to cut through the noise with your blog, you might get a deal out of it, sure. But don't count on it or plan your career around the possibility, or it will lead to tears and recriminations.

Classes. One of the most obvious things an aspiring writer can do is to take writing classes. There are plenty of seminars and such you can take, many taught by successful and knowledgeable writers, and there's no reason *not* to do this—your worst-case scenario probably still involves some fresh perspectives, some new techniques, and maybe a slightly wider reading list. There are workshops that span a few weekends and cost just a few hundred bucks, taught by published authors with real experience. A workshop or seminar isn't going to transform your career like a lightning bolt, but it can't *hurt*. It's not going to send you *backward*.

But do you *need* a class? Probably not. The best way to learn the craft of writing is to read a lot and write a lot. Try to copy the great ideas you encounter. Then try to shape and rub at those stolen ideas until no one can tell where you got them; then they're yours. Ask most writers the best thing you can do to get better at writing and they will immediately say *read more, read widely*. Very few will start their advice with "sign up for a workshop."[11]

---

10 Although it seems to me the book deals are being distributed to parody Twitter accounts these days, mostly—which fits, since Twitter is technically a microblogging platform.

11 If you are interested in workshops, you can start simply by searching for "writing workshops" and adjusting your search for your local area. If there aren't any formal workshops, local writers

Workshops and classes are also structured and public—which is fine, but consider your personality. Some people love collaborating, exchanging ideas, and engaging in public debate. Some don't. If you're not excited about discussing your work with strangers in a public setting, you might not get much from a workshop—after all, many writers, myself included, gravitated toward writing precisely because it's a solitary, solo exercise; I hate working with other people.[12, 13]

In all fairness, I've never attended a workshop. My experience with writing classes and groups came during my college years, where, if you recall, I took as many creative writing classes as I could because they were more or less guaranteed passing grades.[14] My brief experience in those classes left me with the impression that workshops can actually be harmful, because a certain level of groupthink sets in, and the specter of Challenge: Accepted! Syndrome.

Will you get something out of a workshop? Maybe. But you don't *need* one to finish or publish a book.

Collaborators. This leads directly into my final thoughts on what you *don't* need to write and publish a book: anyone else.

Look, I'll repeat myself a bit here: Writing is solitary. It is *gloriously* solitary and is one of the few art forms that requires absolutely no one else to pursue professionally. Will editors, agents, cover artists, proofreaders, and beta readers improve your work and your chances? Yes.

---

often organize "meetups" (www.meetup.com is as good a place as any to start), which offer some of the same benefits.

12 If you're looking for an online workshop for the convenience and lack of actual interaction with your fellow shaved house monkeys, *Writer's Digest* has a bunch on offer: www.writersonline workshops.com.

13 In my professional career I have collaborated with other authors three times. I co-wrote the story and script for the comic book *Sliders: Blood and Splendor* with Jeof Vita, which was fun and lucrative. With the incredible Stephen Blackmoore, I co-wrote a short story titled "Crossed Wires" in the anthology *Urban Allies*; I was paid pretty well for that, which inspired a spirit of collaboration (and Stephen is awesome to work with). The third instance was a series of videos with author Sean Ferrell called *Two Men Have Words* (twomenhavewords.com), which involved writing scripts in a collaborative fashion sometimes. That's it. I can only work with people who regard whiskey as a food group and who look very confused when they hear the phrase "six in the morning."

14 I am starting to think my next nonfiction book should be *How to Get a College Degree Without Doing Anything (Unless Drinking Counts as Doing Something)*.

Are they *necessary*? No, and that's amazing. I can write, format, edit, and publish a book without speaking to another human being, or leaving the house.[15]

You might want a collaborator, a co-author, a second brain to bounce things off of. If so, don't let me stop you. But you don't *need* one.

All you *do* need, as I think I've made pretty clear, is an idea and the ability to write sentences. Everything else is just gravy—and by choice—so don't let anyone, even a successful writer, tell you that you must do this or have that in order to succeed.

---

15 *Or putting on pants!*

12

I'LL TRY THE WHOLE CAUSE AND CONDEMN YOU TO DEATH

YOU ARE THE WORST JUDGE OF YOUR OWN MATERIAL

When I contacted my agent in 2005 to let her know that, through a series of fortunate events, an editor at Warner Books was interested in seeing my manuscript *The Electric Church*, she told me to send her a copy immediately. After reading it, she sent me an accusatory email demanding to know why I hadn't shown her this book months before—or possibly decades earlier using some sort of time machine—our lives could have been so different if only I had gotten my head around temporal anomalies instead of spending my time in high school physics class destroying Slinkies.[1,2] The book was *good*, she said, and she was outraged that she could have been shopping it.

Why hadn't I sent her *The Electric Church*? Simple: I didn't know it was good.

Oh, I *liked* it. I *loved* it. *I* certainly thought it was a great book—but I didn't think it would sell, and I didn't think my agent, who specialized more in thrillers and mysteries, would be interested in it.

Heck, the whole reason Warner Books became interested in *TEC* was because I didn't think anyone would want to pay me for it. When I came across an ad for an internet publisher looking for serialized fiction, I dusted off an old idea and decided to go through their very complex submission process, more or less as an exercise; I'd never outlined or written character biographies before, and I thought it might be interesting to try a different method, especially with a book I wanted to revise but couldn't find my way into.

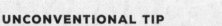

UNCONVENTIONAL TIP

Be critical of your method. Your writing process evolves because it works for you, true, but you're older than you were five minutes ago, or five years ago, and you've changed, making it very likely you're just *slightly* out of sync with a process that has its roots in a much younger version of yourself. Sometimes deciding that you're going to write a book using a completely new process—while doing so might require a lot of effort and may even prove a bit intimidating—gives you a fresh perspective on your work. The worst-case scenario is you will know one more thing you *don't* want to do.

---

1 My high school physics teacher at St. Peter's There But For the Grace of God Academy in Jersey City made the mistake of trying to illustrate wave theory with a bunch of Slinkies. Cut to 7 P.M. and a very weary teacher disgustedly tells me to just go home, he'll buy new Slinkies in the morning. I'd been horsing around with the Slinkies (*they're Slinkies*, for God's sake, how can I *not* mess with them?) and learned a lesson in string theory instead when several Slinkies became entwined with each other. This was a momentous occasion, because it taught me that the universe is random. And cruel. If you don't know what a Slinky is, I feel sorry for your entire generation.

2 I suspect if I ever did acquire time travel technology, I would use it exclusively to prevent embarrassing moments in my life by going back over and over again to make better decisions in specific moments, resulting in me as an aged and withered old man showing up for my first day of high school determined not to let my pants fall down during assembly this time.

If I'd thought *TEC* was marketable, I would never have done it. Because I am what scientists call a *moron*. And so are you, most likely, because there is an *excellent* chance you have no idea how to choose the material you submit or promote. And let's face it: The first step to selling a novel or any other piece of writing ... is to actually write it. But the *second* step is to know whether the finished product is worth submitting—to agents, to publishers, or even to self-publishing platforms.

HARDER THAN YOU THINK

Most writers are also readers. We tend to read pretty widely and deeply, and we read every day. Whether we earned a degree in English or just spent our youth reading everything we could get our hands on, most writers are more than capable of analyzing and critiquing fiction. That's one reason a lot of writers also edit as a side hustle or a day job—because we're good with the words.[3]

So, you'd think we'd be very good at choosing the material we think we can sell, right? And yet you probably aren't, for a number of reasons.

Subjectivity. The simplest reason is the most obvious: Of *course* you like what you've written—you *wrote* it. I certainly hope you're not writing books you hate. It can't possibly be surprising that you enjoy your own work, as it's tailored precisely to what you want to read (or should be). On the other hand—of *course* you hate what you've written. You've never written anything that lives up to your initial concept and expectations; everything is a failure.

The point is, you're very likely not objective about your own work. I fall into the latter category—I rarely think anything I've written matches the incredible idea I started with. Everything gets muddled, the plot meanders, the characters are indistinct. So far there have been nine times when I've been 100 percent wrong—when *totally* objective people have actually handed me a check for something I've written. Even with those successes, it's hard for me to point at one of my manuscripts and say, "Yep, this is great." Impostor Syndrome is real, people.

---

3 The other reason is, of course, because The Man insists we do useful labor in exchange for food coupons, i.e., money.

Lack of Expertise. There's a reason you and I are writers, and it has to do with a near-total lack of any other marketable skill; the list of professions that pay better and more regularly than writing is pretty long. If you're like me, you're also pretty clueless about the market in terms of novels—what's selling? What's not? Why? I have no idea. I barely understand how to balance my checkbook, much less how to peer into the murky future and decide what books will be flying off the shelves in two years.

That's why agents and editors exist. One big reason I pay my agent her percentage is because she's very smart,[4] and her opinion on whether or not a book will sell is usually right. The point is, when I write a book, it's usually because I'm inspired, but inspiration doesn't always mean the book has a market of people willing to buy it, so I need professionals to help me determine which of my manuscripts has potential.

I'm also pretty clueless when it comes to trends. As mentioned previously in this book, trends in publishing are pretty subterranean; editors plan their lists years in advance. By the time I notice that there are a lot of novels about people traveling back in time to become their own grandparents, editors have already moved on to novels about grandparents using time machines to leap into the future to murder their own grandchildren.[5] Which also means that the book I wrote last year might just be on trend for two years from now, but I'd never know it.[6]

Complete and Total Chance. We don't like to think that chance matters much, because we'd all prefer to think that we are masters of our universe and in charge of our destiny—but chance really is in charge. Think about the sheer number of coincidences that had to happen in order to produce you or me, and then the sheer number of things that had to go a certain way to produce your novel. So it's not

---

4 Another is because I fear her. Which is good. Fear is a great motivator.

5 Note to self: Write that book. It's gold, Jerry!

6 It also means I obviously have a deep obsession with time travel, since I keep bringing it up. Things I would do if I had a time machine include going back to 1983 and telling myself to put my baseball cards into plastic sleeves so they'd be worth something today; going back to 1993 and telling myself to buy Apple stock; going back to 2003 and making a better, more legible map to that buried treasure; going back to 1986 and having a long talk about fashion with myself; and if there's time, going back to 1925 to kill Hitler.

WRITING WITHOUT RULES

crazy to say that sometimes you don't know a book will sell, because selling a book requires a crazy series of crazy events to happen—and when they do, it's mysterious and a little disturbing.

UNCONVENTIONAL TIP

Luck doesn't cancel out hard work. When people offer career advice in almost any field, they will usually focus on two concepts: The confirmation bias that tells them because *they* did something that something is *why* they succeeded, and the idea that hard work is all that's necessary. This is because people don't like to think luck had something to do with their success—but this is the wrong way to look at it. Luck happens outside of your control—but it's hard work that puts you in a position to benefit from luck. In other words, just because you catch a lucky break doesn't mean you didn't work your tail off to be in the right spot at the right time. In fact, hard work is 100 percent necessary for luck to kick in—at least most of the time.

NOT FORCING IT

Choosing material isn't necessarily something you do after you're finished writing—in fact, if you think about it, you're choosing material to eventually submit and sell when you decide what projects you're going to work on. From the moment you open a new file and type *Chapter One*, you've made the decision that this is potentially the next manuscript you're going to foist on your agent, on every editor in the universe accepting unsolicited submissions, or your poor suffering fans.

Once you think about it that way, there's a natural temptation to nip problems in the bud and work only on novels you think have a good shot—based on premise and genre—of selling. That's a huge mistake. Preselecting your material might seem smart on paper—after all, why waste your time and energy on a book you don't think has a chance of selling?—but your writing should always come from a place of honest inspiration. You should always be writing something that excites and interests you—and unfortunately, that means you will sometimes write entire novels that have very little chance to sell. On the flip side, there are always examples of novels that seem like unlikely candidates for publishing—and yet there they are, on the shelf.

UNCONVENTIONAL TIP

Not everyone cares about selling their material, but there's nothing wrong with wanting to earn a living with your art. Literary merit and money are not mutually exclusive. Plus, blind luck plays a part here, too.[7]

For some writers, that's a huge problem, because they work slowly. I work fast; I usually have several projects going at once, and it's not unusual for me to finish two or even three first drafts in a year, along with a dozen or so short stories and even the oddball novella or other project. But not every writer is like that; some writers agonize a bit more over every word, spend a long time preplanning their novels, or endlessly revise. The idea that you might spend three years on a writing project that you didn't think would sell at the outset seems insane.

But, look back at what I just said! *You are a terrible judge of your own material.* Just because you don't *think* an idea will sell does *not* mean it won't sell. It's that simple. I've personally had that experience of selling a manuscript I thought had no potential—and I've had the experience where I've sent someone a novel I thought was a surefire sale, only to be told that it's kind of *meh* or simply not right for the market. In both cases I was surprised—and in both cases my complete inability to judge my own material was underscored.

So, if you can't judge your material for marketability or for salability, why try? You're going to get it wrong, so just work on things that excite

---

7 For example, in 2005 I submitted a short story to an anthology that a tiny company based in Brooklyn called Contemporary Press was putting together. The anthology, *Danger City*, didn't pay anything. They accepted my story "Ringing the Changes," but I got a big fat zero dollars for it. A few months later I was informed that the story had been selected by Scott Turow for inclusion in *Best American Mystery Stories 2006*, and it was reprinted by *Great Jones Street* in 2016. I ultimately received about $1,000 for the story, so you just never know.

you. When you're excited and inspired, your writing will be better, and good writing can often overcome every other obstacle. You still might never sell that book in the traditional sense, but if you try to calculate and work on a project you think is a sure sale, your chances of actually selling it are probably about the same, with the end result of having worked on a project you're not inspired about for a big chunk of your life.

THE INEVITABLE
PERSONAL EXAMPLE

Part of what qualifies me to write this book in the first place is how many mistakes I've made along the way to selling nine novels. I recklessly decided on a writing career despite knowing virtually nothing about everything involved with a writing career, and then I put very little effort into improving my chances or learning more about my chosen career.[8] So of course I have a personal example of what I'm talking about here.

Back in 2011 I took a meeting with someone who had an idea: They were looking for a specific kind of book, they liked my writing, and they thought I could hit their target. This wasn't a sale, it was just a pitch, and I was convinced for a variety of reasons. They outlined the kind of book they were looking for and left it to me to write it. I sketched out a proposal, they gave it the thumbs-up, and for the next six months I worked on a novel called *Designated Survivor*, which, as you might guess, pivoted off the idea of the State of the Union Address being attacked, leaving an unlikely member of the President's cabinet as the sole surviving member of the line of succession.[9]

This wasn't the book I would have worked on if left to my own inspiration, but I was sufficiently intrigued with the concept to get some enthusiasm for it, and someone else's interest is intoxicating. Having

---

8 Especially once I got an agent, who I regard as part god, part attorney, and part confessor. She really doesn't like when I call her at 2 A.M. just to ask if she believes in intelligent life on other planets or if she's finished painting her apartment yet.

9 If you're thinking this isn't terribly original, you're right; not only has it been done before, it's the entire premise of the CBS television series starring the second-best Sutherland, Kiefer. Seeing ideas you had six years ago turn up on TV or the bookshelves is, sadly, part of the game.

someone whose opinion you respect tell you that an idea has potential can be determinative, after all—you imagine the deal is already half done, all you have to do is commit some words to paper.

I like the novel itself, actually. I took it in a direction that I think is unexpected, adding a bit of a science fiction element. But my contact didn't care for the treatment and that was that—I'd written a book in the hope of a deal instead of from inspiration, and while that book isn't *bad* in any way, it's not part of me the way my other books are. And so it sits on my hard drive, and I don't put much thought into it. In the end, I would have been better served sticking to what I *wanted* to write about for those six months.

THE BLANKET APPROACH

So, what can you do? Obviously, you keep your head down. You work. You write the things you'd want to read, you polish them, you seek opinions that matter to you, and you submit. How do you determine which of your manuscripts is worth submitting? You don't. You submit all of them, or at least I do. I blanket the world with my writing, throwing everything out there, and seeing what sticks.[10]

In other words, I let other people tell me whether a book or a story is marketable.

This approach works remarkably well. On the one hand, I am stress-free. I create what I want, and except for those moments when a pointed rejection comes in asking me to explain exactly why I thought this load of gibberish was worth publishing, I don't worry much about the sales viability of a book. It's a fun way to write.

Some might argue that this is a great way to waste time, but I argue the opposite. It saves me time from trying to figure out on the front end what's going to make a sale and writing to write things that hit this moving, mysterious target of what *might* sell. *That*, to me, is the real waste of time. Instead, I'm writing stuff I'm excited about and

---

10 In 2002, I submitted 107 short stories to paying markets. Not 107 separate stories, but a handful of stories 107 times. Look on my works, ye mighty, and ... buy something, for god's sake.

WRITING WITHOUT RULES

leaving the judgment about its marketability to people who are a bit more objective.[11]

KNOW WHEN TO FOLD 'EM

As with most advice, this approach is easy to apply when things go well. Spend a year writing a novel, toss it out to your agent or editor, and get a positive response (preferably in the form of an eagle or other majestic predatory bird flying up to you with a bag of gold coins clutched in its mouth), and everything is great. You look like a genius. Everyone likes to be told how smart they are, right?

The hard part comes when people tell you that a book you love is terrible. We've been poisoned by a thousand biopics that tell the story of a genius who had a great idea that everyone else considered crazy or plain old dumb. In those stories, the genius always perseveres despite being told by literally everyone they know that their crazy idea will never work, and we in the audience watch this unfold with a smirk on our faces because we're living in the future where the genius is a billionaire and movies are being made about them.[12]

Now, as authors, we're very unlikely to ever be billionaires, but literary history is filled with examples of novels no one liked that wound up being bestsellers or classics. There's *A Confederacy of Dunces* by John Kennedy Toole, which he revised several times on the advice of an interested editor before finally giving up on it. After Toole's suicide, his mother found the book and tirelessly shopped it. After it was finally published, it won the Pulitzer Prize.

Or there's *Animal Farm*, the other book George Orwell's known for. When he tried to get it published in 1944, it was read as a bit too critical of the USSR, then an ally of Britain and the USA against the Nazis, and he was advised to tone down the politics a bit—he was even rejected by none other than T.S. Eliot. When the author of *The Waste*

---

11 People like my long-suffering agent, who gets manuscripts from me on the regular and has a boilerplate email template that reads, "Dear Jeff, you are undoubtedly brilliant, but this book is terrible."

12 Favorite example of this sort of thing is Dick Rowe of Decca Records, who supposedly said of The Beatles in the early 1960s, "Guitar groups are on their way out."

Land tells you to change your book, you most likely pay attention, but nevertheless Orwell persisted.[13]

So the takeaway might seem to be along the lines of *trust in yourself* or something. The dark side of that advice is that there are thousands of aspiring authors around the world at this very moment refusing to look critically at their work after numerous rejections, because they have come to believe that the secret to literary success is ignoring the fools who offer you anything other than praise. The truth is, one of the most difficult things to do is to listen to criticism and objectively sift through it. If the whole point of subcontracting the process of choosing material is to remove your unreliable subjectivity, you have to remove it from your reaction to negative feedback as well. In other words, if the consensus is that your latest manuscript stinks, you should at least seriously consider the possibility that it stinks even if you really, really like it.

Many places along a literary career invite you to pause for a few decades and obsess over decisions. Choosing which material to show the world is one of them, but you'll never get that time back, and you won't get much back from your time investment either. Outsource that decision-making and put your energy into writing.

---

13 You might be tempted to imagine that T.S. Eliot thought a book featuring talking pigs was a bunch of tosh, but let's not forget that Mr. Eliot is the person who speculated that cats have three names, which in turn inspired the Broadway musical *Cats*, which in turn means T.S. Eliot gave up his right to call anything "tosh" long before his passing.

13

BEFORE THE AGENT

IF YOU SELL A NOVEL BUT YOU DON'T ACTUALLY GET PAID FOR IT, DID YOU REALLY SELL ANYTHING?

The old saw goes, "Write what you know." Which is problematic for a lot of writers, because what they know tends not to be the stuff of compelling fiction. When I was twenty-six years old, what I "knew" was limited to beer, a stultifying desk job, unrequited lust, and a more or less comprehensive knowledge of *Simpsons* quotes. If this doesn't sound very promising when it comes to writing the sort of novels people actually pay money for, that's because it's not. And yet that's the raw material that inspired the first novel I actually sold for real money, *Lifers*.

> **UNCONVENTIONAL TIP**
>
> "Write what you know" is responsible for the worst plague to ever afflict the modern literary world: Main Character as Writer. Next time you pick up a book that has a POV character who is a writer of

some sort, you can thank the piece of trash advice known as "Write what you know," which has given permission to dozens of boring people to essentially turn their career frustrations into grist for fiction. I beg of you, make your main character a plumber, a big-game hunter, an insurance agent—anything but another writer.

Lifers is actually the second title for this novel; it was originally titled *Lie in Our Graves*, which is a Dave Matthews Band song. There are two reasons for that original title: One, I was spending an inordinate amount of time drinking in bars with people who were huge fans of Dave Matthews,[1] which meant I heard his entire songbook about eleventy billion times while hammered; and Two: I am terrible at titles. Absolutely terrible.

You don't realize how important titles are until you start submitting fiction, at which point selecting a title for your novel is like naming a child: More difficult than it seems, and subject to public scrutiny and abuse. Titles are also one of those things that are impossible to quantify: Why do some titles work and others don't? What's the line between clever and pretentious? Why can't I title a book after a Dave Matthews Band song?

That last one was just for fun. Dave Matthews Band songs are poor choices for just about anything.

For a long time, I thought I was a genius at titles. My titles tended to vacillate between pithy and brutal, or portentous and poetic. The first nongenre novel I ever wrote, I titled *Shadow Born*.[2] The book I eventually published as *Chum* was initially titled *In Sad Review*, which made my agent laugh-cry in torment before she ordered me to change it.[3] I always felt like the title should reflect the mood and tone of the novel itself, and since my younger self always thought my novels were

---

1 That is, hot chicks.

2 This is the novel containing Lord Kincaid's Farewell Address, mentioned in chapter four. Aside from my brother, no one will ever read it.

3 Actual conversation: **Agent:** This title is terrible. **Me:** Terrible good or terrible bad? **Agent:** *ugly crying*

dramatic, important works, the titles I chose were, of course, self-consciously (and, in hindsight, hilariously) dramatic and important.

UNCONVENTIONAL TIP

An important aspect of pursuing a writing career is *persistence*, coupled with the ability to absorb rejection. A lot of writers give up when their first book fails to sell or attract an agent, but part of playing the game is knowing that 95 percent of your efforts will lead to nothing, at least at first. I've submitted hundreds of short stories to various magazines and websites over the years, and I am currently rocking a 2.5 percent acceptance rate on those submissions.[4] And the novel *Chum*? It was written in 2002, taken on by my agent in 2004, rewritten and reworked several times over the next eight years as she and I circled back to it every now and then with new ideas or feedback from a rejection, and finally sold in 2013. This is why the idea that a project is "dead" because it's been rejected so much is ludicrous: There is *always* someone out there who will think you're a genius. Persistence has sold more books than talent.

Usually I need some kind of outside intervention to persuade me to change the title of a novel or a story, and it's usually my agent, Janet, who takes me out for a whiskey and explains to me that I can't call my latest novel *The Unfathomable Sadness of Jeff*, or something like that. In fact, these days, I purposefully put awful titles on my manuscripts[5] when I send them to Janet,[6] because I know it will trigger a free cocktail, and like all authors, I will literally do anything if it results in something with the word *free* in front of it or *cocktails* anywhere at all. But with *Lie in Our Graves*, I knew instinctively that I'd just screwed the pooch when it came to the title. First of all, if you're going to title your

---

4 That is an actual statistic, arrived at using maths. To quote Donald Sutherland in *Animal House*: "Listen, I'm not joking. This is my job!"

5 My agent insists I sent her this book with the title *You Really Think You Can Sell This?* but I don't remember that.

6 The number of inside jokes I include in every manuscript I send to Janet has grown to such ludicrous proportions that the novels are more inside joke than story at this point.

novel after a song, you should at least make it a song you like by a band that everyone thinks is cool—say, *Sink the Pink* by AC/DC—and second, the novel that eventually came to be wasn't nearly as deep and sad as the phrase "lie in our graves" would imply. Because, you see, something else I do wrong all the time is put the title ahead of everything else.

BUILDING A MYSTERY

Since my earliest writing days I've started with a title. I can't write a word until I have a title, in fact, which often results in lighthearted romantic tales with titles like *The Horror of Horrorville*. One of the main reasons my titles are almost always awful is because I generally have little idea what my story is about when I choose a title. This also sometimes results in some ham-fisted efforts to link back to a terrible, inappropriate title in order to somehow retroactively justify its choice.

Process is mysterious, of course, but part of my process is mystery. I see a phrase or come up with some kernel of an idea, and the whole creative process becomes about discovering meaning. It's as though I'm doing academic research on my own creative process, and in some dusty ancient library, I come across a phrase but no attached story, and I start trying to figure out what that phrase refers to. This is all well and good as far as process goes, of course, but once a story gets off the ground it often leaves the title behind, and that's when you get stuff like hardboiled detective stories titled *Fluffy the Kitten Eats Her Tail.*[7]

UNCONVENTIONAL TIP

A lot of writers come up to me at conferences or after readings and ask me detailed questions about my process. Do I outline? Have I ever used software like Scrivener? What's my research approach? The fact is, process is whatever works for you. There is no right way to write a book. While another writer's approach might offer

---

7 I can do this all day.

some useful ideas, if your process generates finished work, then your process is *fine*.

So, I was twenty-six, working a job I didn't much like, and spending a lot of time in bars with people my own age observing and occasionally being involved in the ongoing soap opera that everyone at that age is engaged in at all times. Everything seemed incredibly important and dramatic. Every evening ended with someone locked in a bathroom, crying, while an Emergency Response Team composed of drunk friends stood outside the door working it like a hostage situation. And every morning began inhumanly early; every hangover was soul crushing. So, when I decided I was going to write a book based on my own life (write what you know, even if what you know is lame, First World drunk problems), *Lie in Our Graves* seemed like the perfect overly dramatic title. I had a vague notion of a shatteringly emotional story of wasted youth and unrequited love, peppered with shocking violence.

That isn't exactly what I ended up with.

As you know, I'm what literary scientists call a "Plantser," but I usually spend the first draft stage making it up as I go along (see chapter four for more details on my writing process and approach, and the glorious term *plantsing*). So I started off with the epically awful title *Lie in Our Graves*, but, as I wrote, the novel became less sad and dark and more genial and fun. I started to imagine what would happen if I burned down my job.

Like I said: *Write what you know*. And I knew that what time I wasn't spending getting drunk and weeping in public restrooms was being spent daydreaming about my place of employment being destroyed. So I started to write about that—the petty drama and the sociopathic daydreaming—and slowly a story emerged of three twenty something friends who were desperate to change their humdrum lives, to somehow change their velocity. And they decide to do so, not by burning the place down—which, in terms of plot dynamics, isn't such a great motivation—but by stealing all the office equipment and selling it, which they imagine will make them rich enough to break free.

"Write what you know" also tends to inspire stories that are basically transcripts of people's daily lives. Don't do that. The advice "Write what you know" is meant to help you find verisimilitude in your writing; instead of pretending you know what it's like to live somewhere, why not set your story in an area you're familiar with— or, alternatively, go live in that other place for a while. It doesn't mean you should literally base your story on the specifics of your life. Unless you are a necromancer or a detective solving cold cases, in which case, carry on.

Free of what? I mean, I was twenty-six. Free from having a job, mainly.[8]

Anyway, at the end of the short novel (it's really more of a novella, *shhh*, don't tell anyone[9]), they've succeeded and have suffered no negative repercussions, but nothing's changed. In spite of all their effort, the danger, the planning, nothing changes for any of them. The characters literally end the book more or less in the same spots. Maybe a little wiser, but that's debatable. As I worked on the second draft, I started to really hate the awful title that had inspired this story, and I started to concentrate on the eternal, unchanging nature of their lives. And I thought, they're *Lifers*, like in prison when someone's serving a life sentence. *Ta-da!* New title!

THE BONFIRE OF THE VANITY PRESSES

Here we pause to describe for our younger readers the phenomenon of the Vanity Press. You see, in the age of Kindle Direct Publishing and similar platforms, it's hard to imagine a world where people actually

---

8 Which is, let's be honest, the main motivation all writers have for writing in the first place.

9 You will generally be told that in order to sell a novel, it must be a certain length, depending on the genre and the potential market. A commonly circulated number of words for a viable novel is about 80,000. *Lifers* is 40,503 words long. *Chum*, published in 2013, is 60,408. Undoubtedly many factors went into making those word counts viable, but word counts are one of those things that publishers (and everyone else) often insist are held to firm rules right up until they aren't. The takeaway: Don't believe anyone who tells you your novel is too short to sell. It might be harder to sell, but that's not the same thing.

paid huge sums of money to sort-of publish their books, but this is a legit business. Here's how it worked: You'd have a manuscript and you'd get the latest *Writer's Market* and make a note of every single book publisher that published your genre and accepted unsolicited manuscripts. Then you'd send 150 photocopies out with cover letters (which, if you're me, you screwed up completely with typos or by sending complete manuscripts to places that wanted only partials, etc.) and then sit back and wait for someone to offer you a million dollars. Which, back in The Day, was still worth nearly one million dollars.[10]

And then you'd get a letter in the mail from a publisher saying, *Congratulations, we want to publish your book!* And you'd pick up the phone to call your job and quit, call your mother and burst into tears, and then call several other people who know who they are and tell them to go to hell. But then, something makes you keep reading, and suddenly you come across the second paragraph of that letter, and it says something about how with the economy being what it is and the book publishing business being so cutthroat, they're sure you'll understand that the author must put some skin in the game, which is all a way of saying that they'll publish your book for something like $15,000.

UNCONVENTIONAL TIP

There was and is nothing wrong with the "subsidy," "private," or "partner" publishing model—as long as you know what you're getting into. The only problem comes when these companies prey on the dreams of young writers by making it sound like paying your publisher is a common practice (it isn't) and mentioning the rare and often misrepresented examples of famous writers who supposedly found literary immortality through subsidized publishing—in fact, those examples are more accurately *self-publishing*, which is a very

---

10 Like I said, clueless doesn't mean lazy: In the dark days before everyone used email or Submittable for this sort of thing, I would have to make photocopies of my manuscript, type up a personalized cover letter, address an envelope and a self-addressed stamped envelope (SASE) so the expensive photocopy could be mailed back to me, then troop down to the post office with my stack of paper and get everything mailed out. I did this a lot. In 2002, I submitted over one hundred short stories via snail mail. The people at the local post office had unkind nicknames for me.

different thing. The Too Long, Didn't Read version is this: If you do the research and decide subsidy or private publishing is your route forward, go for it. If someone is trying to convince you that a new author writing a check for $15,000 in order to publish his book is the same thing as traditional publishing, run away.

This first happened to me when I was twelve years old. I'd written a terrible fantasy novel titled *Cravenhold*, which was an unholy mix of Stephen R. Donaldson, Jack L. Chalker, and probably some other dudes with a middle initial.[11] I submitted it and got an acceptance from a place called The Vantage Press, which old hands in the novel-writing business might recognize. I was just a kid, so I didn't know anything about them or vanity publishing, but I knew enough to write back a cranky letter telling them where they could stick their "acceptance" and asking them to return my manuscript.[12]

So, fourteen years later, I already knew all about vanity presses when I submitted the newly retitled *Lifers* to approximately every publisher in the known universe, four of which had gone out of business several years earlier. As noted, I got a response back from Creative Arts Books, based out of California. They loved the book! And in an eerie letter that was basically the exact same template as the Vantage Press letter I'd received fourteen years earlier, they suggested that with the economy being what it is and the book publishing business being so cutthroat ... you get the idea. I wrote back telling them where they could stick their "offer" and went to go get blackout drunk, which, like all erudite creative professionals, is how I deal with professional setbacks.

Time passed. About six months later, I received a letter from Creative Arts Books. They informed me they had brazenly ignored my instruction to destroy the manuscript and had now reconsidered. A sim-

---

11 A hint of the awfulness: My protagonist in *Cravenhold* is named Kyle Hudson. Further evidence: He is magically transported into a fantasy universe while holding an unspecified assault rifle, which somehow means he can conquer the world. *I was twelve, okay?*

12 They actually had the gall to send me another letter saying that they really, really wanted to publish my book because it was so darn good, so they crunched some numbers and could possibly do it for just $11,000. Oh, and they continuously referred to the book as CRAVENHOLDEN, in all caps.

ilar novel had done very well, which they chalked up to its appeal to Generation X, which at the time (this was 1999) had a mysterious and lucrative appeal in the sense that it meant "young people,"[13] and, as we all know, young people basically throw handfuls of money at things for no known reason. No one—especially those of us officially part of it—knew what Gen X meant, but everyone was certain it would lead to riches. So, since one "Gen X" novel had done well, they went looking for another "Gen X" novel, and found my manuscript hidden away in a file probably marked *Potential Litigation*. The bottom line: They wanted to offer me a legitimate contract, with a small advance of $1,000 and a standard 15 percent royalty rate. The only thing I had to do, aside from sign the contract, was insert a sex scene.

JEFF SELLS OUT

Yes, a sex scene. On the phone with a man who I'd never spoken to before in my life, I was told that while my book was great, it lacked a bit of the old in-and-out, and if I added some sizzle, they'd be happy to move forward. Now, writers are supposed to have integrity. We're supposed to be stalwart defenders of our art and refuse to ever bend our principles. Plus, caving in to craven editing-via-marketing is a surefire way to ruin your book, because it amounts to people who view your book as a Unit-to-Be-Shifted telling you how to write.

But ... did I mention there was $1,000 on the line? In 1999, there was no Gig Economy. I couldn't spend a few humiliating hours on Fiverr to earn beer money. I had to earn my beer money the old-fashioned way, by quickly writing 3,000 slightly damp words to insert into my novel.[14] Which I did.

Now, there was actually a perfect place to insert the scene, and it even ended up having, I think, an important role in the development of the main character. Plus it was based on one of my own sexual experiences, which means that someday it will be extremely important to the Super Advanced Lizard Scientists who are trying to reconstruct

---

13 Unlike today, when it means "old people." Don't get smug, Millennials, it'll happen to you, too.

14 You see what I did there. Oh yes, you see it.

the history of mankind After the Fall. So I don't feel too bad about selling out. I actually think it's a great scene. Mainly because I am a great writer and I once wrote five hundred descriptions of sex toys and every single one was worthy of a Pulitzer,[15] so obviously I know what I'm doing here.

UNCONVENTIONAL TIP

Never be afraid to try something, and never confuse artistic integrity with refusal to consider suggestions. The sex scene in *Lifers* turned out to be a great idea. While I can't say with certainty if my publisher suggested it because they thought it would improve the book or because they thought a sex scene would help *sell* the book, I can say it's a better book with the scene in it. People will always have a suggestion for improving your story. Don't be afraid of them. You can always reject them after giving them a lot of thought—and you can also reject them after trying to incorporate them.

After that slightly embarrassing moment in my literary career, all that was left was to sign the contract and start popping champagne. Although up until that moment I had regularly signed contracts and agreements without reading them, and may technically still be under contract to several entities I can no longer reliably remember across this fair country, I had a moment of Sudden Onset Maturity and decided maybe I should get someone to review the contract before I signed it. So I asked The Duchess to do it. What's that? Was she a lawyer? No, she certainly was not. A literary agent? Nope. She did work in publishing, though it was in Science! publishing, and she worked as an acquisitions editor.

Gurus trying to help you attain your publishing dreams will probably tell you that you should always have your contracts reviewed by your agent or a lawyer, or both. And they're right. Years later, after I'd signed with my agent, she had me dig up the *Lifers* contract, even though

---

15 See chapter seventeen: How Many Words do Eskimos Have for "Lube"?

Creative Arts Books had gone out of business,[16] so she could review it to confirm that I had the rights to *Lifers* back. She was aghast at the contract; while there were no huge problems, she told me she would never have allowed me to sign it if she'd been my agent back then.

However ... I had what can only be called *mixed results* from skipping any sort of sane book contract review. After all, I got about $600 in total payments (the rest of my advance I got in the form of actual copies of my book because there were *so* many copies of my book left over), the book was actually published, it was reviewed in the *New York Times* (more on that later), and the company went out of business, which made getting the rights back super-easy. So, once again, my cluelessness not only didn't hurt me much, it probably helped, because if I'd had someone competent read that contract, I likely wouldn't have signed it, and *Lifers* would probably never have been published. Who knows what kind of butterfly effect that might have had on world events?[17]

THE ART OF DOING NOTHING

Naturally, after having improbably sold a novel without an agent, I did absolutely nothing. No promotional plans, no follow-up with the publisher to find out what *their* promotional plans were, absolutely zip. I had this crazy idea that if some publishing company was going to invest money in my book, they would naturally take care of marketing and selling the book as well, right? Why wouldn't they? They weren't spending thousands of dollars editing, designing, printing, and distributing my book just for chuckles. They wanted to make money on it. So I just assumed they would handle everything, and I sat back sipping whiskey and waiting to hear from the assigned publicist about television interviews, book tours, and

---

16 Shortly after publishing me ... coincidence? Call me Jeff, Destroyer of Publishers. If you're keeping count, yes, this is the second time a book publisher shined the light of acceptance on me and then went under soon afterwards. This trend would continue to the point that I made it a standard joke in all my cover letters.

17 When my agent reads this, there will be consequences for me and they won't be pretty. While I am pretty sure my agent regards my genial stupidity as charming, I suspect that doesn't mean she can necessarily allow me to get too confident in my Incompetence Superpowers.

invitations to the sort of flashy, open-bar events that
television says authors attend all the time.

> **UNCONVENTIONAL TIP**
>
> If you do sell a novel, it's probably in your best interests to assume
> your publisher will do shockingly little to promote it. Maybe you
> will be pleasantly surprised, but if you plan your own promotion
> and marketing, it won't go to waste even if your publisher lavishes
> attention and funds on you; if they don't do anything of the sort,
> you'll at least have something in place.

Needless to say, none of this happened. What did happen, despite my
failure to do anything and (I strongly suspect) the publisher doing
nothing, was the *New York Times* reviewed *Lifers*. And I almost didn't
even know it.

This was before the internet was what it is today. Back in 2001, when
Lifers was published, the internet was dodgy. Our connections were di-
al-up, it took years to download your email, and Napster had just happened. There were no iPhones, and while Google existed, it wasn't anything like it is today, by which I mean you couldn't really sit on Google
searching for your own name endlessly. As a result, the only reason my
wife and I discovered the review of *Lifers* in the *New York Times*[18] is
because an author friend emailed us: "Congrats on being in *The Times*
today. That's great!!! Some writers would kill for that. Do you have a
really clever agent, or what?"

I didn't have a clever agent; I didn't have an agent at all. My wife and
I rushed out and found a copy of the paper, and there I was. It was just a
"Books in Brief," and it was a decidedly *meh* review (the word *noodling*
appeared in there), but it was still the goddamn *New York Times* and my
book had been mentioned in it. We bought a dozen copies of the paper,
and once again I positioned myself next to the phone with a drink in
my hand, prepared for the onslaught of media attention.

---

18 Because I certainly did not actually read The *New York Times*; I am more of a *Mad Magazine* kind
of guy when it comes to keeping up on world events.

To this day we have no idea how it happened. My publisher did send a copy to the *NYT*, but in the usual way: With little enthusiasm and no belief that anyone would take notice. I didn't know the reviewer personally, and I had literally done nothing to promote the book. The only possible explanation is the reviewer just happened to grab it off the slush pile and randomly decided to read and review it. Random. Random, random, random. I did nothing to promote the book, and yet here I was, in the most-respected book review in the world!

So, naturally, I took this golden opportunity and did ... nothing.

Oh, about a year later I had another book coming out, a semi-self-published collection of essays,[19] and so I embarked on a book tour[20] and included *Lifers*, but by then it was a lost cause. If anyone in the world had ever noticed that review in the *Times* (and there is no evidence they did), it had long been forgotten. A few years later, the publisher went belly up.

UNCONVENTIONAL TIP

While doing some DIY promotion for your book is a good idea, modulate your expectations; the signal-to-noise ratio is hefty, making promotion difficult without a lot of (often expensive) help. I discuss my shambolic efforts at book promotion extensively in chapter eighteen.

LESSONS LEARNED

So, what did we learn about being lazy and incompetent from the story of my first novel sold for money?

- Selling out is not nearly as bad as you're told it is. In fact, it can be fun, and it can actually improve your novel, and if it generates an

---

19 This was a collection of articles I'd published in my zine, *The Inner Swine*, which you can read more about in chapter fifteen. The collection was titled *The Freaks Are Winning* and it was printed and distributed by Tower Magazines, which used to be a division of Tower Records. I also have several hundred copies of that book in boxes stored around the house.

20 Which I called The Big-Assed Famous Tour, because I am a marketing genius.

instant check for $334 (which would be nearly $500 in today's money, thank you inflation!), there's little downside.

- You really should have your contracts reviewed by someone who understands publishing contracts. There are always places where you can pay a little money to get such a service done,[21] and it will save you a lot of trouble in the long run. However, this in no way means *you* should understand how to read contracts. I've been publishing professionally for more than a decade and I can't read a contract to save my life.

UNCONVENTIONAL TIP

Assuming you know more than a lawyer or agent is just as bad as not even bothering to read a contract—even if you've reviewed many contracts, a professional's advice is necessary. I once got an offer of $150 from an online magazine for a short story, but the contract they sent locked down every single subsidiary right for the story, meaning I would never be able to do anything else with those 10,000 words every again—for just $150. My agent caught that.

- Promotion is almost always kind of worthless, in the sense that nothing you do will ever be a magical ticket to sales and exposure. Your book can be reviewed in the biggest venue ever and it won't make much difference.
- All my novels should be titled after AC/DC songs. My top ten choices for book titles would be *Beating Around the Bush, Bedlam in Belgium, Crabsody in Blue, For Those About to Rock (We Salute You), Girls Got Rhythm, Let Me Put My Love Into You, Love at First Feel, Mistress for Christmas, She's Got Balls, Put the Finger on You,* and, of course, *Cover You in Oil.*

---

21 The Author's Guild (www.authorsguild.org) offers this service to its members, as does the National Writer's Union (www.nwu.org).

14

AFTER THE AGENT

BRINGING COMPETENCE INTO THE MIX FOR THE NOVELTY OF IT

After a freewheeling youth spent signing dubious contracts because a Tyler-Durden-like hallucination[1] advised me to, I decided in 2002 to finally get serious and find an agent. In part, this was a decision based on the lack of movement in my writing career since I'd managed to sell my first novel *without* an agent; if you recall from about five minutes ago in the last chapter, after *Lifers* was published in 2001, and reviewed in the *New York Times*, I figured things would start to happen.

Things *did* happen. I got married, adopted a cat, and gained about fifteen pounds. My writing career did not exactly explode, and so I started researching agents.

---

1 I originally wrote "Great Gazoo-like" and then had one of those moments imagining anyone under the age of forty reading this and having absolutely no idea what I was talking about. Plus, Tyler Durden is a much cooler reference, and I want to be a Cool Author. Although the idea of a small green man in a space helmet advising me to sign contracts is funnier, if you ask me.

A lot of writers question the value of an agent, which is mystifying to me—in part because my own agent has been an incredible asset, and not just in terms of sales (though, yes, there is always filthy lucre to consider). That might be confirmation bias, of course; it's always easy to assume that because you are successful at something, and you did something else, the latter must be the cause of the former, but sometimes that's just optics.

The doubt about having an agent stems from a basic misconception about what agents do and how they operate. In one version, you get something like this:

JEFF: I have a novel to sell. It's about a guy who signs contracts because an imaginary friend tells him to. The twist is, in the end it's revealed he's actually the imaginary friend!

AGENT: I love it. Here, sign this.

<JEFF Signs>

AGENT: All right! Let's google publishers and make some random phone calls. Eventually I'll get lucky and I'll get 15 percent of your millions.

<AGENT begins laughing standard villain laugh. JEFF bursts into tears.>

And: Scene.

In another version, you get something like this:

JEFF: I have a novel to sell. It's about a guy who stops wearing pants to work every day. He becomes an internet sensation and a religion springs up around him. The twist is, eventually the whole world stops wearing pants, world peace happens, everyone melts their guns, and then aliens invade and we're defenseless, humanity is made prisoners, and ... we're all forced to wear pants.

AGENT: That is ... oddly specific. Okay, I love it. Sign here.

<JEFF Signs>

AGENT: <Picks up phone> Hello, secret publishing cabal? One standard contract, please. Send my money in the form of gum balls. <Mutes phone> How do you want to be paid, kid?

JEFF: Whiskey lozenges.

AGENT: Done!

And: Scene.

In other words, some folks imagine that agents aren't necessary to the process at all and have just set themselves up as gatekeepers in order to skim pennies from suffering authors; and some folks imagine there's a vast publishing conspiracy where only people who play the game get to be a part of it.

Look, conspiracy theories are always going to be popular, because they accomplish a few things. First, they make you feel smart, like you've seen something everyone else missed. Second, they excuse you from having to do the work, because if it's a conspiracy and everything's rigged, you can't win no matter what you do. And finally, it allows you to discredit anything you want, because you can't disprove a theory, so you get to win every argument.

But reducing the role of a literary agent to a gatekeeper is crazy. First of all, people do sell manuscripts to publishers without an agent—I did it myself, in a mysterious moment of semicompetence that will forever frustrate future historians chronicling my life. And second, if you get a good agent, you're not just getting someone who will sell your work; you'll be getting a Competency Coach.

UNCONVENTIONAL TIP

What makes a good agent? Here's your short list of things to look for:

- A good agent doesn't ask you to pay for reading your manuscript.

- A good agent doesn't offer or solicit for-pay editing services to get your mangy old manuscript into shape.[2]
- A good agent has evidence of actual sales and a current roster of clients,[3] which should be clearly and easily available on their website.
- Those sales are to legit publishers who offer actual money.
- A good agent shows actual knowledge of who you are and can articulate why they love your book.[4]
- A good agent name-checks the Association of Authors' Representatives (AAR) and their code of ethics.
- A good agent is easy to get in touch with and responsive.
- A great agent offers to buy you drinks.

MISTAKES, I'VE MADE A FEW

As you may have garnered, I'm rather freewheeling when it comes to things like contracts and money, and if left to my own devices, I will definitely wind up in a drunk tank someplace wearing just a barrel and some suspenders. The fact that I somehow made it through the first three decades of my life without becoming the property of a Saudi Prince or having a corporate logo tattooed on my face is surprising; I was fairly certain I'd eventually be visited by a Future Jeff, desperately using untested time travel technology to warn me about several dozen terrible decisions I was going to make in the next half hour or so.

Now that I'm nine novels in and making a living from writing, one question I get asked a lot by younger writers is, How'd I get my agent? The answer is surprisingly old-school, low-tech, and labor-intensive: I wrote a book (most agents still insist on this), I got a list of agents ac-

---

2 Serious note: This is different from an agent telling you to have your manuscript edited. The key is whether they're trying to sell you something.

3 You can get a lot of info from Publishers Marketplace (www.publishersmarketplace.com), but it's not free to join. You can get some info from Publisher Alley (www.puballey.com) as well, which also isn't free, but some author groups like the Mystery Writer's of America offer discounts. You can also just do some googling—if they actually have clients who have sold books it shouldn't be hard to find evidence, and their clients should also list them as their agents.

4 My agent always answers the phone, "Jeff Somers' Fan Club, how can I help you?" I always answer: "And you're the one and only member!" It's like a secret password at this point. If Janet was replaced by pod aliens, I would be able to figure it out just by calling her.

cepting submissions, I wrote a lot of letters, and mailed out a lot of partials. The whole process might have changed slightly due to the disruption of technology, but it's essentially the same: You get a list, you contact them; rinse, repeat. It's a matter of hard work, as much as anything else.

Like a lot of young writers, I initially thought of literary agents as just This Thing You Do, a formality like showing your ID at a bar. I figured if I could convince some fool to represent me in exchange for the imaginary monies they might someday earn from my work, it would be that much easier to sell manuscripts. And also, frankly, I had nothing else to do, which is actually a frequent motivation for me.

Now, this was back in 2002.[5] Contrary to popular myths about the olds, the internet did in fact exist at that time, but I was still using a print copy of *Writer's Market* and actual letters—printed out and stuffed into envelopes—as well as hard copies of the manuscript (originally titled *In Sad Review*, if you recall from previous chapters, later to become *Chum*). I printed my partial, I wrote a letter, and a few weeks later, I got a response from an agent telling me they'd recently stopped taking on new work, but they'd met another agent at a conference that might be interested. So I printed another partial, another letter, and mailed that off. Here's how the cover letter I sent with the partial started off:

I obviously need supervision. Despite immense talent and latent superhuman powers, I remain largely obscure and poverty-stricken. Please help me. I've completed a new novel entitled In Sad Review *that I'd like to sell, and I'd like to know if you'd be interested in representing me. Your name was given to me by xxxxxxxxxxxxx, who seemed to think we might be a good fit. I hope you agree ... I have attached here a brief bio, which is almost 90 percent true, and a sample chapter from the book for your reading pleasure.*

---

5 As a testament to my accuracy and formidable memory, I have been telling people for years that I got my agent in 2004. The year 2002 was so long ago my agent had an *aol.com* email address ... and I had an Earthlink email address. If you're younger than me, don't feel smug—I'm guessing there's a MySpace or Ello account in your past. *J'accuse!*

And a few weeks later, despite the fact that my cover letter was a rambling, overly long mess filled with jokes and precious little information, despite the fact that my manuscript was full of dumb typos and grammatical errors, I got a positive response. Here's the actual text of my agent's email back in 2002:

> *Dear Mr Somers,*
>
> *I'm pretty sure I'm not cool enough to be your literary agent, but humor my febrile hopes and send me the rest of the novel.*
>
> *You might force that grammarian ... you have on staff there to take a look at it first. You've got some interesting errors that tell me you weren't paying attention in Mrs. PursedLip's ninth grade English class.*

So, to sum up, I sent a mistake-riddled manuscript out,[6] wrote a cover letter that prioritized bizarre jokes over selling myself, and got an agent. Those of you paying attention at home may perceive a pattern here. Some people will tell you that everything has to be perfect—your query letter must be a precise instrument, your manuscript must be read and reread and re-reread several hundred times to ensure not a single extra space exists within it, and you must research and craft until your fingers bleed. Here's the secret: All of this is *sometimes* true. There are certainly people in this world who will dismiss your work over a single typo. There are people in this world who think there's precisely *one* way to write a query letter. And some of those people are literary agents.[7]

But you don't want to work with any of them. Personally, if a potential literary agent wrote back to complain about a typo or a query letter that resembled something the Zodiac Killer might have written, my response would have been simple: I'd have removed them from my list and moved on, because I don't want to work with sticklers. I don't

---

6 Knowing myself as well as I do, it is not out of the realm of possibility that I simply forgot to save the file after running spell-check. Or that I had the language setting in my word processor set to Danish. Or that I forgot to run spell-check at all.

7 They are also: No fun.

want to work with people who can't tolerate sloppiness, because *I* am sloppy, and I want to work with people who won't be judging me constantly.[8]

So, that's how I got my agent: A combination of incompetence, laziness, and dogged hard work. I am a man of contradictions. Or, possibly, a wizard.

WHY YOU WANT AN AGENT

Next in line after the "how did you get your agent?" question is "should I get an agent?" After all, we live in a world of Kindles and disruption, a world where it's theoretically possible to build a blog or a YouTube channel into a juggernaut of Likes and clicks and unique IPs that will make you very attractive to any publisher, agent or not.

Right there is the mistake: You don't want an agent because they can sell your work.

Or, okay, you *do*. But that shouldn't be the only reason, honestly.[9] From personal experience, I can tell you that selling your manuscripts is something your agent more or less does in their spare time. The other things an agent does?

---

8 This doesn't mean you want people who aren't competent to help you. When reviewing the manuscript of this very book, my agent viciously mocked my tendency to confuse "its" and "it's," plus a plethora of other writing sins. She did so in good humor, though, which makes the mindnumbing act of revising a manuscript six hundred times more enjoyable.

9 Much more important than selling your novel is their willingness to buy your drinks every time you meet to discuss something vaguely related to your career. I like to send myself cease-and-desist letters just to have an excuse to stop by my agent's office, where she has a whiskey collection that rivals mine, and pours with a heavy hand. For a few hours, it's like living in a *Mad Men* episode where people soak up booze and then go to work.

Guidance. The publishing industry, whether you're talking about traditional Big Five publishers or self-publishing through Amazon, Barnes & Noble, or Kobo, is an intricate web of lies, misinformation, and subrights. My agent has pointed out aspects of contracts I would never have noticed on my own; she's explained why certain things were happening; she's offered more insider gossip about why publishers are making certain decisions than I could possibly remember. Having a good agent is like getting a power-up in the video game called Writing Career.

Criticism. We've talked about beta readers and workshops and all that, but some of the best writing advice I've gotten has been from my agent. Agents read a *lot*, they know the market, and their advice is often blisteringly objective. At the same time, their success is entwined with your success, which means their advice is usually incredibly helpful and not just an exercise in coming up with something smart to say about your book.

Strategy. What some folks miss about having a literary agent is that it isn't just about one book, or even an isolated series of books. Movies and TV often make it seem like the writer works in isolation (slowly going mad, most likely), then emerges every year or two with a new book, at which point they speak to their agent for the first time in months. The truth is, a good agent has a big picture attitude—yes, they might be trying to sell one particular book of yours, but they are also thinking a bit more strategically.[10]

UNCONVENTIONAL TIP

Having a literary agent is a relationship. You both get benefits from that relationship, and you should be equal partners in it. An agent that dictates isn't the best agent for you, and a client that doesn't take advice is a terrible client.

---

10 For example, this book you're reading. Prior to a conversation with my agent in 2016, it had never occurred to me to write a book about writing a novel. She noted that I'd been publishing articles in *Writer's Digest* and that I had a lot of experience in the area, and suggested I create a proposal for this very book—and then spent months going back and forth with me to craft it. I'd never written a nonfiction book proposal before; you can read the whole sordid story of how this book came to be in chapter nineteen.

Synergy. In movies, it often seems like agents have one client and sit in tiny offices all day, chain-smoking and talking on the phone. In reality, your agent will likely have a lot of other clients, as well as colleagues and peers, plus relationships with a huge swath of the publishing world—editors, publicists, and associations. What this means is that they will likely expose you to opportunities you would otherwise be ignorant of. My agent has pointed me towards anthologies that have published my work, speaking engagements that have led to publishing opportunities, and a bevy of expert professionals, from photographers who know how to make me look halfway sane[11] to social media experts who have tried in vain to make my self-promotional efforts coherent and effective.

I should note that if you're getting the impression that your agent has to be part of a big firm in order to offer all of this, that's not the case: Over the course of our official relationship, my agent has gone from being a one-person operation to being part of a small agency to being part of a larger agency. The relationships, experience, and wisdom she offers never had anything to do with her precise professional status.

DODGING BULLETS

So, obviously, an agent will help guide you through the process of not just selling your manuscript, but negotiating the contract. One of the most difficult things for any author is believing that your work has actual monetary value; it's common for writers to actually believe they're *lucky* to just be published by someone, and we all make the mistake of giving away our work at some point, whether for some perceived "exposure" value, or because we just don't believe our work is worth anything. Early in my career I gave away a lot of short stories to small magazines, because I didn't think my work was worth anything—and having an agent has changed that for me, because my agent has ex-

---

11 I said halfway, didn't I? When I went to get my first head shots taken, I told the photographer—the awesome and talented Barbara Nitke (www.barbaranitke.com)—that I wanted to be blurry so people wouldn't recognize me. This was because I assumed that once my second novel, *The Electric Church*, was published, I would become so famous I would be chased down the street Beatles-style if people knew what I looked like. Everyone—Barbara, my agent, my wife—thought this was insane. I think the photos turned out awesome.

plained to me that my work is essential to these markets. Magazines need stories. Publishers need books. Blogs need posts. The content I create is worth money because it will be used to *make* money, and as the content creator I deserve some of that for my time and talent.[12]

UNCONVENTIONAL TIP

Writing "for exposure" is almost never worth it in terms of making a living (writing for exposure as a *marketing tool* can work, as we discuss in chapter seventeen). Websites and magazines need your content—it's what they repackage and sell to their readers—so they are getting an economic benefit from publishing you—a benefit you should always share in.

My agent insists on seeing every contract that comes my way and often gets paid nothing for review. She sees it as part of her job to ensure that I don't accidentally sign away rights or otherwise cause problems for myself. Her comments on contracts—even ones she ultimately blesses—have been illuminating. I'm still more or less a moron when it comes to stuff like that, but thanks to the tireless efforts of my agent, I am a *slightly smarter* moron than I was in 2002.

UNCONVENTIONAL TIP

Never hesitate to push back on a contract. When someone offers me a contract to publish something, I often experience an irrational fear that if I request any changes they will simply tear up the contract and tell me to get lost. This ties into the fact that authors often struggle to believe their work has value; we feel like contracts are favors. The fact is, if the other entity refuses to negotiate or at least

---

12 In my freelance career, I am still constantly amazed how much money someone will pay me to write something. It's important to remember that writing is a skill layered on top of talent, and the skill part is where the "value add" comes in. I think I had some sort of labored metaphor about being a "carpenter of words" or something, but let's just leave with this: I was once paid $1,000 to write 100 words.

discuss concerns with the terms of a contract, you probably don't want to work with them anyway.

UNCONVENTIONAL TIP

Don't hesitate to use "having an agent" as a negotiating tactic. People sometimes will pressure you to agree, at least in principle, to certain terms or even to simple participation; I find that saying "I have to discuss it with my agent" is a nonthreatening way to stall for time. It's also a 100 percent true statement.[13]

To be fair, giving away your work will sometimes make sense and sometimes be a great idea. I gave my short story "Ringing the Changes" to the anthology *Danger City*, and it wound up in *Best American Mystery Stories* that year, which wouldn't have happened if I'd insisted on only submitting to paying markets. And I've given stories to charity anthologies, which is obviously a good use of your work. Never say *never*—but always think twice, and maybe three times, about giving away stories or other writing.

A good way of thinking about this is simply to ask yourself who's getting paid. When a magazine wants the right to publish your story for free, are they also giving away the magazine? Is everyone involved a volunteer? If *someone's* getting paid, why shouldn't the author get paid for the *content* upon which the whole operation pivots? On the other hand, when a student filmmaker approached me about adapting my short story "The Amazing Martin Landawer" into a film, I had zero hesitation about granting him the rights, because no one was making

---

13 Does this suggest that you should invent an imaginary agent if you don't actually have one, just to use this stalling tactic? It does. I like the name Theodora Royalties for your fake agent. It's got pizzazz.

money off of it—though we did specify that in the option agreement, just to be safe.[14]

UNCONVENTIONAL TIP

Choosing material isn't just about perceived quality or marketability. When approached for a story or essay donation, look back through work you've tried repeatedly to publish; Trunk Stories are also great candidates for nonpaying markets, because if it's been submitted widely, you're probably not going to sell it for money in the first place.

Free drinks. Have I mentioned that my agent often buys me cocktails? I'm not sure I've stressed this enough.

There will always be exceptions to every rule, and confirmation bias kicks in. The fact is, a good literary agent does a lot more than make a few sales calls on your behalf. Have I mentioned they also sometimes offer to buy you drinks? I feel certain I have, but that would require looking back over this chapter again, and I can't bring myself to do it.

14 You can watch Stefan Allen's film adaptation of the story here: https://vimeo.com/162029026. You can read the story on my blog: www.jeffreysomers.com/blather/monday-short-stories/.

15

SELF-PUBLISHING
ZINES & BOOKS, LOSE MONEY, MAKE ENEMIES, HAVE A BLAST

So, should you self-publish?

These days it's one of the most-asked questions when I encounter neophyte writers. Self-publishing has gone through such a transformation in recent years that there's a lot of opinions out there, usually divided between two competing narratives: On one side, you have the firebrands who will tell you that traditional publishing is dying fast and anyone saying otherwise is just a gatekeeper trying to save their job. On the other side, you have folks who will tell you that seeing "CreateSpace" in the publisher category is the kiss of death, the sure sign of amateur hour. On the one hand you'll hear a lot about the Hugh Howeys[1] of the

---

1 When you broach the subject of self-publishing, the two names you will usually hear are Hugh Howey and Amanda Hocking, both of whom have enjoyed considerable success publishing their books themselves on the Amazon Kindle platform. You'll also hear about folks like Andy Weir, who self-published *The Martian*, or Jason Pargin, who originally published *John Dies at the End* on a website as a serial—both went on to a lucrative traditional publishing arrangement once they'd achieved success on their own. Howey is also a very vocal critic of the traditional model, and a very vocal cheerleader for everyone following his self-publishing example. I have no doubt the success they've enjoyed is real, and that others can—and likely are—duplicating

world, and on the other you'll hear about how the vast majority of self-published novels sell about twelve copies.

As is usual with arguments like this, both sides are wrong. And right. Should you self-publish? That depends entirely on who you are as a writer and as a self-promoter. Here's the thing few people like to tell you: Self-publishing is *hard*. It's a lot of work with no guarantees of a payoff. Traditional publishing is hard, too, but in entirely different ways. When wondering if self-publishing will pay off for you, you must ask yourself, How lazy am I?

Me, I'm incredibly lazy. I may be the laziest man you'll ever meet; I haven't found a corner I didn't want to cut. In every aspect of my life, aside from the literal writing of words, I put more effort into avoiding effort than if I just did what I was supposed to in the first place.

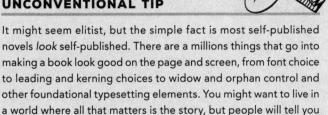

UNCONVENTIONAL TIP

It might seem elitist, but the simple fact is most self-published novels *look* self-published. There are a millions things that go into making a book look good on the page and screen, from font choice to leading and kerning choices to widow and orphan control and other foundational typesetting elements. You might want to live in a world where all that matters is the story, but people will tell you that the professionalism of your presentation also matters. And those people are not wrong.

Which is a challenge, because when it comes to self-publishing, it's like almost 99 percent work. You write a book. This usually takes longer than expected, unless you're me, in which case you start drinking straight from a bottle of bourbon as you type *Chapter One,* then you experience Lost Time,[2] and then you wake up in a hotel in Provence

---

it. I am just as certain that what they do to achieve that success sounds an awful lot like work I don't want to do.

2 Let's talk about my unfortunate habit of Capital Letter Writing as a Technique. I do this so often it would be easy to make a case for a psychological cause, some sort of ancient emotional trauma that still resonates within me, like maybe my parents beat me senseless when I messed

WRITING WITHOUT RULES

wearing a sketchy white linen suit and you have a completed novel on your hard drive.

But for *most* people, it takes longer than expected. Unless you're doing NaNoWriMo, in which case it takes you about thirty days. Thirty days spent guzzling Four Loco until your eyes are permanently bloodshot.

But for most people, yes, it takes longer than you think. And then when you're done, you have to ponder it. You send it out to beta readers, if that's your thing, or you sit on it in agonized silence. You take criticism, you revise and tweak, you set the manuscript on fire and feel relieved until you remember this is just a hard copy and the book still exists on your hard drive, in your cloud, everywhere. So you go back to it, you revise it, you rework it until you forget why you were excited about it in the first place.

At some point—and this is the real challenge for some writers—you have to decide it's done, and then you have to decide what to do with it.

There have always been two options: You try to get it published traditionally—seeking an agent or a publisher—or you self-publish. In the past this wasn't so easy or cheap; your options were to either do everything yourself or hire a vanity press that would do all the design, editing, typesetting, and often the fulfillment for you. The first option was slow and often frustrating, the second was expensive.

But we are living in the "future," aren't we? We now have the option to easily and cheaply self-publish our work, which is no longer a one-way ticket to obscurity and shame. In fact, there are enough success stories concerning writers who self-published their way to riches, or at least respectable earnings, that we can no longer dismiss self-publishing as anything but a legitimate strategy.

But it *is* a strategy, not a religion or a New Way of Doing Things That the Olds Just Don't Understand. There are advantages and disadvantages to both traditional publishing and self-publishing:

---

up capitalizing something. The truth is I probably stole it from some other writer and became overfond of it, much like the time I stole a bottle of bourbon from someone at a college party and became overly fond of that.

ADVANTAGES OF TRADITIONAL	ADVANTAGES OF SELF
• Advance monies (certainty of earnings)	• Full control
• A partner in promotion & distribution	• Bigger percentage of the money earned (usually)
• Someone doing all the stuff you don't know how to do	• Total creative freedom

Your choice may be made for you, of course; while self-publishing is a guarantee, traditional publishing relies on convincing a human being that your book will make them money through awesomeness. If you can't convince anyone of that, then self-publishing is your only way to go. That doesn't mean that self-publishing is the poorer choice—but if you choose traditional publishing because of the advantages it offers and can't close that deal, you have the alternative to explore.[3] If you choose to just go directly to self-publishing, that can be a great decision, too. I know this because I've done both. I've done it all.

UNCONVENTIONAL TIP

You can't reverse the streams; while you can try to sell a novel traditionally and then self-publish it if you're unable to, you usually can't self-publish a novel and then sell it traditionally later. This is mainly because you probably won't sell enough copies, meaning any publisher will look at your sales numbers and instantly become interested in something just over your right shoulder. There are rare exceptions—mainly when a self-published book sells a *lot* of copies—but, generally speaking, if you're going to self-publish a novel, you'd better be prepared to commit to that strategy.

---

3 I am sometimes accused of being elitist when it comes to self-publishing, which is laughable since I've been self-publishing since before most people had ever heard the term—since 1995, to be precise. Back in those days I had to lay things out on a 386 computer and make all my photocopies at work while pretending to do something else. I had to lick stamps to mail out copies, and actually brought hundreds of envelopes to the post office to mail. In short: Haters back off.

MY SELF-PUB BONA FIDES

The Zine. From 1995 to 2014, I published a zine. What's a zine? It's a magazine, except self-published, usually with a very narrow focus. Zines got started as fanzines in the science fiction underground in the early twentieth century and saw a resurgence in the 1970s punk subculture. They tend to be low-fi things, typewritten or laid out simply on a computer, and photocopied and handed out or mailed.

My zine started in 1993 with three partners, friends from school. We were talking one day and I was complaining about the difficulty in selling fiction,[4] and a guy named Rob suggested we just cut out the middleman and publish our own magazine. We weren't the first people to think of it, but it was a new idea as far as I was concerned. The four of us spent the next two years trying to get it together, but in the end we each had very different ideas about what the zine should be, and one by one everyone dropped out until I was left with all the bits and pieces we'd created for it. So I decided to just go ahead and publish an issue.[5]

The first issue of *The Inner Swine* came out in May of 1995. I printed about one hundred copies on the photocopiers in the office where I worked, stapled them together by hand, and mailed them to anyone who I thought might be interested.[6] This was called a *perzine*, or personal zine, which means it didn't focus on a specific subject like music, but was a place where I wrote whatever was on my mind. I published sixty-six issues,[7] and at one point in the early 2000s, I had national and international distribution and was printing two thousand copies four times per year.

Because I'm an idiot, I lost money on that deal. A *lot* of money. I arbitrarily priced the issues at $2 each, but sold subscriptions for $5 a

---

4 I was twenty-one years old. In accordance with the universal law, I hereby apologize for complaining about anything.

5 The fact that I'd been telling people for two years that I published a zine, implying that it already existed, was a motivating factor as well.

6 Including my seventh-grade teacher. Let's just say Mrs. O'Connor wasn't impressed.

7 Each issue was about 20,000–25,000 words, which means I put nearly 1.5 million words out in that zine.

year and $9 for two years. The end result: I had a lot of fun, but lost my shirt and exhausted myself over the course of eighteen years. For a long time there was joy in making that zine, a sense of power. I wrote some regrettable opinion pieces while trying to shock readers, published a lot of fiction, and for a long time had a pretty good following of people who thought I was hilarious.

The thing was, I knew I was doing everything wrong, but I didn't care. I specifically didn't publish the zine to make money;[8] the only reason I charged anything at all was my suspicion that people assume free things are worthless.

UNCONVENTIONAL TIP

Pricing your work appropriately is often challenging. Pricing your work (in self-publishing or freelancing) can become a race to the bottom, and one of the most difficult things to internalize is the fact that your work has value. Many people—even fans of your work—don't really think writing takes any effort; they think we just make it up and scribble it down. But writing is an iceberg—all the reader sees is the tip that gets published, and the research, thought processes, hangovers, and lost weekends that went into your novel are invisible to them. But not to you. While pricing your self-published work can be tricky (market forces are, after all, market forces and no one is going to pay $50 for your novella), remind yourself at every step that you deserve to be paid.

How many issues of *The Inner Swine* did I sell? I have no idea. In the zine world we did a thing where you could offer a trade—someone would send me a copy of their zine in the mail, with a note, and I would send one of mine back. I also kept, like, zero records. Literally, zero. It was a cash business, for the most part—I'd go to my P.O. Box and find envelopes with dollar bills in them, and I'd add that person to the mailing list.[9] And keep them *on* the mailing list long after

---

8 I strongly encourage anyone seeking a career as a writer to get comfortable with this concept.

9 For a long time I just used my personal address for all things zine, but this changed in 2001 for two reasons: One, I had, at that point, moved twice within a few years, and updating everyone

their subscription officially ended. I never wrote anything down. So I might have sold thousands of issues, and I might have sold fifty, I literally have no idea.[10]

In 2014, the zine became a bit of a chore. Between a blog, a freelance career, my fiction, and booze, I was a pretty busy man, and I found I no longer had the need to express my every opinion in little essays, and when I did have that urge, I had a blog. After a lengthy period of internal struggle, I decided to suspend publication of the zine. There's still a website (www.innerswine.com), but it's really just a memorial.

For a long time I thought publishers would be impressed with my zine exploits. I probably shouldn't have just admitted that.

UNCONVENTIONAL TIP

Understanding the scale is important: You have to sell a lot of things to get someone's attention in this business, which is one reason why self-publishing never seems to get any respect: Most DIY publishers simply don't sell enough books.

The Novels. I may have mentioned here my first published novel, *Lifers*, which I sold on my own to a small California-based publisher, Creative Arts Book Company. The publisher bought that novel in 1999, published it in 2001, and went out of business in 2003, which meant the rights reverted to me.

---

connected to my zine was a real pain in the ass. And two, I'd moved in with The Duchess, who was a little freaked out the first time a stack of letters from prisoners arrived at the apartment we were sharing. To explain, in the zine world it's not unusual to offer your zines for free to prisoners. Prisoners at all levels of incarceration are bored out of their minds—they have little to occupy their time. And okay, it's prison and not supposed to be fun, but denying people reading material pretty much guarantees they will never become productive members of society. So I always checked that box, and I was pretty darn popular in prisons. I got a lot of long letters from inmates—thanking me for giving away the zine, endlessly professing their innocence, and occasionally blowing my mind with witty, thoughtful comments on my writing. I couldn't really argue with my wife when she suggested she didn't like random inmates knowing where we lived, so I got a P.O. Box.

10 This is one reason I need an agent. Another reason is the free drinks.

Because I am a dynamic artist, a man of action, and a force of nature, I promptly did nothing about this for eight years.[11]

In 2011, I became aware of this amazing thing known as digital self-publishing, so I decided to put *Lifers* back out there. I pursued this with my usual attention to detail, which is to say I created a cover in about ten minutes and poured the text into a template I downloaded off the internet. And five minutes later, my first novel was once again for sale.[12]

You might ask whether I hired an editor or designer for this project: I did not. Should you? Paying for a copyeditor and proofreader is almost always worth the money.[13] Just remember, your profit margins are going to be tiny, and every dollar you spend on your self-published novel is likely a dollar you will never get back.

I know I keep repeating this, but it's a depressing fact every author should internalize: Most people only sell a few dozen copies of their self-published book. There are exceptions, yes. Sometimes an author already has a platform from which to drive sales and promotion. Sometimes an author has the time, energy, and relentless will required to actually leverage social media and other marketing channels to drive those sales. Sometimes authors are just lucky. Those exceptions don't change the fact that the overwhelming odds are that your novel won't sell too many copies—and even if you do exceed expectations and sell a few hundred copies, you still won't profit much. You should therefore keep your overhead low.

---

11 That's not exactly true. In its death throes, my publisher offered to sell me leftover copies of *Lifers* for $1 per copy, and I decided to buy 1,000 of them. A week later they offered to sell me more for 25 cents per copy and my soul left my body briefly. To this day I have boxes and boxes of *Lifers* in my house. I will sell you one for much less than you might imagine.

12 The role e-books play in keeping out-of-print books available can't be overstated. Whether your publisher has gone out of business or simply doesn't care about your book, being able to re-publish it (assuming you get the rights reverted to you) is a godsend for any author. *Lifers* has only sold a few hundred copies since I launched it on various digital platforms, but that's a few hundred people who wouldn't have been able to read the novel—or, perhaps, even been aware of it—otherwise.

13 Of course, if your wife is like mine and takes a strange joy in finding typos and grammar mistakes, you can have her proofread everything for free! As long as you can handle the shade she throws your way in the form of snarky comments embedded everywhere.

After releasing *Lifers*, I went on to self-publish a series of novellas featuring Avery Cates, the protagonist of *The Electric Church*. This was a classic case of having an idea and running with it: I liked the character and had a beginning of a story, about 10,000 words. There was more story, but I wanted to try something different, an experiment: I wanted to publish a series of novellas—10,000-word sections—as fast as I could write them. And that's one thing self-publishing is great for: experiments. I wrote what was essentially a sixth novel in the *Avery Cates* series over the course of a year, with six distinct stories that connected but stood alone individually, and published them shortly after completion. I didn't hire an editor. I did my own covers. My wife, The Duchess, proofread. It was fun, fast, and successful—I didn't break any sales records, but I made some money and fans of the character got to enjoy another story that featured him, so it was a win-win.

Those are my credentials in the self-publishing world. So, back to the original question, should *you* self-publish?

THE SELF-PUBLISHING LAZINESS MATRIX

You will probably not sell a lot of books. You *might* sell a lot of books, yes. Some people do. The overwhelming majority do not. It's that simple.

Now, you might traditionally publish your novel with a big publisher, get a fat advance and a big promotional budget, be sent on a ten-city book tour and get booked onto radio and TV interviews, and *still* not sell a lot of books. This happens fairly often. So, there are no guarantees in either case.

If you start googling about self-publishing, you will come across a lot of success stories—authors who sold one hundred thousand copies of their novel, authors who earn six figures a year from their books, even authors who sold a lot of books and then leveraged those sales into a traditional contract. And these things exist. They just probably won't exist for you, because those examples are very obvious outliers; the average self-published book sells fewer than 250 copies.

But maybe 250 copies still sounds pretty good to you. Fair enough. Gird your loins, kids, because if you really want to try and make your self-published novel sell, you're going to have to do a *lot* of work—or, if you're me, *not* do a lot of work that you *should* be doing. Because after you write a book you want to self-publish, you have to start thinking about the following: editing, typesetting, proofreading, design, setting the price, managing multiple platforms, marketing copy, and promotion.[14]

That's an exhausting list, but if you're really going to go for it, if you're really going to try to sell some books, you've got to do it all, and the worst part of it is that you can do all of it, and do it well, and *still* only sell fifty copies.[15] Because there's a lot of noise out there, and your biggest challenge is cutting through that noise and getting discovered. And every author who tries cutting through that noise is *adding* to the noise. You see the problem.

Now, you might say that traditional publishing has a similar problem, and of course it does. It's a different kind of noise, though, and more important, *someone else is doing the hard work.* Now, sure, we're living in low times and a first-time author with a modest contract isn't going to get the full-court, Dream Team marketing press, and, yes, you'll be expected to do some of the work of promoting your book yourself. But much of the other work—the designing, formatting, and

---

14 Don't be like me and leave promotion to the end. As previously noted, I'm lazy, so my promotional outreach tends to begin and end with one e-mail sent to about a dozen folks suggesting they read and review my new DIY project. You should really send out review copies months ahead of time, then follow up with personal e-mails. I'm just too lazy and disorganized.

15 You may have heard of Kevin Kelly's "1,000 True Fans" concept. The basic idea is that if you can gain one thousand real fans who have no problem paying you for your work, you're set for life. There's something to this; If you self-publish four novels a year and sell them for, say, $10 each, you can earn yourself $40,000 that way (Kelly's concept assumes you are selling things yourself and therefore keeping 100 percent of the profits, not splitting them with a platform like Amazon). The problems are that, 1) establishing a "True Fan" isn't easy—most people will buy one of your books if it looks interesting, if it gets good reviews, if the cover catches their eye, but they may just as easily not buy your second novel; and 2) keeping up that level of productivity can be daunting. Still, in theory, it makes sense: If you can build a small core of dedicated fans, you can make a go of things.

delivering—gets done for you. It's much less exhausting. Plus, there's usually money up front.

If your agent doesn't retain subrights like translation rights (or if you don't have an agent), publishers will also seek to sell those subrights for you, and when they do, you'll get a bit of money for that,[16] too. The Avery Cates series was translated into a few other languages,[17] and that meant money just showed up on my royalty statements without me having to do anything, which is precisely how I like money to be.

So, when I self-publish, what do I do? Not much. Because I'm lazy. And to me, that's the secret about self-publishing: You either have to be willing to make selling and promoting your novel your job, or you have to accept that you're not going to set any records with your DIY sales.[18] I approach self-publishing with a guerilla tactic: I do it fast, when inspiration strikes. I have fun with the parts I enjoy (the writing and the cover design, mainly), and I skip the parts I don't enjoy much (I think I've forgotten to send out copies to potential reviewers at least five times[19]), and I don't lose sleep over how many copies I sell.

The bottom line is this: Self-publishing is neither a consolation prize for novels you can't sell traditionally nor a magical New Way that will

---

16 Subrights are always fraught with drama. Years ago no one thought to nail down the digital rights for books because there was no use for them. When e-books became A Thing, there was a lot of garment-rending in the publishing world. If you're signing a contract, think about the subrights you're being asked to assign and what they might be worth—but also consider whether you have any chance of selling them yourself. I once had a contract specify the amusement park rights, which was kind of surprising, but then I asked myself whether I was going to come up with a Jeff Somers Wild Ride any time soon. The answer, surprisingly, was no.

17 Producing some of the craziest cover art I've ever seen, frankly; the Italian cover for *The Electric Church* still haunts my nightmares, the German covers for the books are terrifying, and the Russian cover makes the book look like it's set in the Halo universe.

18 Can you game the self-pub system? Of course—various schemes exist, involving complex systems of five-star reviews purchased on Fiverr, fake accounts, and "pump and dump" schemes designed to get your title to number one in an obscure and sparsely populated category. A famous recent example is Lani Sarem's novel *Handbook for Mortals*; she and some co-conspirators placed large orders with bookstores that reported to the *New York Times* and managed to land at #1 on the Young Adult Hardcover Books best-seller list—for twenty-three hours, which is how long it took the *Times* to figure out the scam. Not only do these schemes cost you money, they're also almost more work than just trying to sell your book honestly.

19 If you're keeping score at home, yes, I've self-published eight books and neglected to send out review copies for five of them. It doesn't say "Marketing Genius" on my homemade business cards for nothing.

make you rich through some sort of technological voodoo. It is a strategy and should be treated as such. The most important question to ask yourself when deciding whether or not to self-publish is, How lazy are you? If the answer is, *about as lazy as Jeff Somers*, then self-publishing may not be your best choice—unless you know what you're getting into.

16

SUPPLEMENTING INCOME & PROMOTION WITH SHORT FICTION

GUIDELINES ARE FOR SUCKERS, A SHORT STORY BY JEFF SOMERS

I needed new glasses.

This was becoming increasingly obvious whenever I sat down to write, as my eyes slid across the screen; reading the flickering pixels of my manuscript was like trying to walk across a frozen lake. Everything seemed to be in place—the physics were right, gravity was there, my limbs were moving as expected. The only thing absent was friction, making every step a treacherous project. On the screen, the words were jittery, requiring extra concentration to focus.

I was getting old.

This was the new refrain, and an unoriginal one at that. Everyone begins complaining about being old starting at about age twenty-five—hooting ironically into the dense tavern air—and then slowly shaves away the irony and humor until you're me, sighing disconsolately at the sheer chasm of time that has expanded between the way you see yourself and the way you *are*.

And then there's the book.

"Writing Without Rules" indeed. I glance down at the bunny slippers on my feet, the cat sleeping in my lap. I'm wearing a pair of tattered khaki shorts, a Too Much Joy concert T-shirt, and my often-bent, severely abused glasses which have served as a chronicle of my decrepitude. Where once they had been the solution to my eyesight woes, now they were a monument to physical decline, a line in the sand I couldn't see any more.

I sighed. *Chapter sixteen*, I thought. *I seem to recall assuring an editor somewhere I had plenty to say about short stories and self-promotion.* Maybe there's a funny footnote I can put there, something about a time I had to think fast in a meeting with an editor and pretend I had a whole plan for a book when I didn't.[1] I'll think of one later. I love footnotes.[2] I scratched the cat's ear, and she mewed luxuriously and squirmed so I could transfer the scratching to her belly. Her name was Coco. Like all cats she was an aristocratic capitalist and thus a parasite.

Well, I thought. *Short stories. Heck, everyone should be writing short stories.* A lot of writers view short stories as either more difficult to write than novels, and/or not a profitable way to spend their time. It's easy to see why; if you check out what magazines and websites and the like pay for short stories, it ain't much. The professional rate is usually considered to be about six cents per word, which is what the Science Fiction Writers of America sets as its minimum for qualifying works when you apply for membership. So if you have a 3,000-word short story, and you sell it for six cents a word, you're going to get a check for a whopping $180.00.[3] That might seem like a fair deal until you crunch the numbers and realize you'd need to sell about a half million words of short

---

1 This actually describes his entire modus operandi when it comes to pitching freelance articles, but that comes later in the book.

2 He does love footnotes.

3 Obviously, he knows that $180 is a fair amount of money, and the value of that $180 varies depending on where you live and what your lifestyle needs are. Since Jeff's lifestyle revolves around cats and premium whiskies, $180 does not go very far. Most of it, in fact, will go to kitty litter.

fiction every year in order to make a really low salary; if your stories are all about 3,000 words long, you'll need to sell more than 150 stories per year to keep the lights on.[4] The most I've sold in a single year is *four*.

Be fair, I thought, pushing the cat gently off my lap and standing up, my back popping as I stretched. *Short stories scare some folks.*

As I walked down the stairs from the second floor of the Somers Manse, I pondered this. The house was a well-known Mystery House, a structure begun in 1898 when the widow of a wealthy local brewer had inherited the family fortune and an unfortunate case of mental instability. Construction on the house continued for fifty years as she added rooms without windows or doors, doors that led to the open air, numerous basements, and several ballrooms just large enough for two people to stand awkwardly in. I'd acquired the house for a steal due to the fact that it was obviously haunted by spirits that had learned how to affect matter in the corporeal realm, in addition to being overrun by a colony of feral cats that resisted every attempt to drive them out.

"Novels," I said to the cats as they gathered around me on the first floor, "even though more complicated and longer than short stories, are actually easier in many ways to write. There's a lot of room to play with. Can't figure out your plot? Just noodle about for a few thousand words. Can't see the ending? Just have your characters wander around. In a first-draft scenario, you can just keep writing and writing until you see your way to the goal posts. But with short stories, which range anywhere from 2,000 to 10,000 words, you can't just meander about until you figure out what your story is *about*. That constraint can be frightening."

The cats, used to these monologues, sat on their haunches and studied me, contemplating the possibility that the ape-like god they worshiped had gone insane, and whether a mad god was better than no god at all.

"The thing is," I said, opening a bag of kibble and doling out scoops to the bowls, "there are two fundamental reasons every novelist should

---

4 And that's assuming you only put the lights on when you have company, and otherwise spend your time in the darkness. It also probably assumes you eat a lot of canned tuna and Ramen, possibly a lot of cat food.

be writing short stories. One, the constraint is, by itself, a useful tool for developing your craft. Two, and this is important—"

The cats were already nose-deep in the bowls of kibble, and I might as well have ceased to exist.

"—you can leverage short stories for marketing and promotion, and they *can* provide extra income while you write your novel."

A black cat, named Homer, glanced up from the bowl of kibble in front of him and licked his chops, as if to say, *Preach, you handsome man.*[5] Sometimes, late at night, after a few glasses of whiskey, I imagined that the cats spoke to me—truly spoke to me, whispering in purrs and mewl syllables that almost seemed comprehensible. This was madness. I knew that, and reminded myself of it every day.

UNCONVENTIONAL TIP

"Pro rate" is an arbitrary metric set by certain writers organizations. As noted above, the pro rate for fiction probably won't provide a living wage to you no matter how prolific you are, and if you were paid money for a story, it doesn't really matter what rate per word you received—you're a professional writer. Pro rates are useful as a guide to just how good or bad the rates offered by a market are, but I've sold plenty of stories for one cent per word.

FOR THE CRAFT

The next evening I wandered the house, trailed by a parade of cats, tails in the air. Candlelight flickered, making everything impressionistic.

"I write a short story every month," I said as we searched the house—harder than it seems, because of all the staircases that go nowhere, the doors that lead into the open air. It's possible to take a wrong turn and enter a room with no obvious exit; it's possible to become lost permanently in the basement tunnels. "I've mentioned this before, and I do it

---

5 He's already admitted elsewhere in this book that he talks to the cats when he's alone. The question of whether he thinks the cats are replying to him remains open.

for two reasons. One, it acts as a sort of Super Notebook; instead of just jotting down random thoughts and phrases as ideas for stories—ideas I may not recognize months later when I flip through my notes[6]—I actually develop those ideas into a complete story, with characters, setting, and a plot."

The cats suddenly broke away and gathered at the bottom of a huge bookcase filled with remaindered copies of *Lifers*.[7] I wandered over and raised the candle until it illuminated the top shelf, where an unopened bottle of ten-year-old Glenmorangie sat, gleaming with potential mischief.[8]

"Good gods," I said, setting the candle down on the floor and stepping over to the bookshelf. I studied it, judging its sturdiness, its attach-

---

6 This is no joke. He has occasionally tried jotting down moments of inspiration in a small notebook, emailing ideas to himself, or making audio notes on his phone, and the results are always disturbing. Here are a few 100 percent real examples from that notebook—he is not making any of these up; these are real notes he made in the full expectation that Future Jeff would understand them.

- "gods of gohan"
- "action sequence—coats"
- "the restarted"
- "dust bunnies but future"
- "everything in parentheses"

In case it's unclear: Future Jeff did not understand them.

7 Sadly, this bookcase also actually exists.

8 There is a short list of things every adult must have. One, purpose. Two, ethics. Three, a standard drink to order in any tavern no matter the circumstances. Jeff's is whiskey, and if he's really thinking fast, it's Glenmorangie 10 Year. Yes, you are welcome to purchase some for him.

ment to the wall, the strength of the individual shelves. The cats pushed between my legs, purring encouragement. "This," they seemed to say, "would be a great night, an epic evening." All I had to do was climb one measly bookshelf. As I contemplated, I muttered to my audience.

"Aside from the preservation of inspiration, though, writing a complete story every month also flexes the creative muscles, keeps the gears from getting gummed up. Writing is an art, but it's also a craft; as with any craft, you can develop certain confidences in approach. Sometimes staring at a blank page and trying to just *start* a story is intimidating, but if you do it every month, it gets easier. You get comfortable with the blank space."

I stepped up close to the bookshelf and reached up to grasp the sides, putting one foot on the bottom shelf. When it didn't immediately collapse, I started to climb. The cats arranged themselves in a loose semicircle and mewed encouragement.

"The other bright side to writing a lot of short stories is that you have a deep backlog of material you can polish, revise, and expand into stories you can then submit. Believe it or not, you *can* make some money from short stories—maybe not a fortune, but enough to make it worth your time."[9]

The cats followed my slow ascent.

"Not only that, but when you publish a short story, you can draft on the publicity—if nothing else, it's something to promote, to tell your fans about. And the audience for the magazine or website is exposed to your writing, which might encourage them to seek out your other work. Wait, something's—"

Gravity shifted, and I realized the bookshelf was pulling away from the wall. The cats scrambled, nimbly vaulting out of the way as I crashed to the floor, the heavy bookshelf falling on top of me.

---

9 The most he's made from a single short story is $1,262. Sadly, that kind of money isn't very common. Much more common is the least amount of money he's made on stories: $0.00. Writing is glamorous.

UNCONVENTIONAL TIP

Producing a lot of material gives you more options for marketing and selling your writing. If you have one novel you've been working on for decades and it doesn't sell, you're stuck. Not every writer is comfortable working on stories, novels, and blog posts simultaneously, but if you can train yourself to do so, you'll find your options for making a dime and seeing your work discussed increase exponentially.

FOR THE FILTHY LUCRE

I came to slowly, uncertain of my surroundings. I was looking up at a mosaic of lines and spiraling cracks, ringed by several solemn triangular faces, whiskers and sharp angles. The ceiling, the cats. I tried to sit up, but the heavy bookshelf had me pinned to the floor.

"Go get help, guys!" I whispered hoarsely to the cats. They stared at me, blinking slowly, placid. One of them turned and sauntered away. I had the feeling he wasn't going for help. The rest licked their chops, yawning and shifting their weight from paw to paw.[10]

I sighed as best I could with several hundred pounds of books on my chest. I knew I was going to be trapped there for some time, so to stave off madness I did what I always do: I talked to myself.[11] More. I talked to myself *more*.

"The key to making money from short stories," I mused, studying the plaster above me, "is twofold. One, you have to write—a lot. You can't sell stories you haven't written. And two, you have to submit those stories—a lot."

I glanced at the plump cat sitting near my head, looking like a fat man in a tuxedo. His name was Pierre. "People get hung up on guidelines. Every magazine and website that solicits fiction submissions has

---

10 Cats are certainly not the animal you want on hand for protection or home security. While contrary to popular belief, cats are quite affectionate; they also identify secret hiding places in your home within moments of their arrival, and when terrorists burst in to kidnap you, those cats will be hidden so well that it will require a special scanning machine to locate them.

11 Whether this technique works is up for debate among everyone who knows Jeff.

a complex guidelines document that sets out what they're looking for and how to submit, sometimes going into a surprising amount of detail concerning the formatting of manuscripts and such, or lengthy philosophical treatises on the style and substance of the stories they want. My advice is, don't bother reading the guidelines. Just submit your story to any market that broadly seems like a match in terms of genre. I say that for one fundamental reason:

"**Editors think they know what they want, but they're usually wrong.** One simple fact of life is that people tell you the things they *wish to be*. When someone tells you they're tough, a no-nonsense person, that's what they want you to think of them; whether it has anything to do with reality is another matter altogether. It's the same for fiction markets. An editor will tell you they want X, but as often as not, you show them Y and they go for it.

"There are no guarantees, of course," I admitted to Pierre as he washed himself, licking his paws and scrubbing behind his ears. "But genre is flexible. Style is arguable. Content is a range, not a discrete value. As a simple example, a guideline might say, 'no science fiction.' Fair enough—but what if you've got this genius George Saunders-style short story that involves time travel and clones, but is as literary as they come? Do you not submit it just because of a broad generalization in the guidelines? Of course not. And once you start down that slope, it's impossible to take any of it seriously. So just submit. Submit widely; submit recklessly."

UNCONVENTIONAL TIP

Guidelines and other admonishments to adhere to specific market needs simply outsources editorial control and puts the burden on the writer to decide whether the story is what they're looking for, when the fact is you can't read minds. The only way to find out if an editor wants to buy your story is to have them read it, period.

The cats mewed a rolling chorus of complaints because, I realized with some mild alarm, it was feeding time. It was *always* feeding time.

"Guys, I'm trapped. I can't feed you right now."

I tried to think who might notice my absence first, who might come around to investigate and save me. My alarm grew as I realized the list was extremely short. I looked at the hungry mammals around me. My voice seemed to be calming and distracting them, so I kept talking.

"Submitting short stories can be a job unto itself. I use a spreadsheet. I find a market that pays for short stories,[12] I send a story that's in the same ballpark as the genres and lengths they're seeking. If it's rejected, I immediately find another market to send it to. I try to keep all the stories I've polished for submission in circulation at all times.

"In the past, I've managed more than one hundred submissions per year this way—and the year I passed one hundred was back in the days before you could email submissions, so I was actually sending photocopies in envelopes, which meant I had to include a self-addressed stamped envelope (SASE) with each one—a lot of work.[13] There was a time when no one accepted email submissions, but these days it's pretty common. In fact, I don't consider any market that requires a hardcopy submission, simply because it's too much work."[14]

UNCONVENTIONAL TIP

Don't pay submission fees. It's not unheard of for legitimate and even respected markets to ask you for $3 just to submit a story, but this violates the most basic rule of being a professional writer:

---

12 *Writer's Market* (www.writersmarket.com) remains the gold standard for market listings. Duotrope (www.duotrope.com) is also a good resource, with the added bonus of data concerning response times and acceptance rates. Free resources include The Submission Grinder (thegrinder .diabolicalplots.com), which was launched as a free replacement for Duotrope when that site started charging for access, and Ralan's Speculative & Ralan.com Webstravaganza (www.ralan .com), which can be a little difficult to navigate but offers tons of science fiction and fantasy listings and information about those listings.

13 Anyone who says they want to time travel and live in the past has not thought it through. The past is a terrible wasteland, and there is no Netflix.

14 Jeff's not alone in this attitude; best-selling author John Scalzi has been very clear about how he considers magazines that don't accept email submissions to be foolish, and he has a theory as to why some still require snail mail submissions: He thinks they use that postage stamp as a way of filtering out at least some percentage of nonserious writers (a "bozo filter"). That may be their justification, but if so, it is an extraordinarily lame one.

> **money should always flow to the writer.** Your story has *value*. You're doing them the favor of offering it up for sale. Submission fees at *best* reduce the amount of money you earn if you sell the story and at worst monetize their slush pile so they don't actually have to bother getting readers—and fundamentally imply that your story has no value and they're doing *you* the favor of letting you pretend to be part of some exclusive club. In other words, an editor's time is not more valuable than the writer's.

"Over the years I've sold dozens of short stories and never once regretted submitting widely like this. You might think it's a bit of wasted effort, that a more focused approach might yield a higher return. That might be true, but all that does is shift the work you're doing from submitting to researching. It's simply not worth it."

The cats began sniffing around me. Pierre, the fat tuxedo cat, pushed his wet snout under my arm, growling, hungry. I tried to swallow but my mouth was dry.

FOR THE PROMO

I thought, *keep talking.*

"You won't get rich selling short stories," I admitted. The cats were prowling around me, their soft cries mutating into growls, less and less friendly. "But the money is just part of what you get from selling stories. You also get a golden opportunity to self-promote."

Another cat pushed its snout against my arm, sandpapery tongue lashing out to taste me.

I whimpered, then collected myself. It occurred to me that even if some adventurer or debt collector came looking for me, the Mystery House would stymie them, sending them wandering in circles for hours, days, until they gave up—or became trapped just like me.

I was being digested by a building, with cats as enzymes.

"The thing about promotion is, you need grist for that mill. You need something to talk about in the first place; otherwise, you're just a self-promoting jerk. You have to think about the unwritten contract you have with your readers—their support and interest in you is predicated on the work you produce, the entertainment or insight you offer them. That goodwill can be stretched a little, but constantly promoting older work, work your readers have probably already seen, gets old fast. While some promotion might be evergreen, the most effective marketing will always involve new material for people to read. There's a reason, after all, that people stop reading blogs that don't update often. They get tired of waiting for new stuff."

The cats began mewling in a rhythm, almost as if singing a rondelet, slowly pacing around me. I imagined the epitaphs my friends and acquaintances would write; the problem with having so many writers as friends is they are so reedy and malnourished that they cannot save you after you have become trapped under a heavy piece of furniture, but they will compose clever epitaphs after your own cats have eaten you.

"That's an excellent point," I said. "You can just post stories on your blog and use that to justify your constant self-promotion, can't you? Except that's not very exciting. Part of the glamor of *selling* something is getting some other person to objectively bless your work. Sure, on the one hand, it would be nice if everything were judged purely on the artistic merit of your fiction, but, in reality, getting through the noise and getting people's eyeballs requires you to have a platform, and generally if someone is willing to pay you for a story, they're willing to put some resources behind it, that means something. Plus, you get the magnified reach of social media platforms, increasing the number of people who will potentially read your story. And as we've discussed previously, many people assume if something is free, it has no value. Like it or not, people take your writing more seriously when you're getting paid for it.

"The great thing about short stories is that there's usually no charge for the reader beyond a subscription they're already paying—and often on the web, there's no charge at all. Instead of exhorting people to spend money buying your books, you're offering them an ostensibly free piece of entertainment which can act as a low-pressure introduction to your work."

I paused. It was difficult to breathe under the weight of the books, and the constant brush of noses and whiskers against my skin was tickling me. Without warning, portly Pierre leaned down and put his teeth on the fat part of my arm, making me wince. Then he turned to study me, as if assessing my ability to defend myself, or to see if I would end this charade and feed them before they were forced to eat me as the law of the jungle dictated.

I closed my eyes. I'd always known this was how it would happen.

"Sometimes a free story can work for promotion, however, if it's directly connected to the novel you're promoting. My novel *Chum* was published in 2013 and exists in the same universe as my 2001 novel *Lifers*. So to promote it, I wrote a "lost chapter" from *Lifers* that was a crossover short story, called 'Up the Crazy.'[15] It's not necessary to read it, but it's a fun bite-sized introduction not just to my writing, but to the universe of the novel, which is not for everyone—as well as a nice extra for anyone who bought and read *Lifers*. In other words, it's both an enticement and a reward for readers.

"And this is where all that writing of short stories, despite the low income profile, pays off. By practicing your short game all the time, you'll be able to dash off a story quickly. This is great in two scenarios:

- "**STORY & ANTHOLOGY INVITES**. Every now and then you'll be invited by an editor to contribute to a theme issue or an anthology, and if you don't have anything that fits the overall theme, being able to scratch a story out in a few weeks' time is like a superpower—a superpower that might earn you a few bucks."
- "**QUICK PROMOTION**. Like my 'Up the Crazy' story, if you have a longer work or more ambitious project you want to draw eyeballs to, whipping up a short work that is thematically connected to it is an effective way of doing so that has the added bonus of building goodwill between you and your audience."

The cats growled in hunger. There were more exploratory bites.

"Writing short fiction preserves and develops your ideas, strengthens your skill set, and gives you material you can turn into a little income and a lot of promotion—it's a win-win."

---

15 You can download it (www.smashwords.com/books/view/350566), if you're interested.

The cats howled.

Several sets of small, sharp teeth sank into my flesh. I shuddered and laughed a strange, nervous laugh as adrenaline spiked. "I wonder," I gasped, "which of us is the protagonist of this story?"

And then they were dragging me.

The cats each took hold of me and began to strain. The pain was excruciating, their razor-sharp teeth sinking in as they pulled at my skin—I was being consumed. But then, suddenly, I was moving. Inch by painful inch, I was being pulled out from under the bookcase.

"Oh my god!" I croaked, the floor sliding beneath me. "Yes! Good cats! Terrific cats!"

The pain was almost too much, but it would be worth it to be free. The bookcase shifted as my legs were pulled free, but I found I couldn't move anything below my waist.

The cats kept dragging me.

"You can stop now," I whispered, the pain finally overpowering my consciousness. "I'm free now."

They continued to drag me down the hall, into darkness. As my vision swam to gray, I saw Pierre staring at me as he pulled at my shoulder. *J is for Jeff*, I thought, *devoured by cats.*

17

SUPPLEMENTING INCOME & PROMOTION WITH FREELANCE PIECES

HOW MANY WORDS DO ESKIMOS HAVE FOR "LUBE"?

A lot of neophyte writers who are just starting to wonder if they might be able to write for a living have a very strange concept of what that means. The range goes from people who are amazed to discover you *can* get paid for writing a novel—people who assumed they would have to wash some editor's car or pick up a lot of dry cleaning in exchange for that publishing contract—to those who think you can sell your book and immediately purchase an island on which to build your Bond Villain Estate.

Are there examples of writers who could retire after selling one book? Sure. Just a few years ago, Garth Risk Hallberg scored a $2 million advance for *City on Fire*, not to mention the sale of film rights before the novel had even been *written*. You can certainly retire on

$2 million, even at Hallberg's tender age, if you follow some decent financial advice.

The vast majority of writers, however, don't get that kind of money; the average first novel advance remains stubbornly in the $6,000–7,000 range. I sold my first novel, *Lifers*, for a measly $1,000.00.[1] My second novel, *The Electric Church*, sold to a larger outfit when I had an agent, was in many ways still a first novel for me, because *Lifers* came out of such a small publisher. I got a $6,500 advance for *TEC*, paid in two parts over the course of several months. Now, subtract 15 percent to my agent and a big chunk for taxes.[2] I signed that contract in late 2005. The book did not publish until mid-2007. Conclusion: There was no private island.

It should be noted that things have ever been thus: Jane Austen received £110 for *Pride and Prejudice* in 1813 (she was already a successful author after *Sense and Sensibility*). How much would that be in 2017 dollars? About $8,700, give or take. Plus, Austen sold the copyright for that, meaning she never earned another dime from the book. In short, writers have been on the wrong end of the stick since the dawn of time.

UNCONVENTIONAL TIP

Keep in mind that the concept of "making a living" as a writer means different things to different people. Your geographic location, lifestyle, and personal situation all come together to form a unique equation. Some people will be able to live off of income from novels that others would consider nominal, so when you read about a "full-time" novelist, consider the possibility that they need much less money than you do.

---

1 As stated in chapter thirteen, I only wound up receiving two-thirds of that. The only reason I got that much of my advance is because my wife, The Duchess, made it a personal project to call my publisher every day for two weeks, demanding he honor the contract. I can personally tell you that when The Duchess makes you her personal project, you are in trouble. In the future, after a religion has formed around my legend, people will threaten each other with the phrase, "The Duchess will make a project of *you!*"

2 A professional would have calculated the amount of taxes he paid on this advance. I used the phrase "a big chunk." Draw your conclusions.

I made more on future books, but even so, the nature of the business of writing novels means you're a) unlikely to ever get a huge payday, and b) always waiting for money to trickle in. Finding ways to pay the bills with your writing that don't involve waiting for advance or royalty checks is always going to be a good thing—and if you can combine making a few extra dollars with promotion that drives some book sales, that's what people smarter than me call "synergistically leveraging your opportunity vectors."[3] Or something.

Make money promoting your novel? You might think such a beast doesn't exist, but it does, and it's called freelance writing.

JEFF GOES RONIN

I think every writer who has a day job at some point looks around furtively and wonders if they can't make a living doing what they love: Writing. When I was a young'un, this daydream often took the form of writing a column in a magazine or alternative newspaper, like Carrie Bradshaw in *Sex and the City*,[4] which is a TV show supposedly rooted in reality. I say "supposedly" because the show implies that Carrie can afford a roomy apartment at a rent-controlled $750 per month on the salary she earns from writing *one, weekly single column*. Obviously what appealed to this lazy, ruined youth was the nothingness involved—I liked to believe that I could scrape together, say, 1,000 words per week on some subject I was intimately familiar with,[5] thus requiring no research, and get paid handsomely for it.

As I aged and life stripped me of my innocence, I admitted that this was probably not a realistic idea, and I began to piece together what freelance writing as a profession really is:

---

3 One thing freelance writing has taught me is how to write Corporate Word Salad. It pays well, and means nothing.

4 I also often daydreamed about lying around in my underwear chain smoking. Make of that what you will. Also, to be fair, Bradshaw, like the woman who invented her, goes on to write for *Vogue* at a really great rate of $4 per word, and then publishes five successful books, so really this complaint is focused solely on the earliest seasons of the show.

5 I'll just come out and admit my dream was to write a column about myself. It would be called "What's Jeff Up To?" and it'd be syndicated nationally. In this dream, I also have washboard abs without exercise, and my body metabolizes food into alcohol.

- Pitching ideas on a constant basis.
- Getting paid by the word, ranging from a penny to a dollar or more.
- Writing about things you might not know or care much about.
- Conforming to someone else's style guide.
- Writing a lot of lists, known in the business as Listicles. A *lot* of Listicles.

UNCONVENTIONAL TIP

Listicles ("Top 5 Books You Should be Reading Right Now!") are actually brilliant, because they allow you, the writer, to easily break down any concept into what I like to call High School English Paper Mode:[6]

1. Introduction, ending with thesis statement.
2. Three supporting paragraphs (or in this case, *five* supporting paragraphs, but usually with less depth than your average high school English paper, so it's a wash).
3. Conclusion, reiterating thesis.

Once you get into a groove of thinking about every subject in the history of everything as a high school English paper, writing Listicles becomes so easy it's barely work.

Eventually I was inspired to dip my toe into freelance writing.[7] I started off with what's referred to as a "content mill" website; these sites are easy to get started on and pay minimal amounts of money for blog posts and the like. Generally speaking, a content mill is a bad place to work because the pay is awful and you'll be doing nothing but anonymous work-for-hire, but I had to start somewhere; contrary to what some might believe, being a published author doesn't mean I had a Rolodex filled with editors' names.

---

6 Veronica Roth, of *Divergent* fame, once wrote a brilliant blog post about how the dialogue on *Grey's Anatomy* is basically all high school English papers with this structure. Read it here: https://veronicarothbooks.blogspot.com/2010/10/what-i-learned-about-dialogue-thanks-to.html.

7 Translation: My day job and I got a divorce.

UNCONVENTIONAL TIP

Beware of scams. Content mills and freelancer platforms like Up-work[8] are rife with folks who will ask you to write a free sample as a job interview. Very often the free sample is the piece they needed written in the first place, and once you supply it, they either disappear or inform you that they aren't hiring you. Always remember: You should be paid for your work, even if it's part of a job application (unless, as will be discussed, you're making a strategic promotional decision).

The first gig I landed was actually kind of fun: I wrote humorous blog posts for a wedding-themed site, two articles a week, 500 words a pop, one penny per word. Yes, if you do the math that's $10 per week. But it was kind of fun, and it proved to me that I *could* in fact make a living at freelance writing—it was just a matter of scale.

My *second* job was less fun and makes the point that freelance writing is a *job*, not a dream. It was actually a job writing a lot of different things for a lot of different clients, but the one that sticks out the most was writing catalog copy for sex toys.

Yes, you read that correctly. Believe me, I spent most of my time coming up with synonyms for the word *lubricate*. It sure wasn't inspiring,[9] but it paid (some) bills and forced me to dig deep and find ways to be creative even when I wasn't exactly inspired by the subject matter or the format.

So I worked at it, and slowly built up that side of my career. I also learned something really interesting: Freelance writing not only pays the bills, it promotes your fiction.

---

8 You'd be surprised to discover just how many freelance writers started off on Upwork (www. upwork.com), formerly oDesk. We all hate the site, but we also wouldn't have been able to get started without it. When I used the site from approximately 2012 to 2013 (short terms like this are pretty common since it's a pretty bad place to get writing work), the main recommendation was ease of use; you could create an account and get your first paid writing gig the same day.

9 Though it did provide me with this hilarious anecdote, which I roll out at just about every social occasion. The reactions to it range from mildly shocked and titillated (nonwriters) and very curious about what synonyms, if any, I discovered (writers).

THE BYLINE

The key here is the byline—you need to have your name on the article. This is actually easier than it sounds! Here's the thing with writing on the web, which is where I do most of my freelance work and where it is much easier to get a foot in the door: All those websites out there need content—written content that is actually coherent and has some value for the reader. For this, you can thank Google, which has been waging a war against crappy websites trying to game its algorithms for years now. About five years ago, Google made a change to the way it ranks websites that prioritized the *quality* of the writing instead of simpler metrics like links and keywords. And so any business or blog that wants to draw traffic to their site (and thus needs a solid Google ranking) needs the one thing you and I can provide: Good writing.

That means there are more opportunities for a byline, because part of the whole "quality" thing is having real, actual humans writing their content. Landing a job writing for a blog that allows for a byline, and perhaps a brief bio, means that every time someone reads, and presumably enjoys, something you wrote, they're exposed to your name, the title of your book, and a bunch of other potentially useful bits of information. For example, my bio on the Barnes & Noble website, where I write about books on a near-daily basis, reads:

"Jeff Somers is the author of *We Are Not Good People*, the Avery Cates series, *Lifers*, and *Chum*. He was first sighted in Jersey City, New Jersey, after the destruction of a classified government installation in the early 1970s; the area in question is still too radioactive to go near. Jeff has published over thirty short stories, including 'Ringing the Changes,' which appeared in the *Best American Mystery Stories 2006* anthology."

Every article I write, I get paid for—and then it acts as a soft advertisement for my writing. Obviously, I don't write about my *own* books, as that would be a huge conflict of interest that would decimate whatever shreds of integrity I have left. But the subliminal repetition of my name, my titles, and my writing style combines into a powerful pro-

motional tool that I don't even have to think of *as* a promotional tool—
and that I get paid for.

FANTASTIC BYLINES AND WHERE TO FIND THEM.

Getting freelance writing gigs is a lot easier than you think. Here are
the ways I've landed jobs over the course of my freelance career:

Advertisements. People tend to imagine that the only way to get a
good job writing is to know someone; but the fact is, I've gotten some of
my best-paying jobs just by answering an online ad. I look for ads that
speak my language—ads that are funny, a little irreverent, and, most
important, that focus on the joy of writing for money instead of a soul-
killing list of requirements.[10]

Networking. That said, it isn't unusual to have a friend-of-a-friend
give your name to someone who's looking for a writer, and I've landed a
few decent jobs that way. I always deprecate the value of networking in
general, but that doesn't mean I view it as value*less*; the thing about gigs
like this is that you can't really make them happen—they just sort of *do*.

Cold Invite. On one occasion, I've actually just been straight up recruited. I got a phone call—someone needed a writer, we did a sort of
informal interview right then, and the next day a contract was in my
in-box. Obviously, these sorts of opportunities tend to happen once
you've started to make a name for yourself.

Cold-Calling. I've also reversed that and simply emailed an editor at a magazine or website and suggested I write for them. I don't do
this often, but it does sometimes work, and if a platform seems like an
ideal spot for work—why not?

---

10 Some good places to look for these ads are Mediabistro (www.mediabistro.com), Indeed
(www.indeed.com), and ProBlogger (problogger.com). *Writer's Digest* (www.writersdigest.com)
has a lot of information about finding and landing freelance work, as well. Some folks will tell
you to check out Reddit or Craigslist, but in my experience, the former tends to be a duplication
of what you'll find elsewhere, and the latter is a disorganized way to get scammed. As always,
your mileage will vary.

UNCONVENTIONAL TIP

It never ceases to amaze me how often potential employers will spend the entirety of an ad describing the many responsibilities you, the writer, will have—the many skills you must have, the many personal attributes, the drive and passion to work very hard and always be creative—and not *once* mention how much you might actually earn. With very few exceptions, if an ad for a writing job doesn't even *mention* paying you, it's not worth applying for—even if it's a cool website or a well-known company. A lack of thought about compensating the writer likely means they don't value the writer.

In other words, you're not going to launch a freelance writing career by waiting around for people to recognize your genius and hand you money and platforms. You've got to pursue freelance writing like you would any other job or project. If you want your freelance to do double duty as self-promotion, you've got to look for the following in every job you consider:

- A byline, preferably with a bio.
- Subject matter that syncs in some way with your genre or style.
- A decent platform—writing for a blog that gets a handful of views every week won't help much in the promotion department.

Of course, if you're looking for freelance work to support yourself, these become lower priority—but they should still be there, in the background, informing your decisions about the work you take on. Whether it's a side hustle or your main source of income, freelance writing can help your fiction career in a number of ways:

- Burnishing your professional cred—nothing says *I am a professional writer* like a byline and a paycheck.[11]
- Getting in front of a new audience—unless your personal blog gets a lot of traffic, exposure on other sites or print venues means new eyes on your name.

---

11 Not even business cards that literally read *Jeff Somers: Professional Writer*, which everyone assumes is a joke, for some reason.

Identification as an expert within a genre or field—if you're able to find freelance platforms that sync up with your fiction's style and category, being regularly published on those platforms can establish you as an authority.

> **UNCONVENTIONAL TIP**
>
> Unless the point of the piece you're writing is to promote a book, don't make your self-promotion explicit. If you're being paid to write something, injecting a blatant plug for your own work is a great way to never get another opportunity, so it actually works *against* you. The difference between someone enjoying your essay and checking out your books, and someone feeling like you suckered them into reading an advertisement, can be a single, self-serving sentence.

THE EXPOSURE

Back when I was publishing my zine, *The Inner Swine*, I regularly came up with weird experiments designed to amuse and/or annoy my readers.[12] One such scam was Swinebucks, which is exactly what you're thinking: It was a running gag where I would offer increasingly preposterous amounts of a currency I'd created on my computer in exchange for goods and services. I even photocopied some Swinebucks and sent them to subscribers, pledging that they could pay them back to me for stuff at some point in the future.[13] If I were to repeat that ramshackle social experiment, I would probably call my fake money *exposure*.

Once you start freelance writing, you will undoubtedly be approached at some point about doing some writing in exchange not for the bourgeois concept of filthy lucre, but for that magical substance known as exposure. In fact, as a writer at any level, you've probably been asked to write for exposure or offered exposure in exchange for something you've already written. And I sincerely hope you refused,

---

12 Don't forget, I thought I was edgy. This from a pudgy man who wore glasses so large he could see the future, and who thought it was socially acceptable to drink lite beer.

13 Number of people who sent me Swinebucks to extend their subscriptions: All of them.

because the most important thing you can internalize as a writer is the fact that your work has value, and the second most important thing you can internalize is that *exposure* is meaningless—usually. If you're looking to write in order to earn a living, exposure is a terrible idea and you should punch anyone who suggests it to you. People offer exposure because they don't think your writing has any value—they think their *platform* has value. In other words, they think you're hiring them, not the other way around.

However ... if your goal is to promote a novel or other writing, then exposure might make sense. I've written essays and blog posts for no money—in fact, most writers promoting a book have done so, whether as part of a blog tour or as one-shots. Usually these efforts are suggested or guided by a publicity department at a publisher, a private publicist, or the author themselves and the many voices they hear in their heads on a regular basis. As an example, when my novel *We Are Not Good People* was about to launch, my publisher suggested I write an essay for a site called Off the Shelf. So I wrote a piece titled "My Magician Is Better Than Yours," about my dislike for characters in fantasy stories who are just born with immense magical talents, unlike the hero of my novel, who literally has to bleed for his powers. That essay was then picked up by The Huffington Post, retitled as "These Magical Worlds Are Even Better Than 'Harry Potter.'" The potential audience for an essay on these sites is huge, and I was perfectly happy to write something for the potential exposure.

UNCONVENTIONAL TIP

Exposure is fine compensation if it's your choice and your idea.

I call this "loss-leader" writing; you're not getting paid, but you're hoping to get an indirect benefit from it. The key for loss-leader writing is the platform: The audience needs to either be huge or very targeted toward people who theoretically will love your fiction; or, of course, both.

TAKING THE WHEEL

Okay, so you're sold—freelance writing can be a great, subtle way to promote yourself. How exactly do you go get started?

Well, you could start the way I did, by taking on some fairly low-level writing work, getting paid a pittance, and slowly working your way up. That takes a lot of time, and you'll spend most of that time writing anonymously as you build up a network and, ironically, make a name for yourself while developing the skills needed to be a freelance writer.

That's a good approach, as I discovered, when you're in it for the long haul. Doing time in the trenches of low-level writing trains you in the fundamentals of freelance writing—everything from managing your own time to generating endless ideas for articles—and those fundamentals apply no matter how big the platform is and whether you're writing 300 words for a penny each or 5,000 words for a dollar each.

If you're looking at freelance writing as a promotional tool and you're not terribly concerned with making money or creating a steady stream of work, however, you can take a different approach and simply cold-email some targeted publications or websites. This can be done in three steps:

- **HAVE A CONCEPT.** Never approach a site or magazine without an idea for an article in hand. No one wants to get a vague "hey, I have a book to promote" email—they want you to solve the problem of getting eyeballs *for* them. Obviously, if your goal is to promote a novel or your writing in general, you should try to shape your article idea with that in mind—in my essay that wound up on the *Huffington Post*, I wrote about an eye-catching piece of pop culture (Harry Potter) that would get clicks, and combined it organically with the premise of my own novel.
- **FIND A PLATFORM.** So, if you have an idea for an essay that perfectly promotes your work while being hilarious and informative, where do you take it? You can start with the websites and magazines you already read—it's usually a good assumption that if you're a regular reader, it's in the perfect Venn diagram of your writing and your potential readers. Look for a "write for us" link or, failing that, the editorial emails, and make contact. You can broaden this approach just by googling that phrase "write for us" and adding some keywords to narrow the results. Keep in mind that traffic matters—use sites like EasyCounter.com or Alexa.com to get an idea of how many views a website gets, because if you give away (or even sell) a piece of writing and no one sees it, have you actually accomplished any self-promotion?
- **PITCH LIKE DON DRAPER.** Once you have an idea and a target platform (or fifteen target platforms), you have to *pitch* the idea. A pitch is your idea, the subject, and the slant you're going to apply to it. Your pitch has to be specific, it has to make clear the "angle" of the

piece—the unique approach that will raise it above the noise—and, most important, it has to explain why the essay will bring in traffic and eyeballs.

UNCONVENTIONAL TIP

A pitch should be brief—just a few lines. A short introduction with some credits and other bona fides, then a sentence or two explaining the concept and the twist you're putting on it. Put simply, if you can't pitch the idea in three or four sentences, you haven't refined the idea enough.

You won't always get a response; sometimes you'll get a nibble that comes with a lengthy list of alterations to your concept and sometimes you'll get a robust acceptance. If you get the green light, the next step is obvious: Write your piece. Read the site or magazine's style guides; pay attention to any tweaks they asked for in the concept; hit the word count and the due date. There aren't any favors in the freelance world, and if your essay stinks or doesn't conform to the site's templates, it won't make the front page.

Once it *does* hit screens or pages, promote it. Because you'll also be promoting all your other work.

THE PROMO

We'll be getting into detail on the subject of my unconventional approach to self-promotion and social media in the next chapter, but let's lightly touch on the best way to leverage a freelance writing assignment into promotion for your novel or your writing in general. The key word here is *subtle*.

No one wants an assault of *Buy my book!*-style tweets and posts, not even if there's a free and entertaining article associated with them. Instead, you have to adopt a more oblique approach that prioritizes the piece you've written *and* the platform that's hosting it. They bought or accepted your writing because they thought it would draw some eye-balls their way, so it's your job to drive as many of those eyeballs as possible. Best practice here is to not mention your book or your other writing at all, and focus 100 percent on the specific article you're pro-moting. Let your byline, bio, and association with a larger audience do the work for you. The whole point, after all, is to impress people with your hilariously informative article, inspiring them to look up the rest of your work. Trust in that dynamic, because a more aggressive approach will backfire on you.

UNCONVENTIONAL TIP

Sometimes a website will offer payment linked to page views, where you'll get a small amount of money for every click your article gen-erates. This isn't uncommon, and while the payout is usually very small, there's always the possibility that your piece goes viral and you might get a decent payday out of it.

The thing to keep in mind when using freelance writing for indirect promotion is that such articles offer a long tail. You'll (probably) only be directly paid once (and you'll only have a short window when your article is new and can be promoted as such), but as long as your arti-cle is on the internet, people can—and will—come across it. That sort of passive promotion can last for years, slowly driving traffic to your personal website or stores where your books are on sale. It might not seem sexy, but over time it can become a significant force that moves books off of shelves. And hey, if you get paid for that writing as well, that's just a bonus.

18

SELF-PROMOTION
THE WORLD IS A VAMPIRE AND YOUR SOCIAL MEDIA KUNG FU IS WEAK

I once read to an empty store.

This isn't exactly a highlight of my career,[1] but it's a great story that combines my two favorite elements for anecdotes: my own humiliation and my own fiction. It was 2002, and The Duchess and I had organized a DIY book tour in support of *Lifers* and a collection of essays called *The Freaks Are Winning*, published through Tower Magazines. We set up a six-stop tour over the course of a few weeks, with two readings in New York and one each in Chicago, Philadelphia, Morristown, New Jersey, and Washington, D.C. We did it all, from identifying the stores to contacting the people in charge of events to contacting local media to arranging travel and accommodations.

---

[1] I didn't have my agent yet when this happened, but she laughs really hard when I tell this story.

UNCONVENTIONAL TIP

The key to any promotional event is some kind of media attention. Local radio, newspapers, websites—whoever you can get to interview you, write about the event, or mention you in an events calendar will help. Making these connections months in advance is crucial. If you don't get any media attention, you are like a tree that falls in the woods that no one hears, even if hundreds of people show up—because out of those hundreds of people, approximately five will actually buy a book. This is true of virtual events as well—all those blog tours certainly can't hurt, but don't imagine they will result in a surge in book sales.

Some of the readings were huge hits, especially in New York, Philadelphia, and Chicago.[2] Some were less great; the Morristown event was kind of sleepy. But nothing in my life, before or after, has ever compared to the disaster that was my reading at Olsson's in Washington, D.C., on June 8th, 2002, because literally no one showed up.[3]

I don't know who to blame for this. We did everything we'd always done. I'd reached out to local press, emailed everyone I knew in the area, sent out newsletters announcing my presence. I mean, I didn't expect a crowd, really, but a handful of loyal fans would have been nice. Instead, no one but me, three friends, The Duchess … and my Mom, who no doubt expected some moments of pride in her successful writer son. Instead, we all stood around awkwardly until the manager suggested I just start reading, to see if maybe some randos shopping in the aisles might walk over.

---

2 I read at Quimby's (www.quimbys.com), which if you've never been, please god make arrangements, as it's a fantastic bookstore if you're into zines, alternative press stuff, and just wonderful weirdness. Quimby's has always had a strong zine connection, and so they were a perfect venue for my reading, and we got a great crowd.

3 I did have one other reading that no one came to; it was in 2007 and was right around when *The Electric Church* was published. My publisher, Orbit Books, wanted to set up a reading, and asked me where I'd like to do it. I'd done a reading at a bar called Rocky Sullivan's in Manhattan a few years before that had been a big success, so I suggested we do it there—without realizing that Rocky Sullivan's had moved to an area of Brooklyn as far away from civilization as possible in the intervening years. End result? No one outside of my publisher, literary agency, and immediate family showed up. Technically, it wasn't as bad as the Olsson's gig because there were like thirty people in the room, but still.

And that, my friends, is self-promotion in a nutshell. It's awful, and even when it goes well, you probably won't sell many books as a direct result.

A SUPPOSEDLY FUN THING

The trick with self-promotion in general is that nothing works and no one knows why. It's all about the aggregate; no single event, tweet, or special project will sell a significant number of books or get you the kind of attention that leads to book contracts and agents hiding in your bushes seeking to sign you. *But*, if you keep doing all these useless, pointless things that have no impact, slowly but surely you'll build a platform.

It's like the criminal scheme from *Superman III* or *Office Space*, in which computer programs are used to steal tiny fractions of pennies. By itself, one-eighth of a penny isn't noticeable or useful. Steal a few billion of them, however, and it starts to look like real money. That's self-promotion.[4]

Now, some people make it look easy. Some folks seem to effortlessly gain thousands of followers, their tweets go viral routinely, and they sell a lot of books. And while those things *are* all related, they're not quite as directly related as you might think. Even those folks don't see a one-to-one relationship between, say, a viral tweet and book sales. You almost never see any significant, measurable bump in sales stemming from a single social media or other self-promoting effort.

I've done lots of readings. The Olsson's experience aside, I've had dozens of people show up just to hear me read, to say hello, and buy a

---

4 The true test of nerd cred isn't *Star Trek* versus *Star Wars*, or even being able to say something in Dothraki. It's being able to explain the criminal scheme from *Superman III* coherently.

book. I think the most books I've sold in one reading is about fifty, and that was a pretty unique evening. Usually I'm lucky to sell five copies at a reading; readings are generally a lot of effort for a very small payoff. The time I sold fifty copies was my debut novel, *Lifers*, and it was the one reading I did that year, which helps explain the success—when you have a new book that's just come out, and you plan a reading with enough lead time, you can have a big night. But I'd argue that most of those people would have bought the book anyway. They came to the reading to be supportive, to share in the excitement. If I hadn't planned that evening, they would have bought the book some other way.

The simple fact is, nothing I've ever done has had a noticeable impact on sales. And I've done it all:

- Readings and signings,[5] as mentioned, including signings at huge events like New York Comic Con, where my publisher gave away dozens of copies of the book to anyone who wanted one.
- Panels, where I am reliably witty and entertaining.[6]
- Interviews (print, Skype, web, live).[7]

---

5 I did a reading once at a Barnes & Noble in New York City for my first novel, *Lifers*, where I shared the bill with Dito Montiel, who was already famous for being the lead singer of Gutterboy and a notorious New York personality. Dito had just published his book *A Guide to Recognizing Your Saints*, which would be made into a film starring Robert Downey Jr. He showed up with an entourage and a camera crew that was filming him for a documentary of some sort, and after I stuttered and sweated through my reading, he pulled out a guitar and put on a show that made me look pretty boring. At the end of the event, I went over and told him most of the people who'd come for me were probably downstairs buying his book. He smiled and said most of the people who came for him were probably downstairs *stealing* my book. I was, in other words, completely outclassed. Dito is now in Hollywood, writing and directing films. I recently found a dime on the sidewalk and felt pretty pleased with myself.

6 I once arrived at a New York Comic Con panel twenty minutes early and was the only author there for about fifteen minutes. I chatted with the crowd and led them in chanting my name; then randomly during the panel, when I asked the crowd to chant my name, they did. I wish I could live in that memory.

7 The glamorous world of radio interviews: In 2007 and 2008, I was twice a guest on the Joey Reynolds Show on WOR 710AM in New York. My publisher set it up, and each time I had to be at the studio at an ungodly hour—like 2 A.M. or so—ready to be witty. No one explained to me that my microphone wouldn't be live until Joey officially turned his attention to me, so I spent half an hour making comments that no one could hear and wondering why everyone was staring at me.

- Videos (book trailers, skits).[8]
- Guest blogs.

Some of these things are more fun than others, but none of them have ever resulted in significant, measurable sales spikes. The world wants entertainment, and everything you do just gets swallowed by a black hole, and then it's as if nothing ever happened. Is it possible I'm just not good at it? Sure, it's possible. But I'm so awesome at other things,[9] it isn't likely.

So why do any of it? Because there are plenty of benefits to self-promotion—you just have to understand that a direct link to sales or advancing your career isn't one of them. There's nothing *direct* about self-promotion. It's all about the long tail.

IT TAKES A VILLAGE

As I've said, you won't sell a whole lot of books as a direct result of self-promotional efforts, but that's okay; what you *will* accomplish is even more important. You'll build a brand, and you'll forge a relationship with your readers. Don't have any readers yet? Self-promotion can take care

---

8 I have my own YouTube Channel, "Jeff Somers Rocks You Like a Video Hurricane" (www.youtube.com/user/jeffsomers), where I post book trailers and a series of videos called "Ask Jeff Anything," which ought to be self-explanatory. I also participate in Sean Ferrell's "Two Men Have Words" (twomenhavewords.com), where we have fun making literary-infused skits that muck about in the absurd. So in case you're wondering just how handsome I am in person, you can watch some of those videos and discover that the answer is: very.

9 Including—and possibly especially—self-deception.

of that, too. Just because someone doesn't buy a book right there in the moment doesn't mean a good experience with you won't convince them to buy a book later. The main thing you're trying to do with your self-promotional efforts is to define who you are for people—what you write and what your public persona is—and to entertain them. For free. Because that's part of the deal.

In fact, the more heavily you lean on the "buy my book" aspect of self-promotion, the less effective your self-promotion will be. At the same time, you do *need* to do the whole "buy my book" part, because otherwise people might not notice that you're a writer with a book to sell. People don't mind that you let them know about your book and the fact that they can buy it—they really don't—but they also don't want to be hit over the head with it every five seconds.

After twenty years of readings, interviews, videos, and tweets (oh, so *many* tweets), I've boiled self-promotion down to three golden rules:

- **BE COMFORTABLE**. Don't bother doing anything you don't enjoy doing. Enjoying yourself is as important as your readers enjoying themselves. If everyone's having fun, your chances of making an impact are much higher. Don't listen to anyone who tells you that you have to do something. If you aren't comfortable reading in public, don't do readings—focus on making videos, or writing pithy tweets instead.

- **STOP COUNTING**. I've written some blog posts I thought were brilliant, penned some tweets I thought were absolutely perfect, and made some book trailers I thought should win awards. Usually the actual performance of a bit of self-promotion is directly inverse to how amazing I think it is. The only way to stay sane is to create your bit of self-promo and move on, paying no attention to the Likes, retweets, or other interactions used as a  metric for its success.

UNCONVENTIONAL TIP

Don't forget, while internet-based stuff like videos, social media, and blogs may not be forever, they *do* have a pretty long tail. That means that even if something doesn't have the impact you were hoping for right away, it still has value over time, as it passively soaks up a trickle of further interest and interaction.

- **BE READY TO SAY NO**. There's pressure, sometimes, to say yes to every opportunity, whether it's a chance to read at an event or an invitation to write a guest post. It's almost like we all imagine there is a finite supply of people out there potentially interested in your writing, and if you skip an event, you'll permanently lose your chance to connect with that group. But don't forget, you're not likely to directly sell too many copies anyway—and your time is valuable. If you've been invited to do something, it's because the host gets some benefit from having you there, so it's not about you—which means you can say no if you don't see a benefit for yourself or just aren't in the right frame of mind. It's similar to the rule about being paid for your writing—the opportunity to promote yourself somewhere is likely not a favor, so don't treat it like one.

THE INTROVERT'S PARADISE: SOCIAL MEDIA

The fact is, the easiest, cheapest, and often most effective self-promotion involves social media platforms. They're (generally) free, have a theoretically infinite reach, and often take very little effort to utilize. Anything I can do without standing up or putting on pants is my jam these days—though I won't deny that I've never been the most forward-thinking person.

The first person I knew who owned an iPhone was my friend Ken.[10] This was right after Apple released the first model, and I remember being all sorts of unimpressed. Ken has always been the type to love a good gadget, so the fact that he bought what I saw as an unnecessary toy made perfect sense. But I wasn't interested in it, and was, in fact, kind of mean and dismissive about it.[11]

I've always had a weird relationship with technology. On the one hand, I love it; I love collecting gadgets, and I started monkeying around with operating systems and programming languages years ago. On the other hand, I am deeply suspicious of it and its role in my life, and so I sort of willfully ignore any new development. For example, I didn't possess a cell phone until 2005, when my day job gave me one. And I didn't get anything resembling a smartphone until 2011.

I also didn't have any social media accounts until 2009. In fact, prior to 2009 I made several regrettable public statements about never ever having a Twitter or Facebook account,[12] because, once again, I was certain this thing called "social media" was a fad for the kids and I would never have a need or desire to take part in it.[13] Since those halcyon days, when I didn't know what *vaguebooking* or *subtweeting* meant,[14] of

---

10 I swear there is a point to this story.

11 As Ken will tell you, I can be mean and dismissive a lot. He once punched me because of that. But we're still friends.

12 I probably should have called this chapter, "In Which Jeff Is Wrong about a Bunch of Things."

13 It's a very good thing my job description includes several references to hard liquor and no terms, like *futurist* or *cutting edge*.

14 If you don't know what they mean, I advise you to revel in your innocence.

course, I've been forced to not only establish a beachhead on the shores of social media, I've also been forced to make an attempt at mastering the art of promoting yourself there.

Now, I am far, *far* from an expert on social media. My wisdom on this subject is, in fact, limited more or less to what *doesn't* work—which *is* wisdom. So here's the skinny on what doesn't work when it comes to social media promotion: Everything. *Nothing* works.

EXPECTATION MANAGEMENT

Before we go any further, let's define our terms. When I say what "works" on social media, I mean specifically in terms of, you know, selling books. Social media is *terrible* for actually selling things. What it's good for is raising your profile and putting you in front of other people. Social media is this weird virtual world where nothing means everything and you're doomed to failure even if you succeed.

Take Twitter. Twitter is very easy to set up and start using, but using Twitter effectively requires that you master several microskills:

1. The ability to be pithy and coherent in 280 characters[15]
2. The ability to use hashtags and other tokens to capture traffic
3. The ability to be in the moment and think on your feet
4. The ability to be a consistent presence every day

In other words, you have to overcome the challenge of being entertaining and interesting on a very awkward platform, you have to figure out how to put your thoughts in front of other people, and you have to do it every single day. Easier said than done; the kicker is that even if you get very good at it and start getting lots and lots of retweets, favorites, and quotes—even thousands of them!—you still won't sell more books.

Facebook is even worse; Facebook has made it its business to restrict your access to the people who have chosen to Friend you, and anyone who has ever tried to promote themselves on Facebook has been faced

---

15 As I tweeted when the character limit was raised: "2007 Me: 140 characters is a ridiculous limit! My thoughts are far too complex. 2017 Me: 280 characters is an infinite void that frightens me."

with posts that get thirteen views—and a notification from Facebook offering to let a few hundred more people see it for a small sum of money.

Why then, if social media is so terrible, is it all the rage? Why are there so many social media experts trying to teach you how to use it effectively? There are a couple of reasons:

1. No one understands it.
2. It's (largely) free.
3. The audience is (potentially) huge.

Those three factors sum it up, actually. The first one is why everyone wants to explain it to you, usually for a fee or through a book they're trying to sell you.[16] The second one is why every author in the universe is on social media, kicking the tires and trying to make it do wheelies. The third is why we all keep thinking that if we just keep shouting into the void, eventually it will translate into book sales or a raised profile, just because of its sheer size. The former, unlikely. The latter? Maybe. But the secret to social media promotion is to stop thinking about social media promotion, because the simple rule is that no one buys a book or offers you a publishing contract *for* a book because you're good at posting Instagram photos.[17]

---

16 Smell that? My ears are burning. *Oh my god, my ears are burning!*

17 Unless, of course, it's a book of Instagram photos.

I've had meetings with a number of supposed social media gurus—smart, hard-working people who usually offer the same advice, some of which I'll repeat here, because it makes sense on a practical level. But I'm convinced that no one really knows how it all works, *because* so much of the same advice gets passed around, and every meeting I've taken on the subject has a low-level hum of awkwardness, because everyone knows that no matter what I do I'm unlikely to suddenly become a social media star, ever. I mean, come on: *Look at me:*

Photo by Barbara Nitke

So why bother? Because social media doesn't equate to sales in the traditional sense, where you shake a hand, look someone in the eye, and convince them your book is worth $15 or that you're a talent worth investing in. It's much, much weirder and more confusing than that, a sector where nothing is directly related. Social media is like string theory. Everyone is pretty certain it's a powerful, fundamental force of the universe, yet no one can quite explain how it works. When you take a less scientific approach, however—when you give in to your natural inclination to be lazy about things—suddenly it all works out. I don't claim to be a social media expert, but I can tell you I've figured out how to have fun and indirectly promote myself and my work there. All you have to do is three things.

JEFF'S THREE STEPS TO SOCIAL MEDIA DOMINATION[18]

It's a lot easier than you think and doesn't require too much of your time. If you want to make an impact with your social media on whatever platform or platforms you enjoy, do these three things.

1. **Post Every Day.** This is actually not that hard—it just takes a little planning. Being active is part of the whole deal; no one comes back to a blog that's never updated, and no one follows a Twitter account that behaves like an ancient volcano that may or may not erupt at some point in the near future. People have a lot of options when it comes to spending time online, and they aren't going to waste it hanging around your dormant social media accounts unless you're already very famous and proven to be interesting.

So, you have to show up every day and put in some work. Don't worry about being brilliant—I haven't said a single brilliant thing on social media since I signed up. I may, in fact, be the most boring person to ever have a Twitter account.

I don't let that stop me, though. I show up every day, and I get involved. This might seem exhausting, but I follow a very simple strategy that makes it pretty easy:

- **SCHEDULED TWEETS**. I use a free service called TweetDeck to schedule tweets every week. This takes me about a half hour on Sunday morning to set up. I pick a theme for the week—say, short stories I've published or hilarious photos of myself, and I set up fifteen to twenty tweets for the week, in the morning, afternoon, and early evening. This isn't meant to be comprehensive or exciting, it's meant to ensure that if I get caught up doing other things and forget to attend to my social media duties, at least *something* goes out. Scheduling your social media can be a powerful tool—but be mindful that you might

---

18 As long as we agree that, in this context, the word *domination* translates to "mild success," we'll be fine.

want to cancel or edit content if something happens. For instance, say you have a joke about a famous writer queued up and then that writer passes away; you don't want a tweet that makes fun of them to land at that moment.

UNCONVENTIONAL TIP

Don't set up your tweets to cross post to Facebook or any other automatic replication. It seems like a good idea but that assumes people only live on one social media platform. Most people have accounts on several platforms, and if they start to see the same posts—word for word—everywhere they look, it might seem robotic. Also, it's annoying to be forced to read the same thought four times in the space of five minutes. If you want to ensure something hits every possible platform, take the time to at least word it differently.

- **SPONTANEOUS POSTS**. Don't overschedule your posts; the scheduling is just to ensure that if you are buried under rubble or taken hostage at a bank robbery, your social media will continue to remind people that you are still alive and your books are still for sale.[19] Flesh out your social media presence by commenting on reality in real time. These could be posts of random bon mots or just those that jump on a rising hashtag bandwagon.

- **INTERACTION**. If you use social media as a bullhorn for shouting your message at everyone, it gets old fast. The word *social* is not in there for nothing—people expect a little actual interaction. You don't have to get into lengthy arguments or discussions with folks. A few Likes or retweets, with the occasional comment or endorsement, are appreciated and go a long way toward making people feel like you're part of a community instead of a soulless advertising presence. In other words, your social media content shouldn't

---

19 The risk here is obvious: If you really are buried under rubble, people will see your tweets and think, oh well, he's fine, and not bother checking on you until long after you've starved to death. Or have been eaten by cats.

be endless appeals to buy your book; it should also include some actual conversation.

2. **Have a Persona**. Do not, under any circumstances, believe for a moment that your social media should actually represent you as a person. For many people, of course, it is; they post their intimate moments, deepest feelings, and personal opinions. The thing is—and this can be confusing—they're also probably not promoting a book or a writing career in general. Do you have the *right* to be yourself on social media? Of course you do. You just shouldn't. You should become someone else. I'm a guy who drinks whiskey for breakfast and wanders the neighborhood without trousers, carrying a cat around like a broke-ass Bond villain. You don't have to be that, but for god's sake don't be yourself. You should have a persona and a brand—and those can be modeled *very* closely on your actual personality and life, but the distinction between the two is crucial—you *control* your brand and can shape it at will. You can't do that with actual personality.[20]

3. **Conflict Avoidance**. Again, you shouldn't be using your social media as a way to express your personal opinions and inner feelings. Or at least I don't think you should. Some people do just that and get away with it. For some people, that *is* their brand. Some people get pulled into arguments and get buried under controversy, and there has been more than one writer forced to shut down their social media because they expressed a political, religious, or other opinion. Your career won't necessarily become an unrecoverable quagmire just because you got into trouble on Twitter, but it won't *help*. When tempted to tell someone they're crazy about something on the internet, remember this simple fact: No one has ever won an argument on the internet. Ever.

Much of this is advice that just about anyone with some experience online will offer you. The key is to apply it in your own way. For me, Twitter is a place where I can be a little crazy. I don't have the attention span or energy to monitor Twitter constantly, so I tend to tweet a large volume of thoughts all at once—this is called a "tweetbomb." I have a number of folks who always check to see what I'm rambling on about at

---

20 At least I hope you can't. If you can, please spare me when the culling begins.

4 P.M. on weekdays. In a strange way, it's like having a broadcast show that people tune in for. My tweets rarely go viral; they're often just random thoughts about whiskey and writing and what's irritating me that day, but folks like them, and that's why I do it.

Someone will likely tell you I'm doing it 100 percent wrong. But then, *someone* will *always* tell you you're doing something wrong, won't they?

UNCONVENTIONAL TIP

Social media can become exhausting if you let it dominate your thinking. Relax. You may not become the next Snapchat star, but you *can*—and should—have a little fun. And fun, oddly enough, is often what sells people on your social media channels.

THE KNOWN UNKNOWNS

One of the most common questions that comes up in regards to promoting a book or a career is how can you possibly rise above the noise and be *noticed*? There are literally hundreds of thousands of tweets, posts, and other pieces of content posted online every day. Your clever piece of wordplay or complaint about burritos gets thirteen views, while someone else posts an animated GIF they didn't even make themselves and gets 500,000 Likes.

It's mysterious, believe me, I know, because as I may have mentioned, no one knows how any of this works.[21]

This is where the advice to have fun comes into play: If you're going to fail miserably at promoting yourself or your books, you should at least have some fun doing it. I've tried a few experiments that didn't exactly make me into a social media star but were fun to play with.

---

21 Whenever I tweet something that gets thousands of impressions and hundreds of interactions, I am always surprised; when I try to replicate it, I get fifteen lukewarm impressions. It's almost like the owners of the social media platforms are manipulating things ... to make us ... pay for something. Hmmnnnn. ...

Twitter Stories. Back in the dark ages of 2009, I was, like everyone else, desperately trying to figure out the *why* of Twitter. *Why* did we want to microblog? You could, after all, use existing social media like Facebook to write very short posts if you wanted to. Why did we need a whole other platform for this?

I'm sure I didn't think of this on my own, but the inspiration escapes me: I decided to tweet a short story. I created a separate Twitter account for this, called Somers Story (twitter.com/Somers_Story) and I selected a short story, titled "The Black Boxes," that I had written recently and liked. I edited the story so it was a series of 140-character chunks, and I laboriously input each chunk into a scheduler. Then I told everyone, and my publisher told everyone, and to this day I don't think the account ever had more than five hundred followers. Maybe that's because no one actually wants to read a short story 140-characters at a time. Lesson learned.

Text Adventures. I loved playing interactive fiction games as a kid, and I found out there's a programming language created to write such stories. So I downloaded the compiler and wrote a text adventure based on the third Avery Cates books, *The Eternal Prison*. It was a lot of work and the end result was a little wonky, and I can't swear it sold one more book than I would have otherwise, but I had fun creating it, and that's all I need to consider it worthwhile.

Ask Jeff Anything. I started making a series of videos where people would email me a question about anything, and I would answer it. Naturally I always tried[22] to be funny when I did this, to be as absurd as possible. I've slowed down on these because they take a lot of time to put together, but I had a blast making them and always got a great response from people. Or *a* response, which is really all I need.

Self-promotion is thankless in many ways. People will happily accept your videos, blog posts, tweets, and photos, and then merrily refuse to buy a single book. But over time, if you keep at it, you can build a community of fans who will in turn act as the best advertising you can ask for—people who enjoy and recommend your work.

---

22 Word choice matters. I *tried*.

19

THE RECURSIVE CHAPTER ON SELLING THIS VERY BOOK

CONTAINING A RECURSIVE CHAPTER ON SELLING THIS VERY BOOK

Inspiration is a funny thing. I once had a sudden epiphany about a problematic novel while sitting in the audience at a performance of *Mama Mia!* on Broadway.[1] I wrote a key scene for *We Are Not Good People* in a state of panic and terror after attending Bouchercon and convincing myself I would never publish again. I wrote a novel based on a single sentence in a zine I read thirty years ago and haven't seen since.

We've discussed ways to find ideas for novels, but sometimes it sort of just happens. A synapse fires—or *mis*fires—and you have a notion. It festers, it sprouts, and before you know it, you're writing a book. Or at least that's how it happens *sometimes*. Sometimes you sweat, strain,

---

1 My wife still hasn't forgiven me for standing up and shouting *"Everyone be quiet! I need to think!"*

and force an idea to gel into a novel. And sometimes someone else hands you an idea, like a gift.

THE LONG TAIL

Books—novels and nonfiction alike—usually have lengthy incubation
periods, those years when they're nothing more than an idea and some
random notes. They're like icebergs; all a reader might see is the published book in 2018, without ever knowing that you had the original
inspiration for it in 1994.

I've published a lot of books. Here's the length of time between initial inspiration and published book:

Lifers: 6 years

The Electric Church: 16 years

We Are Not Good People: 18 years

Chum: 12 years

As you can see, most of these books took a long
time to develop from original inspiration.

This book that you're holding in your hands is no exception, really; it has its roots in 2014, when I was invited to give a presentation at the Writer's Digest Annual Conference in New York City. I'm not sure how the invitation to the conference came to me, though I can imagine there was some corporate synergy involved; my novel *Chum* is published by Tyrus Books, which was at the time owned by F+W Media, which also owns *Writer's Digest*. That, plus the fact that I live in the New York City area and thus wouldn't need to have travel and hotel expenses covered, is likely how it came together. In other words, I was a cheap date.

I developed a presentation called "Take Off Your Pants and Write!" all about plotting and pantsing (and plantsing) a novel, and it was a hit. I was invited back the next year, and the editor-in-chief of *Writer's Digest* magazine attended the seminar and invited me to pitch article ideas to her for the magazine, which I did. I had an article in each subsequent issue of the magazine after that and was invited to give the presentation a third time.

One day in 2016, my agent suggested I come by her office for a drink and a strategy session.[2] I had some digital-only novellas coming out in my Ustari Cycle series, and she had a novel of mine she was going out with to publishers, but it's always a good idea to get together and make sure you're on the same page and working with the same information. So I went to my agent's office one afternoon, she poured us each a few fingers of bourbon, and we sat in the conference room, chatting.

One of the best things about having an agent—a good agent—is that they're simultaneously smart, experienced, and connected in the publishing world, *and* a huge fan of your writing. Having an advocate who knows the trends in publishing, who knows the editors and the situation at every publisher, is a superpower. Having someone like that who also thinks your writing is amazing is, well, amazing.

---

2 I think she said "strategy session," though to be honest all I heard was "drinks" and I accepted the invitation, then spent the intervening week wondering what I'd agreed to discuss.

WRITING WITHOUT RULES

So we were chatting and my agent asked me how I liked writing for *Writer's Digest*, and then she got this look in her eye and asked me if I'd ever thought about writing a nonfiction book, a guide to the writing craft.

See, for me, writing those articles about writing was fun and personally helpful, because they offered the opportunity to organize my thoughts on the subject of writing and publishing.[3] Plus, I was hearing from lots of writers who appreciated my advice and my point of view; it was nice to think I was helping out, paying back a little. It would never have occurred to me to expand on those ideas and leverage this new platform I'd developed. This is because I'm a writer, not an agent or a businessperson. I saw an opportunity to be creative and make money with the words, nothing more.

My agent, however, saw the possibilities. She saw me establishing myself as an authority—finding an audience for my unique blend of boozy experience, hilarious pants-related jokes, and wide-eyed incompetence.[4] She saw me strengthening a relationship with a publisher. She also saw an opportunity to get a book in print when I didn't have anything else scheduled to come out. This is another reason why literary agents are key: Aside from all the *other* stuff they do, they often see your career from a slightly different point of view than you do. For example, I think the conversation went something like this:

AGENT: You should totally write a book about the craft of writing. Call it something like *Unpublished, Drunk, and Pantsless Is No Way to Go Through Life*.

ME: Sounds like a lot of work. All those words, and I'd probably have to, you know, remember things and maybe google something. Hard pass.

AGENT: Probably a little money in it.

---

3 As evidenced by this book, I apparently have a lot of such thoughts. Which surprises everyone, including my wife, who has informed me that when she heard about this book, she expected it to be a lot of "rambling stories" and "weird jokes." That's what we in the marriage business call "support."

4 Now, that's a brand!

ME: I do have debts because I invested all that money in internet memes. Slightly softer pass.

AGENT: No more refills unless you agree to think about it.

ME: How about *Writing Without Rules*?

AGENT: Good. Go home and work up a proposal.

See, I'm usually not smart enough to think in terms of *career*. I'm usually thinking in terms of what would be really cool to write; in fact, like a lot of writers, I often work on novels that excite me instead of ones that seem likely to sell, which means I wind up with a fair number of manuscripts that don't have huge potential for selling thousands of copies. Sometimes what you need is for someone else to suggest you write something you'd never think of in a million years, go home to work on that proposal, and slowly build excitement as you see the potential to have fun, make something great, and write something no one else has ever done.

INDECENT(LY SHORT) PROPOSAL

Now, I'd never actually written a book proposal before. I'd written synopses of books that hadn't yet been written, I'd sketched out four novels' worth of future plot—but I'd never actually sat down to write a document designed to compel a publisher to hand me a check and make some room on their schedule. It's a whole different way of thinking; with fiction I usually start with the assumption that I have an awesome idea for a story and leave it up to the publisher to figure out how to sell it. Trying to reverse-engineer that was a refreshing and challenging experience that I failed at almost completely.

The proposal I sent was two pages long and was essentially a glorified table of contents. It was funny, and the material described was what eventually evolved into this book, but looking back it was pretty naïve of me to think that all I would need to do was sketch out some good ideas and a publisher would commit to investing in the project. After all, when I sell a novel, it's usually completed, ready to be edited, and put into production—often we're talking about years of work before the book gets in front of an editor. My brief proposal offered no assurances that there would ever actually be a book to publish, while simultaneously making several jokes about my habit of day drinking and falling asleep in front of my keyboard.[5]

My agent, hilariously blunt as always, replied with the following email:

"Well ... no.

This isn't quite what I need. I'm not sure if you've ever seen a nonfiction book proposal before. So, before we go any further, here's an example. Follow it.

Questions today are free. Stock up." [6]

The proposal she attached was *15,000 words long.* I had to pour myself a drink.

UNCONVENTIONAL TIP

A real, actual writing career is a lot of work, and involves a lot of rejection—and that rejection is not always going to be gentle. It's key to remember that everyone involved is investing time and effort, so they can't waste either on half-developed ideas, no matter how brilliant—and they don't have time to be particularly *nice* about it. If you're not willing to work on the proposal, why should they think you'll work on the *book*? That's why the end-all, be-all advice is always very simple: Do the work. Don't complain, just do the work.

Then, I got to work.

I wrote a detailed overview offering a glimpse of the style and substance of the book. I researched the potential audience. I wrote up some compelling reasons why folks would actually buy this book. I offered up potential endorsements, and I researched competing titles (sometimes referred to as "comparable titles" or "comps") and offered argu-

---

5 People keep telling me that constantly joking about being drunk and incompetent is not a sound career strategy, but I'm usually too drunk and incompetent to pay any attention.

6 She likes to use this line a lot, but trust me ... questions are never free. Note: When reviewing this manuscript, my agent put in a note: "Questions are free. *Answers* on the other hand cost money. Correct answers are more expensive. There's a sliding scale." Duly noted.

ments as to why my book would sell better and why it fit a niche the others didn't cover. I wrote about my platform and my specific qualifications, I fleshed out the proposed table of contents, and I wrote two sample chapters.

In the end, I wrote about 15,000 words just for the proposal. I went from being fairly clueless about the process to being painfully aware of it in about a week.

UNCONVENTIONAL TIP

You can't know everything. When in doubt, just take your best guess—someone will correct you. For example, if you don't write the proposal because you're not sure how, then you'll never get the feedback necessary to learn. Bottom line: When unsure, just move forward.

I sent it off to my agent, feeling pretty good about myself ... until the revisions began. I'm used to revisions. Writers have to be, that's literally half the job. We went through ten revision cycles on the proposal, trying to sculpt the pitch and refine all the descriptions so it would be irresistible.[7] When we decided it was the best proposal it could be, though, it felt good. I was confident we had a winner and waited eagerly to hear back on the offer.

Here's a basic rule I always forget about: When I get overconfident about selling something, my intuition is almost always dead wrong.

The acquiring editor called me up to discuss the book; she thought I'd strayed a bit from the core idea I'd outlined in our initial discussions, and so I had to ponder the content and tweak the chapters a bit to get it back in line with the original vision, which obviously required an *eleventh* revision. Which I did, cheerfully, because feedback that

---

7 The only other time I spent this much effort on a writing project before even typing "chapter one" was when I created the pitch for *The Electric Church*, described in chapter nine of this book.

amounts to "change these three things and we have a deal" is *literally* the next best thing to a deal.[8]

I had a pretty short timeline for writing this book, which isn't unusual. Luckily, not only does the book have roots that go back three years, I've also been doing freelance writing for so long that the idea of coming up with 80,000 words in a few months doesn't bother me in the least; it's what I do every day. Plus, I was already well on my way to plantsing, even though there isn't a plot, so to speak, in this book. Because I'd spent so much time writing the proposal and working on the table of contents, I already knew exactly what I'd be writing about in every chapter. I was able to hit the ground running and write in a naturalistic, spontaneous way—just as if I was pantsing the story of my writing career and lessons learned from it—because I'd already done the plotting.[9]

UNCONVENTIONAL TIP

Sometimes the whole point of doing some plotting is to enable yourself to pants your way through the actual writing. Plotting is like marking a trail through the woods so you can run the way back.

LESSONS FOR NOVELS

So, this is a nonfiction book. And yet there are some good takeaways from all this for novel writers:

- **BE OPEN TO IDEAS.** An idea is not a book, fiction or nonfiction. It's a kernel that has to be worked over, a starting point that needs you to layer on ideas, words, time, and thoughts that will slowly ag-

---

8 The lesson here is simple: You will mess up. You will make the wrong assumptions, you will forget details, you will forget that your big, important call is actually a Skype meeting and sit in front of your computer without a shirt on. That last one actually happened to someone I know, at his job. He got fired. Don't be that guy, or at least don't be that guy until you have established your brand as "person who shows up for Skype meetings without a shirt."

9 I started writing this book on January 2, 2017. I finished the first draft on April 2, 2017, exactly three months later. I spent another three weeks revising and had a final version by May 2, 2017. Not quite NaNoWriMo, but not bad.

gregate to book size. Writers as a group have a tendency to be very protective of their ideas (hence the endless hand-wringing about copyright and online piracy) and also very certain that *their* ideas are the *best* ideas. Very often—if not all the time—however, your ideas are really built on someone else's ideas, and sometimes it's someone else's idea that turns into a successful book. Bottom line: Don't get hung up on the precise source of an idea. It's never the *idea* that matters—it's what you do with that idea.

- **DO THE WORK**. Sometimes writing is easy, and some writers seem to think it should *always* be easy. If you expect to be able to sail through 80,000 words and never once hit a moment of uncertainty—a moment where you're pretty sure you've just wasted three months of your life—then you're not taking the craft of writing seriously. The difference between a finished manuscript and a bunch of *un*finished manuscripts is usually the ability to regroup and keep moving forward, even when you're frustrated or disappointed in your own execution. Often the most difficult aspect of *do the work* is dealing with feedback and revisions—you've worked your butt off on something, and all you get are lengthy edit letters detailing your failures. Get over it. Start at the beginning and attack your manuscript again—and again, as often  as necessary.

UNCONVENTIONAL TIP

Doing the work when it comes to feedback, Edit Letters, and the like *doesn't* mean you have to do everything someone says. You can—and should—disagree with feedback, even if it comes from your editor. Yes, if you simply refuse to make any changes you'll damage that relationship and jeopardize the book, but I've yet to meet the editor who won't have a conversation about revisions with an author. Do the work, but stand up for yourself, too.[10]

---

10 For example, in an early draft of *We Are Not Good People* I killed off one of the protagonists, and my wife told me I was making a huge mistake. I resisted changing the story until my agent read the draft and agreed. I can barely stand up to either of those women alone; united, they are

- **DON'T PAY ATTENTION TO GURUS.** If there's one lesson I hope everyone takes away from this book, it's that there will always be people who set themselves up as experts in the field of writing and publishing. Many of them are sincere, and many have good, useful information and experience to offer. I certainly hope I do. But never hesitate to ignore folks like me. The key to writing and publishing experts is that their experience is usually singular. If your experience matches up with theirs, then that advice will be golden and very useful. If you're on a different track, it won't match up at all, and it will become very easy to imagine that you're doing it wrong because you're having a different experience. The fact is, if you follow a guru's advice and don't see results, you just need to find a different guru. No one knows *the* secret. We all only know *our* secret.[11]

THE RÉSUMÉ

Like a lot of people, writers or not, I have a tendency to self-aggrandize a little.[12] Part of that is an unconscious pretension that I wrote this book simply because someone convinced me it was a good idea. But the fact is, I was able to write this book because I put in thirty years of writing and publishing, including dozens of completed novels, hundreds of completed short stories, thousands of submissions and rejections, and many, many hours spent drinking whiskey and thinking about writing. Or just drinking whiskey, which I count as work, even if my accountant refuses to claim liquor as a deductible on my taxes.

The point is, I couldn't have written this book ten years ago, or even five years ago. Part of the whole "guru" thing that annoys me so much is the way people often fudge the amount of effort and work they put into their craft in order to make it look effortless, to make themselves look

---

unstoppable. On the other hand, they have both advocated giving Avery Cates a love interest for years, and I've so far managed not to do that.

11 In a related note, that should probably be number four on this list: If someone, or several dozen someones, tries to convince you that making 33 percent of your book's content hilarious footnotes is a bad idea, ignore them. Ignore them so hard you actually increase the footnote content of the book to 50 percent.

12 For example, my business cards currently read "Jeff Somers | I Invented Words."

like geniuses. The fact that so many people believe that what makes a genius a genius is that they don't have to do the work is a problem. Genius or not, you have to do the work. You have to accumulate the years. You have to get the rejections, learn the lessons, and develop the skills.

The point is, it's a process. If you're not quite able to finish a novel, or can't get anywhere with your submissions, don't despair; don't assume you just don't have "it." I was twenty-four when I sold my first story for actual money,[13] and a year later I co-wrote a comic book with my friend Jeof Vita for a lot more money—but then it was years before I sold anything else. I wrote my first real novel when I was about fourteen, but I didn't sell a novel until I was twenty-eight—and then I didn't sell another until I was thirty-four. It takes time, and those intervening years seem *long*.[14]

That's why ideas are the least valuable part of a novel. Ideas are as easy as letting your mind wander. It's everything else—the work, the time, and the suffering—that makes a book.

---

13 "Glad and Big," *Aberrations Magazine* #34, 1995. I was paid $7.50. I never cashed the check, because I was twenty-four and stupid and thought I should keep it as a souvenir, which I regretted years later when I was broke and starving. Which in turn reminds me of Jeff's Law that I forgot to enshrine in these pages: *Always cash the check.*

14 Which is why there is whiskey.

WRITING WITHOUT RULES

20

CONCLUSION

SUMMATION AND NAKED PLEA TO BUY MY NOVELS OR POSSIBLY LOAN ME $50

So, here we are. The end of the book. Unless you read it out of order, like some sort of animal, in which case all I know is that you have no idea how to read a book properly, which is all I *need* to know.

For a long time, I thought I didn't know how to properly *write* a book. Or, more accurately, I thought I didn't know how to *be a writer* properly—the writing part I've been mostly confident in my whole life. But when I met other writers, they would always talk about aspects of the craft and business of writing I'd never found important, or never bothered to do; they always made it sound like it was a given that every writer who considered themselves a professional did these things. I would sit there and nod along and wonder, *Is that* really *necessary?*

There's a great story about Dustin Hoffman and Sir Laurence Olivier when they were making the film *Marathon Man* in 1976.[1] Hoff-

---

1 It's a good movie, but an even better book (by William Goldman). For a long time in my early adulthood, I took a strange pleasure in discovering that films and TV shows I'd seen as a kid had novels as source material, and this was one of those moments when I was browsing a used-

man, a method actor, prepared for the torture scenes in the film where his character is exhausted, terrified, and sleep-deprived by not sleeping for days beforehand, forcing himself to stay awake so he would be right there in the moment with the character. When Olivier—who was not a method actor, but rather classically trained—heard this, he looked at the younger actor and said, "My dear boy, have you tried *acting*?"

That's how I sometimes felt when discussing writing with other authors. They'd talk about their intense research, the lengths they went in order to create accurate details, and I would think, *My dear boy, have you tried* making stuff up? And then I'd wonder if I was missing something fundamental, if I was, in a word, a *fraud*.

That's where this book came from. The slow realization I've had that there is *no* right way to write a novel has been freeing and exciting. Every writer starts off thinking there must be some sort of formula, some rules. How many of *X* can be in every novel? How much of *Y* do you do to promote yourself? Slowly, I've come to realize that there's no such thing as a "right" way. You write what you want to write, and you try to sell it the way you want to sell it. It might work; it might not.

Other people can offer you advice and guidance, sure. And sometimes it will work. But the daylight between, "You have to do this to succeed," and "This worked for me, your mileage may vary," is where this book lives.

I hope it's helped. As someone who has self-published, sold books to houses big and small, who's given away short stories and sold short stories, and written every kind of freelance material under the sun, this entire book could be boiled down to one piece of advice: You do you.[2]

---

book store and stumbled on an ancient paperback copy of this title, and my mind exploded. Because it had never occurred to me that the movie had been adapted from a book. As you can see, I am truly a deep man.

2 I sincerely hope you aren't standing in a bookstore having flipped to the last page out of curiosity, and now you're about to put this back on the shelf because I just saved you some time and money. *Dammit, Jeff, think before you write!*

THE KING WORM

A final anecdote:

When I sold *The Electric Church*, I was pretty excited. It was listed pretty prominently on the publisher's front list, and I got a lot of attention for it, making me think we were onto something.

Then the publisher asked to see ideas for sequels.

I never think about sequels, or series. Every time I write a novel, I intend it to be a stand alone, which is dumb because—especially in the science fiction and fantasy genres—no one thinks in terms of stand alones. After all, if you have a successful first novel, why wouldn't you want to write endless sequels?

So, when my publisher asked me for ideas for sequels to *The Electric Church*—before the book had even published—I was at a bit of a loss. As far as I was concerned, the novel was self-contained.[3] Instead of thinking about how I was going to leverage this book sale into a career, I was busy pondering all the free booze my publisher and agent would buy me.

But the wheels started turning, and I had an idea. I quickly sketched out a plan for two more books, making the Avery Cates series into a trilogy—the second book would be *The King Worm* and the third book would be *The City State*. It was a bold concept, in my opinion, and I started working immediately. I wrote the first sequel quickly, burning up with inspiration. At no point did I choose to share my concept with my agent or my editor, because I have a superstitious belief that if you explain a novel's plot or premise to someone before you write it, it loses its power.

At one point the publisher invited me to a party, at which I got pretty inebriated (because these things are usually open bar[4]), and I started to brag to my editor that I'd already written the sequel and it was great.

---

3 I felt this way despite the fact that the novel ended on what is clearly sequel bait. To say I am not and have never been self-aware is an understatement.

4 Did I stand up on a table and do the *Titanic* "I'm king of the world!" bit? I don't remember, and The Duchess has destroyed all the video files. She delights in informing me that I did shout, "I'm a rock star!" several times on the walk home.

This was true. Or at least the first part was true, and I firmly believed the second part. But when I finally sent *The King Worm* to my editor, she rejected it, saying—accurately!—that it was repetitive, with a plot modeled very closely on the first book. This was on purpose, but my editor wasn't wrong, either. I'd made a terrible mistake.

UNCONVENTIONAL TIP

Always remember: A publisher has a different agenda than you do. You want to write a *great* book that *also* sells; they want to publish a book *that* sells. The difference can be subtle, it can be imperceptible, it can be clear, but there is *always* that divide.

My publisher still offered me a book deal for the sequels, and I went back to the drawing board and came up with two story ideas that my editor loved (and we eventually did two more books, bringing the series up to five). And, in the end, I loved the new ideas more, and I think the five-book Avery Cates series is much better than the trilogy I'd originally imagined.

So what's the point? Two of them, actually. On the one hand, I once again did everything kind of wrong. I wrote a book without thinking about career implications. I stormed ahead on a sequel before confirming that it was a good idea. I also got drunk at a party and made an ass of myself, but frankly that happens so often it barely counts.

On the other hand, I learned a lot. I learned a bit more about how the publishing world works and what I can just charge ahead and do—and what I can't (or shouldn't). I learned the value of thinking before I act. And I learned a lot about my character and universe. *The King Worm* won't be published, but the material in there served to help me conceptualize the Avery Cates universe. And my editor's feedback on the book in her (very nice) rejection was instructive, showing me that no matter how great some of the ideas were, the repetitive nature of

WRITING WITHOUT RULES

the plot was untenable. I still think back to that experience when contemplating new books.

So, in the end, getting a book rejected and putting a book deal in peril was exactly the right way to go.

And that's how it is. There is no "right" way. You have to do things the way you want to, learn your lessons, and take your wins. I know I still do things the "wrong" way more often than not, but it all works out one way or another. Either I sell something, learn something, get better at my craft, or, if nothing else, I write something *I* like—even if no one else does. The fact is, there will be plenty of times when you feel like a fraud or an amateur, convinced that every other writer knows more than you do and is playing the game better. They don't, and they aren't. It just seems that way from the outside.

And yes, I still drink too much at publisher parties. Because, in case you missed the key takeaway, they're usually *open bar*.

INDEX

WRITING WITHOUT RULES